# Breakfast at The Beach House Hotel

# Judith Keim

# BOOKS BY JUDITH KEIM

The Talking Tree (The Hartwell Women –1)
Sweet Talk (The Hartwell Women – 2)
Straight Talk (The Hartwell Women – 3)
Baby Talk (The Hartwell Women – 4)
The Hartwell Women Series – (Boxed Set)
Breakfast at The Beach House Hotel –1
Lunch at The Beach House Hotel – 2
Dinner at The Beach House Hotel – 3
Christmas at The Beach House Hotel – 4
Fat Fridays (Fat Fridays Group – 1)
Sassy Saturdays (Fat Fridays Group – 2)
Secret Sundays (Fat Fridays Group – 3)
Finding Me – A Salty Key Inn Book – 1
Finding My Way – A Salty Key Inn Book – 2
Finding Love – A Salty Key Inn Book – 3
Finding Family – A Salty Key Inn Book – 4
A Christmas Star – A Seashell Cottage Book – 1 (Late 2018)
Going Home – A Chandler Hill Book – 1 (Early 2019)
Coming Home – A Chandler Hill Book – (Late 2019)
Winning BIG – a little love story for all ages
For more information: http://amzn.to/2jamIaF

# CHILDREN'S BOOKS BY J. S. KEIM

The Hidden Moon (The Hidden Moon Series – 1)
Return to the Hidden Moon (The Hidden Moon Series – 2)
Trouble on the Hidden Moon (The Hidden Moon Series – 3)
Kermit Greene's World
For more information: http://amzn.to/2qlqKMI

# PRAISE FOR JUDITH KEIM'S NOVELS

## THE BEACH HOUSE HOTEL SERIES

*"Love the characters in this series. This series was my first introduction to Judith Keim. She is now one of my favorites. Looking forward to reading more of her books."*

*BREAKFAST AT THE BEACH HOUSE HOTEL is an easy, delightful read that offers romance, family relationships, and strong women learning to be stronger. Real life situations filter through the pages. Enjoy!"*

*LUNCH AT THE BEACH HOUSE HOTEL – "This series is such a joy to read. You feel you are actually living with them. Can't wait to read the latest one."*

*DINNER AT THE BEACH HOUSE HOTEL – "A Terrific Read! As usual, Judith Keim did it again. Enjoyed immensely. Continue writing such pleasantly reading books for all of us readers."*

*CHRISTMAS AT THE BEACH HOUSE HOTEL – "Not Just Another Christmas Novel. This is book number four in the series and my introduction to Judith Keim's writing. I wasn't disappointed. The characters are dimensional and engaging. The plot is well crafted and advances at a pleasing pace. The Florida location is interesting and warming. It was a delight to read a romance novel with mature female protagonists. Ann and Rhoda have life experiences that enrich the story. It's a clever book about friends and extended family. Buy copies for your book group pals and enjoy this seasonal read."*

## THE HARTWELL WOMEN SERIES

*"This was an EXCELLENT series. When I discovered Judith Keim, I read all of her books back to back. I thoroughly enjoyed the women Keim has written about. They are believable and you want to just jump into their lives and be their friends! I can't wait for any upcoming books!"*

*"I fell into Judith Keim's Hartwell Women series and have read & enjoyed all of her books in every series. Each centers around a strong & interesting woman character and their family interaction. Good reads that leave you wanting more."*

## THE FAT FRIDAYS GROUP

*"Excellent story line for each character, and an insightful representation of situations which deal with some of the contemporary issues women are faced with today."*

*"I love this author's books. Her characters and their lives are realistic. The power of women's friendships is a common and beautiful theme that is threaded throughout this story."*

## THE SALTY KEY INN SERIES

*FINDING ME* — *"I thoroughly enjoyed the first book in this series and cannot wait for the others! The characters are endearing with the same struggles we all encounter. The setting makes me feel like I am a guest at The Salty Key Inn...relaxed, happy & light-hearted! The men are yummy and the women strong. You can't get better than that! Happy Reading!"*

_FINDING MY WAY_- "Loved the family dynamics as well as uncertain emotions of dating and falling in love. Appreciated the morals and strength of parenting throughout. Just couldn't put this book down."

_FINDING LOVE_ – "I waited for this book because the first two was such good reads. This one didn't disappoint.... Judith Keim always puts substance into her books. This book was no different, I learned about PTSD, accepting oneself, there is always going to be problems but stick it out and make it work. Just the way life is. In some ways a lot like my life. Judith is right, it needs another book and I will definitely be reading it. Hope you choose to read this series, you will get so much out of it."

## OTHER COMMENTS

"Always love books written by Judith Keim. From these strong women who go through lots of difficulties and adventure to the Florida beach hotel books. Every book is entertaining and fun to read with plenty of excitement and surprises.

"I was first introduced to Judith Keim's books with her Beach House Hotel series and since then look forward to each new book from this author. Her stories draw you in so you become invested in the lives of her characters and want to know what comes next."

# Breakfast at The Beach House Hotel

## The Beach House Hotel Series – Book 1

## Judith Keim

Wild Quail Publishing

This is a work of fiction. Names, characters, places, public or private institutions, corporations, towns, and incidents are the product of the author's imagination or are used fictitiously. Any resemblance to actual events, locales, or persons, living or dead, is coincidental.

No part of this book may be reproduced or transmitted in any form or by any electronic or mechanical means, including information storage and retrieval systems, without permission in writing from the author, except by a reviewer, who may quote brief passages in a review. This book may not be resold or uploaded for distribution to others.

Wild Quail Publishing
PO Box 171332
Boise, ID 83717-1332

# Dedication

For Joan and Charlie
Thanks for being part of so many happy memories
including riding an imaginary train with me and Mrs.
Eye-Jones.

# CHAPTER ONE

I gripped the armrests of my seat as the jet accelerated down the runway with a roar of its engines. The plane lifted up into the air like an eagle in flight. I let out the breath I'd been holding and told myself to relax, that it was too late to make any changes, and I needed to escape the dreary weather of Boston and the drama of my recent life. And though I felt so vulnerable, so unable to find joy, staying with a total stranger wouldn't be all that bad, would it? Not when it made Liz, my daughter, so happy.

She'd convinced me to fly with her to the Gulf Coast city of Sabal, Florida, to spend Thanksgiving as a guest of her freshman college roommate's mother. I didn't know Rhonda DelMonte, except through emails in which she'd chatted about the wonderful connection her sweet daughter, Angie, had made with Liz and me. She'd seemed friendly, but still ...

Tamping down my anxiety, I turned to Liz. "What are you reading?"

She held up her *Cosmopolitan*. "Not really reading, more like drooling over some sexy soap stars. One of them looks just right for you, Mom. Vaughn Sanders. He's a real hottie."

I gave her a weak smile. After all my heartbreak, the thought of dating anyone made my stomach curl.

Liz gave my hand a squeeze. "Mom, I'm so glad we're making this trip. Dad is being such a jerk, and I can't stand you-know-who."

I gazed out the window at the clouds that caressed the plane with long white fingers. As I stared at the mistiness outside, I wondered what I was going to do with my life. The divorce had happened so suddenly I wasn't ready for all that followed. I couldn't help a snort of disgust. Breaking up with me, Robert had declared he no longer wanted to be a wallflower at the dance of life. As if he'd ever been that poetic! I knew very well it took two to tango, but I'd been caught off guard that he'd chosen a new dance partner—the young, voluptuous receptionist in his office just a few years older than Liz. "Kandie with a K" is what she'd called herself, flashing a smile and a generous peek at her implanted breasts. No doubt Roberts's ridiculous wallflower comment had come from her and one of the silly magazines she constantly read at work.

Liz gave me a worried look. "Are you all right?"

I nodded. But inside, I was anything but okay. The divorce had left me without a home, a job, and with much less money than I'd thought.

Our landing was as smooth as the rest of the flight. Prepared to make the best of the situation, I gathered my things. This was the only vacation I'd have for months, perhaps years, to come.

We deplaned down steps onto the hot pavement of the airport apron. I drew a deep breath of the pungent, tropical air and stood a moment, admiring the tall Australian pines and palm trees lining the Sabal airport. I blinked against the brightness of the sunlight, and my heart lifted. I was so glad to be away from cold, gray New England.

"Hurry up, Mom!" said Liz impatiently. "Angie's waiting."

When we walked into the waiting area, Angie rushed forward and swept Liz into a warm embrace. Watching them, I smiled. With no siblings, they'd quickly become like sisters. I turned to Angie's mother, and shocked, I rocked back on my heels. *This was sweet, shy little Angie's mother?*

Wearing a bright-green, silk caftan and sparkly, gold and "diamond" sandals, Rhonda DelMonte stood before me like a large, tropical bird. Rhinestone-studded sunglasses rested atop her head, and huge diamonds, offset by a deep tan, winked at her ears, wrists, and throat. My gaze traveled up to Rhonda's bleached-blond hair pulled away from her full face and gathered in a knot at the base of her head. Wide brown eyes, surrounded by lashes stiff with mascara, studied me openly.

"So, you made it!" Rhonda boomed, pulling me into a bosomy hug that reeked of *Poison* perfume. "Let's see if we can put some color on that thin, little figure of yours!" She squinted at me. "And a sparkle in those eyes."

Bowled over by her presence, I forced a smile.

She gave me a little jab in the arm. "Boy, have I heard a lot about you! But, don't worry! It wasn't *all* bad." She let out a short burst of laughter and studied me. "Ann Rutherford sounds so formal. I've decided to call you Annie."

"But ... but ..." I sputtered. I *hated* the name "Annie." It reminded me too much of Little Orphan Annie. My own parents were killed in an auto accident when I was just five, leaving my strict grandmother to raise me. "I don't ..."

"Don't pay any attention to me." Giving me a broad grin, Rhonda elbowed me playfully. "I have to dub people in my own way, and with those round blue eyes of yours, you're an Annie if I ever saw one!"

Before I could respond, Liz tugged on my arm. "Mom! You have to come see what Angie got for an early Christmas present!"

She led me outside. A shiny, little white convertible was parked in the waiting zone.

Liz grinned. "Neat, huh? I've always wanted a Beemer!"

"It's just perfect!" Angie gave her mother a quick hug. She

might be a little spoiled, but she was a sweet girl. Dark-haired and quiet, she was a perfect match for my more outgoing blond daughter.

We loaded the car with the suitcases, and I squeezed into the backseat of the BMW with Rhonda. As we drove through town, it was difficult to hear Rhonda's chatter above the rush of wind in my ears, but I strained to listen.

"Palm Avenue is one of the nicest shopping districts in Sabal. They have some beautiful things." Rhonda gave me a meaningful look. "You'll be able to buy some bright, fun clothes, and not be quite so beige."

Dismayed, I glanced down at the simple beige dress I was wearing.

"Don't worry." Rhonda winked. "We've got plenty of time for shopping."

I sat back in my seat, realizing this short visit wasn't going to seem short at all.

We left the commercial area and drove along a winding street lined with large, palatial homes. Angie slowed, entered a drive between two huge pillars, and pulled up in front of an enormous stucco mansion. Liz and I exchanged looks of amazement. Awed, my gaze swept across the extended façade of the house, and I wondered how many rooms it contained.

"This is The Beach House," Rhonda announced proudly, indicating the lovely estate that belied its simple name. "It used to be a small hotel at one time, but now it's where we live. Someday I may turn it back into a hotel—a kind of place for classy people. Your kind of place, Annie. Come on in! Manny will get your bags."

Angie shook her head. "Mom, Manuel and Consuela are off for the holiday."

Rhonda gave a hearty laugh. "Oh, yeah. I forgot." She

turned to me. "Manny is my right-hand guy. You know what they say, every woman needs a Manny around the house!" Rhonda roared at her own joke, and I couldn't help chuckling.

We entered the house through double, carved-wooden doors. As I stood in the tiled entry, I looked across the living room through a wide expanse of sliding glass doors that led to a lanai. It held a magnificent spa and an infinity-edge pool that appeared to be one with the sparkling blue water of the Gulf of Mexico just beyond. I was captivated by its beauty.

"It's wonderful, Rhonda!"

She grinned. "Get comfortable. Then we'll swim and have lunch." With a flash of green silk, she disappeared into the back of the house.

Angie took the suitcase from my hand. "I'll show you to your rooms."

She led me upstairs into a sizeable room overlooking the broad expanse of beach and Gulf water. The walls, a rich cream color, were enhanced at the baseboards and the ceiling with wide, carved wooden moldings painted a contrasting stark white.

I set my bag down on the bed. The green in the plush, quilted bedspread was repeated in the mini-print draperies and, again, in the cream, patterned carpet.

"Lovely," I murmured.

"A professional did it." Angela gave me a knowing look. "My mother would go for pink flamingos on the lawn if you know what I mean." Even as the corners of her mouth lifted, unconditional love shone in her eyes.

I smiled. Angie and her mother seemed as close as Liz and I.

Angie left, and before I unpacked my suitcase, I yanked off my beige, knit dress. I'd never wear it in Rhonda's presence again. No doubt she'd order me to take it off. The woman had no idea about boundaries.

After settling in, I pulled on my new bathing suit, loving the thought that, while Robert and Kandie were coping with sleet and an early snow back home, Liz and I were able to enjoy tropical warmth in a gorgeous setting far away from them.

Standing on the balcony off the bedroom, I gazed down at the pool. The waterfall at one end sent glistening ripples dancing across the pool's surface. The sound of the tumbling water was almost drowned out by the lapping of the Gulf on the broad, white beach beyond the house. Peace such as I hadn't known for a long time wrapped around me, and the headache I'd developed after meeting Rhonda eased.

Downstairs, I walked outside and blinked rapidly from the glare off the water. I was pleased now I'd splurged and bought a new beach cover-up. After the cool November days up north, the sun felt especially hot.

"Hey, Mom! Come on in. The water's great!" Liz looked up at me from the pool with a happy grin.

At her smile, I was happy I'd agreed to come to Florida. The divorce had rocked her too. I dipped my toe in the sparkling water and let out a contented sigh. It was pleasantly warm. I took off my cover-up and opened my bottle of sun block.

"Is that a new suit?" Liz asked.

"Yes. Do you like it?" I'd chosen a tasteful, black, one-piece bathing suit.

Liz wrinkled her nose. "Mmm, not exactly."

Rhonda approached us, munching on a carrot stick and carrying a plate of sandwiches. "It looks like you're going to a beach funeral. You'd look great in a bikini! Why are you wearing that?"

For a moment, I was too surprised to say anything. "But it's a nice traditional suit."

"I bet that's just the kind of thing your ex liked to see you in. Right? From what I've heard, he was an uptight asshole."

A furious retort died on my lips as old memories came back. It was true. Robert had a fit if I wore anything he considered too "daring" at the country club pool. Especially after one of our neighbors, drunk at a party, told Robert he was lucky to have me in his life and in his bed.

"I knew it!" Rhonda gave me a smug look. "Tomorrow we'll get you a new suit. I'll even pick it out." She grinned. "Boy, have you got some changes coming. You're going to have a ball! Or should I say balls?"

I swallowed hard as Rhonda roared with laughter. What, I wondered, had I gotten myself into with this visit? Rhonda and I were like night and day, totally out of sync with each other. I could almost hear my grandmother say, "You're in trouble now, young lady." And, for once, she'd be right.

Rhonda threw an arm around me and grinned. "I knew we'd get along."

"Yes, of course." I ordered myself not to roll my eyes and wondered how many hours until my flight home. Our first day together was not half over, and I had another five to go.

By the time I crawled into bed that night, I was too tired even to continue counting the remaining hours of the visit. The sun had overheated my skin, and my trying to remain an enthusiastic guest as my grandmother had taught me had fried my mind.

I awoke and stretched. The sun peeking through the drapery caused my lips to curve happily. It was another beautiful day in paradise. Vowing to relax and get along with my hostess for the next few days, I climbed out of bed and got dressed.

Downstairs, I took in the view from the living room and let out a sigh of pleasure. As I walked into the kitchen, Rhonda greeted me with a smile. "Today, we'll go to the Shops at the Lagoon for a bathing suit for you. It's time to liven you up a bit."

I could well imagine what Rhonda would pick out for me and pressed my lips together. The neon pink tank top she was wearing outlined every one of her curves, and her orange shorts were ... well, too short.

"Yeah, Mom, liven up, as Rhonda says." Liz beamed from Rhonda to me. "I've tried to tell you ..."

At my warning look, she stopped talking.

Rhonda rose and put an arm around me. "I just want to see you have some fun, hon. I know what it's like, following a divorce. Now, do as I say and go take that skirt off. We're wearing shorts today."

"But ..." I looked down at the filmy skirt I'd bought on sale last summer—I'd been so excited about a chance to wear it.

"Go on now," urged Rhonda.

"Hurry, Mom! Rhonda's taking us out to breakfast."

Deciding not to make a scene, I headed back upstairs praying I could make it through the next few days without coming to blows with Rhonda. She was so ... so ... damn ... bossy!!

Thanksgiving was another beautiful, tropical day. I pulled on shorts and a T-shirt and padded downstairs. Rhonda was already in the kitchen finishing a pumpkin pie.

"Happy Thanksgiving! Can I help?"

Rhonda shook her head. "Maybe later. Right now, I'm ordering you out of the kitchen. Go for a walk on the beach, and then you can relax by the pool."

More orders. I took a deep breath. Two and a half more days to go. "Okay, let me know if you need me to do anything." It was, I now knew, useless to argue with her.

As I strolled along the beach, the sound of the waves lapping against the shore eased the tension in my shoulders. The cry of a gull swooping above me caught my attention. I waded into the water, letting the salty froth wash over my feet and cool me before I headed down the beach. My muscles stretched as I picked up my pace. It felt so good.

After a quick bite to eat back at The Beach House, I changed clothes and lay on a chaise lounge next to the pool. In my new, lime-green bikini—the skimpy one Rhonda and the girls insisted I buy—I immersed myself in a book, unwinding for the first time since I'd arrived in Sabal. The television blared from the kitchen, announcing cold, rainy weather for Macy's New York Thanksgiving Day Parade. I thought of all Robert had done and hoped it was just as miserable in Boston.

Liz took a seat on the lounge chair beside me. "I love being down here in Florida. How about you?"

I nodded. The thought of still being at home, facing my first big holiday as a single, sent a chill racing across my warm skin.

"It hasn't been so bad then?" Liz studied me.

"Rhonda drives me crazy, but I'm glad to see you happy." I was learning to cope with Rhonda's bossiness. Growing up as I had with my strait-laced grandmother in Boston society, Rhonda's salty language still jarred me. Rhonda didn't even notice, and I doubted she ever would. But she was tender-hearted, and that went a long way with me.

Later, Rhonda came out to the pool. "All right, ladies, it's time to go upstairs and get dressed for dinner. Wear something nice for the holiday. We're celebrating!"

With thoughts of Thanksgivings in the past, I slowly climbed the stairs. It would take me a long time to get used to all the changes in my life. I undressed and stepped into the shower. The cool water felt good on my skin as I soaped my body, removing the last of the suntan lotion.

Drying off, I glanced at my reflection in the glass shower door. Though the big four-oh would happen in another two years, I didn't look close to my age. At five-three, and with my shoulder-length black hair hanging straight, I looked more like an older sister to Liz. Had I been such a disappointment to Robert? We'd married young, right after I discovered I was pregnant. I'd accepted that time had cooled things down. But after all I'd done for him as a lover, a mother, a business partner, I'd thought our marriage was solid.

I pushed aside the lingering doubts that rubbed my mind raw, dressed in my frothy skirt and a sleeveless top, and went downstairs. The girls had set the dining room table. Crystal water goblets, white wine glasses, and sparkling silverware lay at each place atop the white damask tablecloth.

My mouth watered as I slid onto the plush dining room chair Rhonda indicated for me. Tantalizing aromas had wafted from the kitchen all afternoon. She left and reappeared with a golden brown turkey on a huge platter.

"It looks wonderful, Rhonda," I gushed. Her cooking was great.

"Thanks." She set the platter down, then handed me an opened bottle of white wine. "How about taking care of this, Annie? Just make sure you fill mine to the top." Her lips curved impishly. "Leave a little for yourself."

Relieved to be able to do something useful at last, I accepted the bottle and poured the wine out just as the girls finished carrying in the side dishes.

We ate in peaceful silence, each morsel of food worth every calorie.

"I hope Kandie burned their turkey," Liz said out of the blue, and we all laughed. Kandie, the twit, couldn't even heat up something properly in a microwave.

Rhonda raised her wine glass. "Here's to us!"

We clicked glasses and smiled at each other before sipping our wine, well aware of the pain each of us had endured.

At the end of the meal, I took the last bite of my pumpkin pie and dabbed my mouth with my napkin. The girls hastily excused themselves and bolted to meet some of Angie's friends. Sipping coffee, Rhonda and I remained at the table. There was still so much I didn't know about her. With the girls around, we hadn't had much time alone with each other.

"Everything was scrumptious," I said, meaning every word. The woman was a whiz in the kitchen.

She grinned. "It's something creative for me to do. And I have to tell ya, I get bored easily. With Angie away, it's hard for me to fill my days—other than ladies' lunches and that type of thing." She leaned forward. "How about you, Annie? What keeps you busy with Liz away at school?"

"Well, recently I've been struggling with the divorce." A long sigh escaped me. All the changes in my life suddenly felt like a blow to the belly. "In the past, I've helped Robert with our business—consulting for companies regarding their benefit plans. And I've done volunteer work at the local library. Now, I need to find a place to live. Then, I'll have to find work elsewhere to bring in money; I can't trust Robert's support to last. He's promising to make things easy, but I'm sure it's just to keep things simple while he and Kandie set up housekeeping."

"Yeah? What kind of work will you look for?"

Rhonda's interest encouraged me. "I'm not sure. I've been very much a part of Robert's consulting practice, but it was more or less in the background. I don't know if I'll be able to convert that into a paying job."

She gazed at me thoughtfully. "Something will work out, hon."

More comfortable with her now, I blurted out, "After all those years with Robert, I thought my life was settled." I shook my head. "Delivering the news, he was so darn smug. It was bad enough that he'd been fooling around, but, with Kandie? If it weren't so painful, it would be laughable. It's such a typical story—the boss and the bimbo." Tears stung my eyes. "He all but crowed like a rooster when he told me Kandie was pregnant, and they were going to be married as soon as possible. I've always wanted more children, but it never worked out."

Rhonda clucked her tongue. "That's terrible. I thought I was all settled too. Sal and I started out together in high school. Who knew things would get so screwed up?" She rose. "Come on, Annie. It's a beautiful evening, and we can talk some more outside."

I followed Rhonda outside.

She stopped and turned to me. "Men are bastards, aren't they? Let's have an after-dinner drink and toast them, 'cause, bad as they are, I want 'em around."

I wasn't at all sure I'd ever feel that way again. I just wanted to succeed at whatever I chose to do as a single woman, proving to Robert and everyone else I could do very well on my own.

Drinks in hand, we stretched out on long, comfortable chaises by the pool. The early evening air, full of the tang of salt was pleasant as gentle, onshore breezes whispered by us.

"What is your ex like?" I asked. No further mention had been made of him by either Rhonda or Angie.

"Sal? He was a skinny little kid, a real loner in my neighborhood at the Jersey Shore, where we grew up. My brother, Richie, used to bring him home for supper now and then because he lived with his mother, and she worked late. We married right after I graduated from high school. My father wasn't going to put up with Sal just hanging around me, you understand. Not if he wanted to be part of our family's business." She smiled dreamily. "Sal was a really good lover, and we were happy—living in Jersey, working in my family's butcher shop."

"What happened?"

"You don't know?" Rhonda sat up in her chair and faced me with a broad grin. "One hundred eighty- seven million dollars is what happened. That's what!"

Shocked, I rolled to a sitting position.

"Sal and I put aside some money for a vacation in Miami Beach," she explained. "I bought a lottery ticket there. 'No way you're gonna win, Rhonda,' Sal tells me. But I've got a feeling I just might. 'If I win, it's all mine,' I tell him. Sure enough, that Saturday night, they called out my numbers. Sal just sits there like a dummy while I shriek my lungs out. I tell him I'm sick and tired of the cold weather up north, that I want to give the butcher shop to my brother Richie, and come live in Florida."

Rhonda's smile disappeared, replaced by a hurt look I understood all too well. "Money turned Sal into a real asshole. We left the family business, came to Florida, and bought this house, thinking it would be fun to fix it up together and turn it back into a hotel. But he wasn't interested in that. Not really."

She let out a sigh that spoke volumes. "One day, he

announced he was moving to Palm Beach with a young girl he'd met in Fort Myers. Guess those girls saw dollar signs when he drove them past the house, 'cause he let everybody think he had all the money. But, he didn't; I'd been advised by my brother's lawyer to keep all of it in my name, in a trust. Sal told me he didn't care; he'd take enough money to live well, that he just wanted out of the marriage so he could be with someone young and new."

I recognized the haunted look in Rhonda's eyes and reached over and squeezed her hand. "I'm sorry, Rhonda. I really am." I knew very well how much that hurt.

"Me, too. It sucks, don't it?"

I couldn't stop a giggle. All of a sudden, we were laughing together, letting out our pain and sorrow in great, gulping guffaws.

Rhonda leaned over and flung an arm around me. "Ah, Annie, you're not as bad as I thought."

My heart warmed. They were the nicest words anyone had said to me in a very long time.

# CHAPTER TWO

Perhaps because I dreaded what awaited me, the flight home seemed to take no time at all. Too soon, the captain announced preparations for landing. Determined to be strong in the days ahead, I gathered my things—the next few weeks would not be easy. The gray, gloomy weather outside added to my sense of unease.

The girls and I collected our luggage and took a cab to my home in Wellesley, where the driver unceremoniously dumped us and our bags onto the front walkway of the large house I'd always loved. Robert had inherited the house from his parents, but I'd always thought of it as mine. I now understood what a huge mistake that was.

I stood a moment observing the house's height and the Colonial design that had always given me a sense of stability. Sitting so settled on the expansive lawn, it seemed to mock me for thinking I'd live all my days there, protected within its walls from the vagaries of life. The new owners didn't want to move in until after the holidays and a winter vacation, but it still didn't give me much time to undo the house I'd lived in for almost sixteen years.

The next day the girls returned to school, leaving me with a reality I abhorred. I scoured ads in the newspaper, but each time I read about an apartment or townhouse complex, my spirits plummeted, and I was unable to follow through with calls.

The holidays came and went in an emotional blur. Kandie had declared she wouldn't accept second-hand furniture, so

Robert told me to do whatever I wanted with the furnishings in the house; Kandie and he would have all-new, modern furniture as she wanted. Trying to ignore the memories that seeped from every room, I sorted through closets and drawers, preparing to downsize. I still hadn't decided where I wanted to live.

Time dragged and sped up, like a clock whose internal workings had gone haywire. My life, which had seemed so steady and fulfilling, passed in aching loneliness. The friends I once thought would stand by me started to fade away as their weekends and social times were filled with other married couples. My desire to stay close by the neighborhood disappeared, which made my search for living quarters harder.

Surprisingly, Rhonda called every few days, just to say hi. I'd come to understand that her outspoken manner hid a heart of gold and began to enjoy those calls. I think she was lonely too. I hoped, as she did, that she'd find a good man someday. She was a woman who liked having people around her.

One night, I lay in bed staring blankly at a silly reality show on TV. Worry wove through me. I hadn't found a new home, and until I did, I wasn't going to look for a job. Working with Robert was no longer an option.

The phone rang, jarring me out of my whirling, negative thoughts.

"Hi, Annie! It's Rhonda! I didn't catch you in bed, did I? With a man, I mean?" She laughed at her own joke.

I shook my head and chuckled. Rhonda was Rhonda. Only she would say something as outrageous as that.

"Too bad, doll," Rhonda said, catching her breath. "No problem. I've got something to take your mind off men—for a while, anyway. I want you to fly down here as soon as you can. We've gotta talk."

"Rhonda, I can't just pick up and fly down to Florida at a moment's notice. I've got to find a place to live."

"That's why we gotta talk. I'm not going to say anything more until you get here. I'll have my travel agent order you a ticket. How soon can you come?"

"Oh, Rhonda, I don't know ... how can I?"

"Come on! It's beautiful here—sunny and in the low 80's. What do you say? I'm not going to give up until you say yes."

I knew from my past experiences with her that Rhonda wouldn't quit bugging me until I agreed to come. My impatience with her usual pushiness fled. What was the worst thing that could happen to me if I went to Florida for a few days?

Two days later, I sat aboard a flight to Ft. Myers, still amazed at myself for accepting Rhonda's challenge. But then, my whole life had turned upside down. Who was going to stop me from making a rash decision like hopping on a plane at the last minute? Not a single soul. And maybe, as Rhonda said, it was time to have some fun.

As the plane came in for a landing at the Southwest Florida International Airport, I peered out the window. Palm trees swayed in the breeze, welcoming me in their own way. It was such a nice change for me. Curious to know why Rhonda had insisted I come, I picked up my purse and left the plane.

I walked into the baggage claim area and grinned. In a flowing, pastel top and darker green slacks, Rhonda was all but jumping up and down with excitement. She waved, and I hurried over to her.

She threw her arms around me and gave me a good

squeeze. *Funny*, I thought, *after being with Rhonda even a short time, my old friends back home seemed shallow and cold.*

While we waited for my luggage, Rhonda kept grinning at me. I couldn't contain my curiosity. "So, why did you want me to come here?"

She winked at me. "You're not going to believe it! That's all I'm saying for now. I'll tell you all about it at The Beach House."

We stowed my bags, settled ourselves in Rhonda's bright-red Cadillac, and took off from the Ft. Myers airport down I-75 toward Sabal.

Behind the wheel, Rhonda turned to me, her eyes sparkling. "So, Annie, tell me what's happening with your search for a new place. You've found nothing so far?

I shook my head.

"Good." Her mischievous smile made me uneasy. I kept glancing over at her, willing her to spill the news, but she just smiled at me. My curiosity grew. It was so unlike her to hold back on anything.

We entered the drive between the two huge, pink-stucco pillars that secured gilded, wrought-iron gates, and I filled once more with admiration for the home Rhonda casually called "The Beach House." It had, I knew now, thirty-two rooms and stood like a palace, regal and splendid, at the water's edge. We pulled into the circular driveway, and Rhonda parked in front.

At the sound of car doors slamming, a short, wiry man hurried toward us from the side lawn. He wore a loose, white, short-sleeved shirt over dark pants. A straw hat perched on his head shielded his tan face from the sun, but it was unable to quell the sparkle in his dark eyes as he drew closer, a broad smile on his face.

"Ah, here's Manny." Rhonda grinned. "My Manny around the house."

Manny laughed good-naturedly. "Welcome." He gave me a little bow and took my suitcase, carrying it around to the side of the house.

Rhonda and I climbed the front steps. Inside the entry, I took in the view across the white and black marble floor, across the cream-colored Oriental rug in the huge living room, and through the series of sliding doors out to the large pool. Seeing the pool and the sparkling blue waters of the Gulf again, my admiration grew. It was everything I'd remembered—and more. I took a deep breath of salty air, feeling the stress of the last few weeks ease.

"You're in the same room as last time. Hurry, Annie! Go get changed. I'll fix a light lunch for us, and then I'll tell you what's on my mind. We have lots to talk about."

I climbed the stairs and walked into the room I'd come to think of as mine. My suitcase was already resting on a luggage rack in the room. I took off my winter clothes, slipped on a pair of light shorts and a T-shirt, and happily wiggled my bare toes in the warm air.

"Annie! Annie! Aren't you ready yet?" Rhonda called from the bottom of the stairs. "C'mon! I've got lunch ready! We can eat and talk at the same time! Hurry!"

I felt like a young girl as I all but skipped down the stairs. It was good to be back in Sabal. Looking at the splendor around me, I felt less in awe of the luxurious surroundings than I had during my first visit. The house, though impressive in size and décor, had a surprisingly homey air.

I walked out onto the pool deck.

"Sit down, Annie. We gotta talk." Rhonda indicated a chair at the glass-topped table.

Plates laden with chicken salad, sliced tomatoes, and

frosty-cold, green grapes sat at each place, along with a tall glass of iced tea.

I'd no sooner taken a bite of my chicken salad than Rhonda said," Okay, here it is. My plan is for us to open The Beach House as a bed and breakfast, or maybe a small, boutique hotel, the two of us, with you living here on the grounds."

I choked on the salad and reached for the glass of tea. *Starting a new business? Rhonda and I working together every day? Living together? Impossible!*

"It would be a whole new start for each of us. You've got the class, and, from what you told me earlier, you have the business experience. I've got the place. Whaddya say?" Her voice rose with excitement. "It's time for me to do something meaningful with my life. I've dreamed of running a place like this since I was a kid, cooking with my mother."

Trying to come up with a polite way of saying no, I took another sip of iced tea.

Rhonda leaned forward. "Listen, Annie; I need you. Money alone can't make it work. I know that. You're the other half of the equation. I'm not afraid of hard work, but I need guidance, and, God knows, I'm bored to tears with Angie away. C'mon! Whaddya say? Huh?" She squeezed my hand so hard I winced.

My mind raced. The idea was intriguing, but it would never work. Not with the two of us.

But ... the idea of turning The Beach House into an elegant bed and breakfast place, or better yet, a small hotel, was very enticing to someone who had no home, no plans, no future. The elegant house with its fine appointments, beach frontage, balconies as part of the individual bedrooms, the expanse of private grounds, all lent themselves to a stunning possibility.

"C'mon! What do you think?" Rhonda's voice rose with impatience.

I reluctantly shook my head. "I don't think so."

Rhonda jumped up, rushed over to me and tugged me to my feet. "Forget lunch. I've got some things to show you. I've been thinking about this ever since you left!"

She grabbed my hand and pulled me through a tall hedge of oleander and hibiscus. A small house, an old caretaker's cottage I surmised, stood in disrepair. Hidden as it was behind the tropical growth, it hadn't been noticeable on my previous visit.

"This is where you can live." Rhonda indicated the structure with a flourish. "I've had an architect look at it and draw up some plans for renovating it. It's yours if you want to buy it for a reasonable price and pay for the renovations." Rhonda flung an arm across my shoulders and grinned. "I knew you wouldn't allow me to just give it to you. You're too damned independent for that!"

Speechless, I looked from her to the cottage, trying to absorb the impact of her words. It needed work, true, but in my mind's eye, I could already envision what it would look like with a new roof, new paint, and landscaping. It could be beautiful! Absolutely beautiful!

"What do you say? And look at this!" Rhonda dragged me by the arm past the front of the main house to the other side of her yard to a multi-car garage. "There, at the end of the garage, is where we can put a laundry and extra storage. And listen to this, upstairs we can create an apartment for Manny and his wife, Consuela. She works for me, too. We even have room for another, smaller apartment for another staff member."

She then hurried me to the front of The Beach House and pointed to the circle of lawn. "A landscape architect came and looked at the grounds. He told me he could plant a putting green in the front circle. And we can have horseshoes and a shuffleboard court behind the garage and new parking on the other side of the garage, south of the tennis court. Thank God, the court is in great condition already. You should see his plans! It's going to be perfect! What do you think? Huh?"

I stood in a daze beside Rhonda, taking in the scene, feeling like a game-show winner having all my prizes described to me one by one. My imagination took over, and I could envision how lovely it would be. It was beautiful already.

The entire property was enclosed by high, pink-stucco walls—tall enough to give total privacy to the lush grounds surrounding the enormous house, whose massive pink and white façade drew my attention. A broad expanse of tiled roof and countless windows lined its front, making the house appear to extend endlessly. Over-sized wooden doors stood guard at the top of wide, marble stairs. Potted palms sat on either side of the door, balancing its height and softening its edges.

"Well, Annie?" Rhonda gave me a pleading look.

It was, I realized, the chance of a lifetime—for anyone else. I let out a disappointed sigh. Rhonda and I, with all our differences and my lack of money, would never be able to make it work.

Not in a tricky business like this.

# CHAPTER THREE

I returned to Boston telling myself I'd made a wise decision not to join forces with Rhonda. But ideas about what The Beach House could be like as a boutique hotel continued to dance in my head. At those moments, my practical side took over, and I forced myself to focus on finding a new place to live. I was running out of time.

Rhonda called every day to check on me.

When I told her the townhouse I liked was sold out from under me, she said, "This is a sign, Annie. You come down here, and we'll work things out. I want you in business with me. You agreed The Beach House would be perfect as a small hotel. Like I said, you're the classy one with the business background. We can make it work together. I know we can."

I listened to her eagerness, and a whisper of hope came to me. Maybe I could make it work between Rhonda and me. As different as we were, I recognized that beneath her bossy manner there was decency, kindness, and caring. It might be just what I needed at this time in my life.

"But I'd need money to become a real partner and buy the cottage," I said, pulled back to stark reality. "I couldn't accept any from you. That's no way to start a business. I have to be able to be a partner in the true sense of the word." My voice caught as the truth of what I'd said hit me like a blow to the head. "Thanks, anyway, Rhonda. That's real sweet of you."

We hung up. My mind numb, I dragged myself to the shower. I had invested the bulk of my small inheritance from my grandmother in Robert's and my consulting company. At the time, I'd happily agreed to use the money in this way. I knew it would please my grandmother that her money was helping to build a strong foundation for a marriage that would last forever. How stupid of me.

The Rutherford Company board meeting was taking place on the last day of the month. I told myself I had every right to be there as I entered the empty boardroom and sat in my usual seat at the large, oval, mahogany conference table. Waiting for the others to arrive, I admired the muted beige and mauve colors I'd picked out for the boardroom a few years earlier. Seascapes of Maine and an oil painting of the New Hampshire Mountains accented the walls and reminded me of a happier time when Robert and I had bought them together.

Other board members arrived. Polite small talk centered on the horrible winter weather that seemed to hang over the city like a gray, wet blanket, making us wish for warm, blue-sky, August days.

My pleasure at seeing the other people evaporated when Kandie walked into the room. I stiffened and wondered what she was doing in this meeting. I took a deep breath and fought the urge to yank her hair out, one dyed strand after another.

A rush of cold air from the outside followed a tall, white-haired man into the room. He stopped and frowned at Kandie, then took a seat beside me.

I warmed to his quick kiss on the cheek. Kevin O'Donnell had always been one of my biggest supporters. He leaned over and whispered, "I want you to know how sorry I am about the divorce. Robert is an ass."

Unable to trust myself to speak, I merely nodded.

Robert was the last to enter the meeting. He stood by Kandie's chair. Jaw flexing, he gave me a defiant stare and laid a hand on Kandie's shoulder.

My stomach flamed with acid. He was acting as if he were showing off a prize he'd just stolen.

Shifting uncomfortably in their seats, the others in the room glanced from him to me and back to him. "Kandie is going to take minutes for the meeting," said Robert, emphatically. "Now that she's part of the family, it's important for her to get up to speed on what's going on."

As Kandie looked over at me with a cutting smile of triumph, Kevin reached over and covered my hand with his. I wanted to cry at the soft touch of compassion.

Robert scowled at us. "Okay, let's get down to business."

I willed myself not to look at Kandie, who sat beside Robert as if that were her rightful place. Bile rose in my throat. For a business course in my sophomore year at Northeastern University, I'd formed a dummy corporation on paper, developed a business plan for it, and designed consulting services to corporations and smaller companies to help them theoretically develop benefits packages for their employees. I'd been dating Robert seriously by then, and he'd liked the idea so much, he'd taken it as his own and set up The Rutherford Company, with himself as President. He'd rationalized that a man in business presented a stronger front and gave me the role of Vice President. We'd worked day and night to get the business up and running and to keep it going. I still owned a large amount of stock in the corporation.

As I focused on Robert's words, alarm grew within me. In the last year, there'd been a dramatic decrease in the number of new clients. Consulting depended in large part on not only what projects you were working on, but what was in the pipeline. And of those projects in the pipeline, at least fifty percent of them would produce less than expected. As Robert continued to lay out a plan that didn't take this into account, I felt I had to speak up. My survival depended on it.

"Robert, I'm concerned we haven't changed the focus of our consulting program. With the need to place a strong emphasis on providing better and more diverse services to clients, shouldn't we be changing our format a bit?"

Disagreements between us were not unknown, but Robert reacted as if I'd slapped his face. He glared at me. His cheeks turned an unhealthy red. Beside him, Kandie huffed and puffed noisily. The others at the table stirred restlessly.

Robert scowled at me. "As I recall, Ann, you didn't attend the last board meeting. If you had, you would've been able to hear for yourself exactly why we're going to continue on our present course. Our clients have traditionally been the big guys, and they have pretty much the same agendas they've always had, with some minor modifications, of course."

I knew his thinking was flawed. The economy had changed, and so had the accepted wisdom in business. Hoping to draw support from the other board members, I prepared to speak again. I knew it would irritate Robert, but I couldn't let it go.

"I'd feel much more comfortable if we explored different ways we can address companies of all sizes, not just the big guys. We need to broaden our base."

A shocked silence filled the room. Robert had never taken kindly to board members questioning him. But I held firm. With the stock I owned in the company, I needed to think of my future.

"Ann may have a valid point there," said Kevin O'Donnell.

"I say she's more or less out of the loop now," Robert responded with barely concealed fury. "Perhaps it's time for her to do something else and stay out of this business."

My lips tightened. Why hadn't I seen how selfish, how childish he'd been in the past? Furious, I gave him a fixed stare. "I hope everyone here realizes that I, not you, conceived the idea for this company."

Robert looked as if he were ready to lunge across the table and strike me. The only sound now was the restless twitching of the Board members stirring in their seats.

I fumed. He was going to let our personal problems override our business association. I barely listened to the rest of the meeting. My worries about the company were sincere. It was essential for us to reassess our *modus operandi* to cope with the changes in the economy—local, national, and worldwide.

"Anything else?" Robert was saying as I focused back in on the meeting. "If not, the meeting is adjourned."

The other board members jumped to their feet, obviously relieved the meeting had ended without another major confrontation between Robert and me. I remained in my seat, fixated by an idea taking shape in my mind. Could I pull it off?

"Ann? Did you hear me?"

I blinked. The others had gone, leaving Robert, Kandie, and me in the conference room.

I rose. "Robert, do you have a moment? I'd like to discuss something with you. Alone."

A pout formed on Kandie's lips. "We're going to lunch, Robert." She patted her round stomach and gave him a smile. "You promised the baby and me."

It took all my willpower not to slap her. I kept my voice low, controlled. "I need to talk to you now, Robert. It can't wait."

Robert frowned. "If you're going to bring up the business

with the mortgage on the house, I'm not going to listen. That's a done deal."

"No, no. This is something else." I silently vowed it would be different, that Robert would never take advantage of me again.

Robert looked at Kandie and shrugged, then turned back to me. "Okay, but you'd better be quick about it."

We went into his office. Forcing myself to arrange my features in a pleasant smile, I sat facing him. My pulse quickened. This had to work.

"Well?" Robert leaned back in his chair and looked at me suspiciously. "I'm waiting."

I swallowed nervously. "I realized you meant what you said at the board meeting about my doing something else. You'd be happy to be rid of me, wouldn't you?"

Robert's eyes brightened. He pulled his shoulders back and gave me a condescending look. "We both know it's not working very well. You've changed. You challenged everything I said today."

I bit my tongue. I remembered only too well how much he'd depended on my opinions in the past, the many discussions we'd had in the privacy of our home, the exchange of ideas he'd sought. My input was one of the reasons the company had been so successful. I'd been proud of my contribution. But how foolish I'd been to let everyone believe Robert knew it all.

"I had to speak up, Robert. I'm not happy with the plan for the year."

Robert's eyes turned dark, unfriendly. He looked at me as if I were a complete stranger.

"If you're not happy with the way I'm doing things, maybe it's time for you to move on."

Elation, warm and thick, flooded through me. Knowing

how perverse Robert could be, I tried not to show it. "Maybe it's time for me to leave the business. But it has to be a fair agreement. And this time, Robert, everything we agree on must be put into writing. Understood?"

"You're serious about this?"

"It might be best," I said, watching a grin spread across his face.

An hour later, Robert and I stood face to face.

Robert shook his head. "You're a fool, Ann. This company is going to continue to grow, and you're going to lose out."

Refusing to take the bait, I closed the door to Robert's office behind me and faced a furious, toe-tapping Kandie. Giddy with relief, I gave her a broad smile and patted my purse. Inside was a signed letter of intent for Robert to buy me out of the business he was too egotistical to change.

# CHAPTER FOUR

"Hey, Annie!" Rhonda called from the bottom of the stairway. "You finished changing yet? You wanna take a walk on the beach? The sun is going to set soon. Maybe we can see the green flash!"

"Hold on! I'll be right down!" I went back to drying myself off with a thick towel. It still surprised me that I'd managed to talk Robert into buying my shares of stock in the company. Even though he would make the payments in installments, it meant I could come to Florida, take part in the hotel business, and fix up the cottage. And, truth be told, I wanted out of the company before Robert realized I'd been right all along, that they had to make some changes or face the consequences.

I slipped a pale-yellow tank top over my head and pulled on a long peasant skirt in a luscious shade of azure and hurried down the stairs.

"What's the green flash?"

Rhonda grinned. "They say if the atmosphere is just right, you can see a bright-green flash at the moment the sun dips beneath the horizon. I've never seen it, but I never get tired of looking for it."

"Sounds intriguing. Let's go."

We walked out onto the beach. Rhonda threw an arm over my shoulder. "You know, Annie, I'm awful glad you're here. For a while, I wasn't sure you were going to make it. I sure am lucky you're gonna be my partner in this project. We'll make a good team. I know it!"

I glanced at Rhonda out of the corner of my eye. It had taken a huge leap of faith for me to come to Florida, but I had little choice. Finding a home and making a living were the reasons behind my decision. I was determined to make it work. Rhonda, too. After being hurt by the men we'd trusted, we each had strong reasons for wanting to show the world we could make something of our lives on our own.

The sand was white and velvety smooth on my bare feet as we strolled along the water's frothy edge. From a distance, I turned and looked back at The Beach House. The mansion's beautiful, pink expanse was awe inspiring. The tall, swaying palm trees lining the beach, the warm caress of the evening breeze, and the oranges and reds of the setting sun, like strokes of paint coloring the canvas of the darkening sky, filled me with gratitude. At moments like this, I wanted to pinch myself to make sure I wasn't dreaming.

"Hi, Rhonda!" A tall, well-built, gray-haired man wearing a bathing suit strode toward us.

"Well hello, Brock," Rhonda smiled prettily as he joined us. "It looks like it's going to be another beautiful sunset on the Gulf. Say hello to my friend, Ann Rutherford. Her daughter, Liz, and my Angie are roommates at Boston University. Ann's going to be our new neighbor."

"Oh? Is that why you're fixing up that little cottage on your property?"

Rhonda smiled and nodded. "She's going to live there."

Brock turned to me. The setting sun cast a golden glow on his handsome, classic features. His tanned, muscular physique was shown to good advantage in the bright-blue bathing suit that clung to his trim figure. His green eyes crinkled at their corners as he smiled warmly at me. His gaze met mine and lingered.

My cheeks grew hot as I realized I'd been staring.

"Welcome to Sabal," he said. "I'm sure you're going to love it here." He turned to Rhonda. "Maybe you two lovely ladies would come for drinks one night this week. How about it, Rhonda?"

She gave him a playful punch on the arm. "Oh, come on! You mean you'd like Annie to come for drinks. I see the sparkle in your eye, Brock Goodwin, and it has nothing to do with me!"

Brock leaned over and gave Rhonda a kiss on the cheek. "Darling, you always bring a sparkle to my eyes."

Rhonda laughed. "Who can resist charm like that? Okay, let us know when, and we'll be there."

"You're on! I'll give you a call." Brock gave me another once-over that sent heat snaking through my body.

As if he knew the response he'd had on me, he winked and walked away, whistling.

"He used to work for a large import company. He still does some work for them, traveling to faraway exotic places on buying trips. When he's here, he's everybody's favorite extra guy. You can see why."

"He's very attractive," I said, watching him stroll down the beach, waving to people. I was still surprised by the way my body had responded to his blatant admiration. It had been a long time since a man had looked at me that way. Not that I wanted anything to come of it. I thought of Robert and all he'd done to hurt me, and a bitter taste coated my tongue.

"He's such a bullshitter, but everybody seems to like him," continued Rhonda. "Being president of the Gold Coast Neighborhood Association gives him a lot of power, and he likes it. That's why I didn't mention the hotel. Not until we get our final permits."

###

Rhonda and I sat in the makeshift office we'd set up in The Beach House library, going over the construction schedule, checking progress against our projected opening. It would be a huge push, but we wanted plenty of time to run the hotel in the off-season to get the kinks out before the winter season began.

Rhonda, in her usual unrestrained manner, had already begun making changes to the house, figuring they'd enhance the value of it, regardless of how the hotel aspect worked out. She'd had an architect design a large dining room and an office, which would be added on to the house behind the kitchen. As far as anyone else knew, she was merely renovating her house and the cottage on her property.

Most mornings I awoke to the sounds of men working. On this particular morning, I rose early, walked the beach and, after a quick shower, shared a simple breakfast of fresh fruit, coffee, and bagels with Rhonda.

She nudged me. "Grab a second cup of coffee, and let's go check on things."

Outside, a crew of men was smoothing concrete on a newly poured pad for the new dining room. Studying the slab, I measured in my mind's eye how many people the room would hold and hoped the day would soon come when we could seat such a crowd for a meal. Without money coming in, each exciting bit of progress on the house added a strain to my nerves.

Going into business, starting the process with a promise of money paid out over time from Robert, was one of the scariest things I'd ever done. But I understood the company couldn't afford to do a payout in one lump sum. And Rhonda didn't want to waste a minute before getting the project started.

We left the workmen and walked over to where the

cottage stood. Gutted, it looked forlorn with no interior walls. Exposed wiring hung on hooks, like threads of a broken spider web.

Rhonda threw an arm around my shoulder. "Lookin' pretty bad, but it's gonna be real nice. I just know it."

"I hope so."

Later, we met with Rhonda's tax consultant. His unpretentious office sat over a clothing store on one of the side streets off the main drag. Kenneth Small looked exactly like his name—short and compact. Close to retirement, he exuded an air of quiet confidence as he discussed the basic agreements in forming an LLC and talked to us about everything from tax impacts to long-range planning. His voice droned on and on.

Rhonda looked as confused as I felt.

Kenneth's expression turned grim. He turned to Rhonda. "You should never have contracted to have the work done on the house without first having your agreement with Ann squared away. You say the lawyer should have that by the end of the week?"

Looking like a chastised middle-grader, Rhonda nodded.

Kenneth looked me in the eye. "I can tell you're not about to take advantage of Rhonda, but that isn't always the case for a wealthy woman like her. The truth is, most of Rhonda's money is tied up in trusts and other non-liquid forms."

"I understand. Believe me; I want to be able to make this project work for both of us," I said calmly, but I felt attacked.

He gave me a look of satisfaction. "All right. Now let's talk about the bookkeeping system you're going to use."

By the time we left his office, I was nursing a headache.

We drove home in silence.

After changing into more comfortable clothes, I sat out on the pool deck with Rhonda. She'd mixed up a batch of margaritas. I sipped mine, trying to remain calm as Kenneth Small's warnings repeated themselves in my mind. The hotel business was risky, and I knew it.

"Do you think we can do it, Annie?" Rhonda gave me a worried look.

Telling myself we had a fighting chance, I pushed aside lingering doubt. "Before I left Boston, I talked to a neighbor of mine, a hospitality consultant. He agreed with our concept in principle. It fills a niche in the marketplace. A small, luxurious hotel like ours will be a nice alternative for people who want to escape their daily routines, unwind in a tropical atmosphere, and stay in a more relaxed, estate-like setting."

The jangling of the phone stopped our conversation. Rhonda answered it and handed the phone to me. "Your lawyer."

"Ann? Syd Green here. We have a bit of a problem. I thought the agreement for the sale of your company stock was all set to sign, but now Robert is claiming that with the bad year they've had, he's had to rethink things. He says the real value of your stock is lower than appraised. He doesn't think you should've been given so much stock anyway because your help in the business was nothing more than secretarial work, even at the beginning."

My headache sprang to life. I grabbed onto the edge of the glass-topped table. "That's not true! He could never have had the company up and running if I hadn't been there, working beside him. And it was a lot more than typing and filing! I set up his whole advertising campaign, from magazine and newspaper ads to meeting with various businesses. I organized all office procedures, everything. It was my original idea to begin with, and I worked to make it real. It was mostly my money that helped give him his start. I want my full share, Syd!"

"I understand, but I'm warning you that the deal may fall through. Your letter of intent is non-binding. It's based on the appraisal. Robert says he's not accepting the appraisal he was given. Trying to fight it would be counter-productive. Let's work with him on this."

Acid pooled in my stomach. Robert had become such a liar I didn't know him anymore.

"What about it, Ann?"

I didn't have much choice. If I tried to fight it, the lawyers would take any gain I might receive. "All right. I need the money to go ahead with this project down here. But I'm telling you, it's not fair!"

"Life isn't always fair, Ann. Think it over. Sometimes, we have to make compromises." Syd's calm voice made me grit my teeth as he continued. "I admit I don't understand Robert's attitude because I'm well aware of all you did to help him out. If it's any comfort to you, I feel he owes it to you to do the right thing. But that's not happening. Let me see what I can do. I'll get you the most money I can."

I hung up the phone and burst into tears. Without the sale Robert and I had agreed on, I didn't know how I'd come up with the money Kenneth Small had insisted we have before beginning the project. Fixing up the cottage was an additional problem.

I told Rhonda the gist of the conversation.

She gave me a pat on the back. "We gotta keep moving forward, Annie. We can't stop now."

"I know." But I felt as if I were swimming upstream in a raging river.

Over the next few days, I concentrated on drawing up a business plan for the hotel. Rhonda had insisted we apply for a business loan, and I wanted to be prepared. I poured my heart and soul into the details of the plan, praying the optimistic projections we made could succeed, and the plan I outlined step by step was not the result of mindless imaginings. I'd made the move to Florida intent on making the project work, and now, I might not even be allowed to try.

# CHAPTER FIVE

After much discussion and many revisions to our business plan, Rhonda and I went to the Main Street Bank. If our meeting here was not successful, I might not be able to stay in Florida as part owner of the hotel. The receptionist took our names, made a phone call, and then an attractive young woman appeared to greet us. She led us into a board room oozing Bahamian charm with its dark-green carpeting, pale-pink walls, and a mural of palms and tropical plants.

"Mr. Rice will be with you shortly," she announced cheerfully and left us.

I wiped my sweaty palms on the skirt of my gray linen dress and paced the room. A leather notebook, filled with our business plan and other documents, lay on the table before me.

Rhonda gave me a pat on the back. "Don't worry, Annie. They know me here."

A tall, debonair man with white hair and a golf-course tan entered the room and beamed at Rhonda. "Good to see you again, Rhonda. Very good, indeed. And who is this lovely young lady?"

"Hi, Bob." Rhonda placed a hand on my shoulder. "This is my business partner, Annie Rutherford."

I shook hands with him and took a seat at the table next to Rhonda, facing him.

"Well, then. What can we do for you today, Rhonda? I must say, I'm curious to know about the business you wanted to talk to me about."

Rhonda explained what we had in mind with such eagerness I couldn't help smiling. She handed him our business plan and continued talking, waving her hands excitedly, flooding him with information. In her enthusiasm, she said a few things that weren't exactly correct, but the documents she'd handed him were. Rhonda stopped talking.

Bob took a few moments to look over my resume and then focused his attention on me. "Interesting, Ms. Rutherford. I'm amazed at all the work you did in setting up the business with your husband."

His smile filled me with pride. After spending years downplaying my role in the business to build Robert up, it had been a revelation to me to see what skills I'd used to accomplish all of it. I took over the discussion with Bob, detailing my business background and experience with more confidence, trying to convince him that what I could bring to the table was valuable. I told him I'd consulted with an expert on the viability of such a project, and the financial projections I laid out for the first two years were achievable.

He gave me a perfunctory smile and turned to Rhonda. "As much as I admire Ms. Rutherford's experience and yours, you understand there's no way we could consider making a loan to the two of you unless we were assured that you would continue to bank with us. And we would need to use the hotel as collateral. Of course, the fact that you have several large accounts here is very important to us."

Feeling as if I'd been kicked in the stomach, I collapsed against the back of my chair. He'd apparently dismissed everything I'd said.

Rhonda glanced my way and turned back to Bob. "So," she said in icy tones, "I keep my money here, and we get the loan. Is that it?"

His cheeks turned bright red. "Well, I didn't mean that in so many words ..."

Rhonda shrugged. "I just want to get it straight ... you know, make sure we understand each other because I can always take my money elsewhere."

His face blanched. "Oh, my! I want to assure you we never considered refusing you a loan. A good customer like you ..."

Rhonda turned to me and rose. "Well, partner, that's set. Shall we go?"

Bob rose to his feet and stood beside the door. "We'll have the paperwork ready for you to sign first thing tomorrow."

"At your best rate and terms." She smiled sweetly at him, and I wanted to kiss her.

"Thank you, Bob," I said, trying my best to be civil. "We appreciate your support."

Outside, I grinned at Rhonda. "You were wonderful!"

She shook her fist. "The prick! What did he think he was doing? It made me sick, the way he treated us!"

I silently vowed that even if it meant working day and night, I'd make the hotel a success.


I arose early and dressed, eager to see the cottage before the workmen arrived. I tiptoed outside and, stretching, took a moment to breathe in the cool, salty air. Another winter storm had hit the north, and Robert would, no doubt, be shoveling snow. Maybe, I thought meanly, he'd have a heart attack and die.

As I pushed through the hedge and paused, a wave of happiness washed over me. The small, stucco cottage would soon be mine. I walked up to it and entered through the front door. A wide-open space greeted me, broken here and there by studs for the new walls. Seeing the drawings on paper start to come to life, I could hardly wait to move in.

Determined to make things right, I returned to the main house to give Syd Green a call. I'd yet to hear from him regarding a compromise with Robert. My heart sank at the thought of giving up my new life in Florida. I greeted Consuela, already at work in the kitchen, grabbed a cup of coffee, and headed to the library to make my call. I punched in Syd's number and waited nervously for him to answer.

"Sorry, Mr. Green is out of the office today and won't be back until Monday," his secretary told me.

Sick with disappointment, I let out a long sigh. If he'd heard any good news, Syd would've called. I calmed myself and settled behind the desk to review our plans—plans that might or might not take place.

Later that day, Rhonda and I arrived at Brock's house just after six o'clock. Several cars were parked along both sides of the street and in his driveway. The sound of jazz floated through the open doorway of the sprawling, single-story, Spanish-style home.

Brock's face lit with pleasure at the sight of us. Rhonda kissed him lightly on the cheek and gave him a playful punch on the shoulder. "I thought it was going to be a small get-together. I had no idea it was going to be an all-out party!"

Brock laughed. "You know how these things grow down here. If you ask one or two people, suddenly it's three or four, and more and more. Anyway, it seemed like a good payback time for all those dinners I'm always invited to attend."

He lifted my hand and kissed the back of it. "Even with all these other people here, I have no intention of ignoring you." His gaze lingered over me. "You look lovely tonight."

My black silk pants and pale-blue silk shirt had seemed plain next to Rhonda's colorful print caftan, but now, I was glad I'd worn them. My skin was a golden brown from the sun, and my eyes were offset by the blue of the shirt. The simple pearl earrings and the strand of pearls around my neck completed an outfit that would win even my grandmother's approval.

After Brock had greeted all his guests, he approached me. "Let me give you a tour of the homestead."

A wing off to the right contained a large master suite that opened up onto the lanai. Two guest suites sat in the opposite wing. The kitchen, living room, dining room, and small library were overflowing with guests, but I was able to see the many art objects displayed in glass cases or placed strategically in niches here and there.

I pointed to what looked like an ancient pottery piece of a god or goddess of some kind, sitting on a shelf in the library. "It's lovely."

He smiled. "Not as lovely as you. I'm hoping we can become friends—very good friends. I'm leaving in a couple of days to go up north. My company needs me, but I'll be back in time for Rhonda's annual spring party. After that, perhaps you'd consent to have dinner with me here, alone?"

At the way he was looking at me, my hands and feet turned cold. I wasn't ready for a real date. Not now, maybe never. "I'd have to check with Rhonda. I'm staying with her for the time being, and I wouldn't want to appear to be rude."

Brock laughed softly and gave me a wink. "Leave Rhonda to me. It'll be okay. I promise you."

I smiled, but my insides did somersaults at the idea of dating him or anyone else.

Our days became filled with preparation for the annual

brunch Rhonda held as a farewell to the snowbirds and a salute to year-round folks. She'd proudly told me it had become a tradition in Sabal.

Under Rhonda's supervision, Consuela and I kept busy in the kitchen chopping, stirring, and tasting the dishes we were cooking and freezing ahead. It pleased me to see us all working together.

As the time of the party drew near, I decided to go into town to look for something new to wear to the party— something more in keeping with the resort atmosphere. My conservative wardrobe from Boston seemed out of place among tropical palms.

The air felt good as I walked briskly, enjoying the exercise. It was a pretty little town, filled with unique shops, galleries, and restaurants. I strolled along Palm Avenue taking in the sights. I stopped outside one of the shops and studied the two-piece outfit in the window. The softly draped, light-green pants were paired with a sleeveless top with a scooped neckline. Sparkling rhinestones were strategically placed among its colorful, tropical, floral design.

I went inside, and a short time later, I walked out of the store with the outfit. Not only did it fit perfectly, it was on sale. Robert would never have approved of anything so flashy, but I was pretty sure Rhonda would.

When Rhonda saw the outfit, she gave me a hug. "You're coming along, Annie. It's perfect for you. Too bad we're not the same size; I'd borrow it from you."

My smile wavered. *Had I overdone it?*

She looked at me, and we laughed together.


The day of the party, Manny was kept busy outside, helping to park cars. A policeman directed traffic on the street. I stood inside the front doorway, amazed by the number and variety of people who greeted Rhonda at the top of the steps with warm embraces. Even the mayor of Sabal embraced her with enthusiasm.

A priest arrived, and after greeting Rhonda, introduced himself to me as Father Hennessey. He stood beside me, a fond expression on his face as he watched Rhonda greet other guests.

"Such a good soul she has," he murmured.

A short, round, gray-haired woman approached us.

"How are you, Mrs. Stern?" said Father Hennessey.

"Fine thanks." She turned to me. "Who are you?"

I smiled and held out my hand. "Ann Rutherford, from Boston. My daughter, Liz, and Angie are roommates at college. That's how I met Rhonda." We'd agreed earlier not to mention the hotel or our business partnership until we had our final approvals.

"I'm Dorothy Stern, and any friend of Rhonda's is a friend of mine. She's been a huge blessing to so many of us." She inspected me through glasses whose thick lenses made her eyes seem as big as golf balls. "Your outfit is stunning. Very Florida," she said before moving away.

Father Hennessey and I exchanged amused glances.

A number of people approached him, and I wandered over to the buffet table. Each tray was garnished with parsley or other herbs or, like the individual miniature mushroom quiches, enhanced with hibiscus blossoms.

"Hello there," came a familiar voice in my ear. "Mmm, good enough to eat." Brock leered at me playfully, as if he'd been talking about me and not the food.

I laughed and felt an unexpected chill race down my spine.

"Let's go outside, shall we?" Brook took my elbow and

guided me through the crowded living room, onto the lanai.

A few people were circling the pool with their drinks. Others were admiring the view of the ocean and the lush landscaping.

"Have a seat here in the shade," said Brock. "I'll run inside and get us each a plateful of food. I don't want to miss tasting a thing. Rhonda's a fabulous cook."

I watched his long, easy strides as he walked away, and noted how many of the women in the group followed him with their eyes. My thoughts drifted back to the time I'd taken Robert home to meet my grandmother. He'd charmed her and all of her friends with smooth talk and easy grace. Robert wasn't as handsome as Brock, but they shared a certain sureness about them that translated into a worldly take-charge manner that most people found attractive.

"A penny for your thoughts," said Brock, returning to the table and handing me a plate with a full sampling of food.

"Just thinking about several things," I answered truthfully.

Brock gave me a pleased grin. "I hope it was something good. I have every intention of enticing you away from here for dinner Monday night. You'll agree to come, won't you?"

I hesitated, then nodded. I had no desire to get involved with anyone else so soon, but it sounded like a pleasant evening.

"I'd love to show you around the area," he continued. "Florida is a surprising place, filled with interesting spots one could miss driving by, except for Orlando, of course. There, Mickey rules."

I laughed. It felt good to chat with a handsome man. I'd almost forgotten what it was like to flirt with someone. But that's all it was, a few moments to enjoy. I had no time for anything else. Not with possible financial disaster hovering over me.

After everyone left the party, I went through the house with Rhonda and Consuela, straightening and picking up champagne flutes and other drink glasses that had been missed.

"What did you think of my party, Annie?" Rhonda said, smiling.

I looked around the room where not long ago a substantial crowd had gathered. "It was fabulous, Rhonda. And now I know The Beach House is perfect, absolutely perfect, for what we're planning."

Rhonda kicked off her sandals, plopped down on the couch and grinned at me. "Told ya."

I laughed and lowered myself onto the couch beside her, feeling more and more comfortable with our decision to go ahead with the hotel.

Later, after Manny and Consuela and the rest of the staff had left, Rhonda and I relaxed around the pool in our bathing suits. The late afternoon sun felt good on my shoulders as I sipped iced tea and dangled my feet in the water.

"Tell me about Dorothy Stern," I said to Rhonda. "She's a big fan of yours."

"Dorothy's something else. She lives in a small apartment not far from here. She has some health issues, mostly with diabetes. I found out that some people living in her building have problems of a different kind, and Dorothy and I sorta helped them out." Rhonda's cheeks turned a shade of pink, and I realized she was embarrassed.

I smiled, liking this new shyer side of her.

# CHAPTER SIX

My heart pounding, I sat up in bed and took a steadying breath. I'd dreamed I was being chased by a monster, and no matter how fast I tried to run, I couldn't move. Not with huge rocks strapped to my feet. I knew the significance of my dream. I still hadn't received money from Robert and was worried I'd fail. I got up and poured myself a glass of water, trying to control the images that wouldn't leave my mind.

During breakfast I kept checking the clock, waiting for a decent time to call Syd Green. I swallowed the last of my coffee, went into the library, and phoned his office.

After exchanging greetings with me, Syd cleared his throat. "'Glad you called. I've worked out a deal with Robert. I hope you'll approve."

I held my breath.

"Rather than the fifty percent of the stock value, we've agreed that your share will be forty percent. Robert wants more recognition for running the business all those years."

"But ..."

"Listen to me, Ann," interjected Syd, not unkindly. "I had to work hard to get even that, by forcing Robert to admit that he continued to seek and obtain your advice on most material financial matters throughout the years. This is far better than doing battle with him. That would cost you more than the ten percent he's fighting for."

I bit back a bitter reply, but I knew now that it was up to me to fight for everything I could.

"What about the payments? I hope that stayed the same." It was difficult to force the words out between my clenched jaws. "He's to pay me one-half now and the second half in three installments over the next twelve months. I will need every penny of it."

"He's agreed to that. Apparently, he's anxious to pay you off. With the birth of his little boy, he has another college education to think of in the future."

I gasped at those hurtful words. I'd wanted more children, but had lost two after Liz.

"As I've pointed out to him on several occasions, he's getting off easy," Syd continued. "With that payment to you, he has no alimony and limited child support. He does have to provide health insurance for Liz and pay for her education, which has already been taken care of with the sale of the house. He knows he's in a good position; he just doesn't want to admit it. So relax and go on with your project. Good luck, Ann! You deserve it!"

I hung up the phone and let out a trembling sigh. Within a year, I'd be free of Robert. Hopefully, I'd never have to ask him for another thing.

Rhonda poked her head into the library. "Ready, Annie? Drew's here."

Drew Carter was the architect Rhonda had hired for the hotel project. Young enough to be flexible, talented beyond his years, he was the perfect person to do the work for us. I'd even hired him to help me with the renovation of the cottage.

Drew came into the room and unrolled the new plans he'd drawn up. He laid them across the large table we'd placed in the library. "I think you'll be pleased with what we've done with the garage."

I eagerly took a look.

He'd placed the commercial laundry room at the end of

the garage closest to the hotel. Above it, he'd drawn the apartment for Manny and Consuela. It was surprisingly large, with lots of storage and an easy flow to the open space. Their apartment even had a nice balcony overlooking the tennis court and plantings beyond it, giving them privacy.

"Wait until Manny and Consuela see this!" Rhonda's dark eyes shone with excitement.

"I'll go get them. They'll be thrilled," I hurried out of the room to find them.

I returned with them and stood aside as they listened to Drew explain what everything meant.

At the hint of tears that coated Consuela's eyes, a lump filled my throat. Standing beside her, Manny nodded his approval and turned to Rhonda.

"You sure, *Señora*, this is what you want? It is so much."

"Are you kidding? It's perfect having you here!" Rhonda exclaimed. "Right, Annie?"

"Right," I said with conviction. Consuela and Manny deserved everything we could do for them. They were two of the best. Having them close by would be a help to all of us.

With a look of satisfaction, Drew packed up his things. "Very good. I'll give you a call when the specs are complete."

Later, Rhonda and I ate a lunch of curried egg salad sandwiches and sipped Consuela's special limeade by the pool.

"I'm going to spend the afternoon with Dorothy," Rhonda announced. "Do you mind, Annie?"

"No, I need to do some work on my own." After the call from Syd, I was anxious to redo my budget. I had to make sure I could handle my share of expenses. The sale of my stock to Robert would barely provide enough to do my share of start-up costs and only if he paid me on time. Bottom line, it would be touch and go. And if we couldn't get the hotel up and running well from the start, it might not make it.

Brock called later in the day to remind me he'd pick me up at six. I hung up and let out a sigh. I had no real interest in seeing him. Not with so much else going on in my life. I'd wanted to cancel earlier, but Rhonda thought it was a good idea if we kept things pleasant between Brock and us , with his being president of the neighborhood association. In order to please her, I went along with it.

That evening, anxiety accompanied my every move as I showered and got dressed. It would be my first post-divorce date, and my stomach felt as if I swallowed a butterfly on steroids. Sitting on the edge of the bed as I slipped pearl earrings into my earlobes, I actually felt sick.

"Annie? Brock's here!" Rhonda called up the stairs.

I swallowed hard and reassessed myself. The blue, sleeveless sundress I'd chosen was classic and was nicely offset by the single strand of pearls I'd slipped around my neck. White strappy sandals completed the look.

My mouth dry, I descended the stairs.

Brock whistled.

"You look wonderful, honey." Rhonda's colorful earrings jangled her approval as she gave me a quick hug. "Blue is definitely your color."

"Absolutely." Brock's gaze caressed me and lingered, making me feel as if he was mentally unzipping my dress. I wanted to run back up the stairs.

Rhonda gave me an encouraging smile. "Have fun!"

I squared my shoulders. "I'll see you later. I won't be late."

"Well, not too late." Brock winked at me, and my body turned cold.

Without so many people in it, Brock's house seemed much larger. He excused himself and headed to the kitchen. I wandered through the spacious living room, admiring the exotic vases and art objects that filled shelves and niches.

The sliding glass doors were open. Trying to relax, I stepped out by the pool and breathed in the mild, perfumed air. The pool area was surrounded by stucco walls covered with bougainvillea and other greenery, giving it a private, lush setting. The sky was clear. The full moon cast its glow on the surface of the pool, illuminating the scenery with soft light. A small table covered with crisp white linen sat in a corner of the garden.

Brock came up behind me, and I turned to him with a smile. "This is lovely."

He grinned and handed me a flute of champagne. "I ordered this night just for you." He raised his glass. "Here's to a wonderful evening."

I took a sip of the bubbly liquid and turned to him. "This is something new for me. I haven't been out on a date since my divorce."

His lips curved. "I'm delighted you chose to make that first date with me." He checked his watch, set his glass down, and fussed with the grill.

Chatting between us about nothing, I stood aside as Brock grilled Mahi Mahi. Then I followed him to the kitchen and helped him serve it, along with a mélange of vegetables and a crisp romaine salad.

We carried our food to the outdoor table and sat in the balmy night air. "Mmm," I said, taking a bite of the tender white flesh of the fish. "I didn't know you could cook, Brock."

"There are a lot of things you don't know about me." He reached across the table and clasped my hand.

I slid my fingers away from his and leaned back in my chair. "Tell me about your work. You have such interesting art pieces in your house."

"As a buyer of imports, I've traveled all over the world for my business. It's afforded me a view of places most people don't get to see. As you may have noticed, I especially enjoy native artwork in any medium. Besides, it's fun to meet new people and learn about their culture."

"Rhonda tells me you're also president of the Gold Coast Neighborhood Association."

Brock straightened in his seat. "Yes. It's very important to have someone watching over things because you never know what somebody is going to try to pull off. In fact, the other day, I heard a nasty rumor about a hotel." His eyes pierced mine. "We need to talk about that, Ann."

I stirred in my seat. We still didn't have all the permits we needed. "What ... what have you heard?"

He shook a finger at me. "I have friends in city hall and in the county offices. You can imagine my surprise when one of them asked how I was going to like a hotel in my own neighborhood."

His look of disapproval shot a cold chill through me. Realizing he wielded a lot of power, I tried to come up with the right words. "Rhonda and I want to turn The Beach House into a small, intimate, upscale hotel that would subtly fit into the neighborhood."

His eyebrows lifted in surprise. "Rhonda never mentioned a word of this to me. She should have, you know." His pique at being left out showed clearly, and I instantly regretted giving him any details.

"Actually, very few people know," I hastened to add. "We're applying for the commercial permits now. Perhaps you can help speed things along. We'd really appreciate it."

"Perhaps." He seemed mollified by my request, and I breathed a little easier. We needed him on our side.

We finished our meal and sat sipping coffee. I gazed up at the stars sparkling in the dark sky and let out a sigh of satisfaction. Despite my worries, the evening had turned out to be pleasant.

"This has been very nice." I folded my napkin at my place. "But I think I should be going back. I have to be up extra early tomorrow morning."

"Oh, but the evening is far from over." Brock rose to his feet. "Let's sit in the living room and settle our meals. I'll put on some music."

Not wanting to appear rude I was resigned to spending a little more time with him. I moved into the living room and took a seat on one of the love seats.

"Just a minute. I'll be right back." Brock left me. Soon soft strains of guitar music filled the room.

Brock returned and lowered himself on the couch beside me. He stretched his long legs out in front of him and faced me. Smiling, he brushed back a strand of hair from my face and then cupped my cheeks.

"You're lovely. Know that?" His gaze told me what he wanted to do.

My body tensed. "Brock, no ..."

Ignoring my plea, Brock placed his arms around me and lowered his lips to mine. His hand cupped one of my breasts.

Panic sprang up inside me. This wasn't what I wanted. I pushed him away. "I'm sorry. I'm just not ready for this."

Brock grimaced as if I'd slapped his face. Frowning, he sat back, allowing me the opportunity to move.

Feeling like a fool, I scrambled to my feet. "It isn't you. It's me. Please, if you don't mind, I'd like to go home. All of a sudden, I'm not feeling well."

"If you insist." His voice was as cold as a winter's day.

Humiliation washed over me, but I couldn't change the way I felt. He'd acted like a creep. The whole idea was totally wrong.

Brock delivered me home in silence and sped off in his car.

I let myself in the front door. Hearing the sound of Rhonda's voice on the phone in the kitchen, I snuck up the stairs.

In my room, I slipped out of the sundress and looked down at my half-naked body. *What was wrong with me?* Tears stung my eyes. I looked normal for a woman my age— even good. *Had Robert's actions stunted me emotionally?* It was all so confusing.

I'd just climbed into bed when a knock came at the door.

"Annie, are you in there?" Rhonda asked. "I didn't hear you come in." She opened the door and stepped inside. A grin spread across her face. "How'd it go?"

I opened my mouth to answer her and burst into tears.

"What's the matter?" Rhonda rushed to my side. "Did he hurt you? If he did, I'll kill him."

I caught my breath with a shaky sob. "No, no, it's just that I got so upset when he came on way too strong. I don't know if I'm ready for all this."

Rhonda put her arms around me. "Awww, honey."

"I mean it, Rhonda, how am I ever going to make it in this crazy, single world? I don't even know who I am anymore. Everything I was before is ... is gone. My whole life is upside down!"

Rhonda looked at me with sympathy. "We all go through times like this. But, Annie, it's different for you. You've got a whole new life ahead of you ... with me and the hotel!"

I returned her embrace, unable to visualize that life. Rhonda and I were so different, and the hotel? I might never be a part of it if Robert didn't keep his word and pay me. And Brock Goodwin was another person who might stop us.

# CHAPTER SEVEN

I was sitting in the library one evening, going over some paperwork when Rhonda burst into the room. "When I needed a building permit for the addition of the dining room and the renovation of the cottage and garage, it was no trouble. Why the problem with a few permits for enlarging the parking areas and building an open-air chickee hut on my property near the beach? Huh? My lawyer said some of the provisions are grandfathered from the previous hotel."

She paced the room. "The Gold Coast Neighborhood Association has tabled our request for their support until the board has had a chance to talk about it privately." She stopped her pacing and turned to me with clutched hands. "Annie, we need their support."

I got to my feet. "The zoning for a commercial property like ours requires us to have a parking space for each room." Acid burned my stomach. We couldn't stand any delays. We wanted to be up and running smoothly by September, October at the latest.

Rhonda's face flushed with anger. "It's all Brock Goodwin's fault. What a bastard! He told everyone we were out to ruin their peaceful lives. It's a damn good thing Jim Worthington was there with me, representing us. He explained we have room to accommodate cars on private property, so visitors would not have to park on the street. And the tropical-style hut was just a place where guests could gather in the shade."

She exhaled. "After the meeting, I pulled Brock aside and

demanded to know just what was going on. You wanna know what he said?" Rhonda lowered her voice in imitation. "'I want to make sure you won't ruin my upscale neighborhood.' How do you like them apples? Pretty nervy, him saying that, after I took this falling-down property and turned it into something real nice, and after you gave him a heads up and asked for his help."

I remembered how angry he'd been with me when I demanded to go home. *Was he that much of a jerk that he'd try to get back at me?* "We'd better make a list of concerns brought up in the meeting so we can address them one by one." Without the Gold Coast Neighborhood Association's support, we might be permanently stalled.

After a restless night, I rose early, slipped on a pair of shorts and a T-shirt, and tiptoed downstairs. Stealing outside to the lawn by the beach, I gazed up at the pale-pink fingers of the sunrise reaching across the gray sky. The mournful cries of seagulls greeted the dawn. I drank in the salty smell of the Gulf and sighed. Hearing the gentle lap of waves that kissed the sand and curled away, I stepped out onto the sand. No one else was nearby.

I loped along the sandy surface of the beach. Lightheartedly, I held out my arms, dipping and twirling like I'd done as a child, lost in the sense of freedom it gave me.

"I hope I'm not intruding," said a familiar voice behind me.

I jerked to a stop and whirled around to face Brock. "What are you doing up so early?"

In just a pair of running shorts, his well-exercised body glistened with sweat. "When I'm in town, I enjoy rising at dawn and having the beach to myself. Well, almost to myself."

He winked at me, and I gathered my nerve. "I was going

to call you today, Brock. I want to apologize for the way I acted the other night. I'm not used to dating yet."

"Yeah, I'm sorry, too. I was rushing you, and even though I knew it, I couldn't stop myself."

I cleared my throat. "We need to talk about the hotel. I thought you were going to help us, not hurt us."

"That depends on you." He gave me a meaningful look. "The gourmet restaurant at The Royal Hotel is great. How about I take you there? We can discuss it then. Sound okay for tonight?"

Feeling trapped, I gulped. "All right. I'll be ready to answer any questions you might have."

"Fair enough." He grinned. "I'll pick you up at seven. Glad I ran into you, so to speak."

As I watched him sprint away, my earlier happiness evaporated.

The doorman at the hotel assisted me out of Brock's sleek, bottle-green Jaguar. I took a deep breath, determined to get through the evening the best I could.

Nattily dressed in white slacks and navy blazer, Brock took my arm and ushered me inside the hotel. As we crossed the marble floor of the lobby, he nodded to an elderly couple walking slowly by us, then waved to another gentleman standing next to the front desk.

When we entered the *L'etoile* restaurant, the hostess beamed at him. "Good evening, Mr. Goodwin."

The maitre d' hurried over. "Good evening, Mr. Goodwin. 'Nice to see you again."

Obviously enjoying the attention, Brock introduced me.

As we were being seated at a table in the corner, a well-dressed couple waved to Brock from across the room. Brock excused himself and left to talk to them.

Alone, I took the opportunity to study the understated opulence around me. The dark, rich tones of the wood-paneled walls were warmed by the polished finish of the lighter-colored wainscoting. Crystal wall sconces shot glitters of light everywhere, reflected by the crystal glasses placed atop crisp, white-linen tablecloths. A female musician sat in the far corner of the room playing a golden harp. Strands of her soft music wafted throughout the room, redolent with tantalizing aromas coming from the kitchen. I let out a sigh of appreciation. It had been a long time since I'd been taken to a nice restaurant for dinner.

Brock rejoined me. "That's one of the city councilmen sitting over there. They're celebrating their anniversary. I had to say hello." He lifted the leather-covered wine list he'd left behind. "Let's have a nice red wine."

Recalling the many times Robert had done the same, I sat by as Brock went through the procedure of ordering and approving the wine.

The appetizers arrived, and between bites of garlic-butter-coated escargots, I opened the topic that had been hanging unspoken between us. "How do you feel about the plans for the tiny hotel Rhonda and I plan to open? I understand you have some concerns."

Brock's expression lost all charm. His nostrils flared as he waggled a finger at me. "You two ladies have to understand the ramifications to the entire neighborhood. It's important to the rest of us that property values not drop. We've all suffered during the latest financial upheavals. For many people, their homes are a major investment." His tone was so hostile I wondered if he was in some financial trouble.

"I understand," I said firmly, "but we believe our project will add value to the neighborhood, not take anything away from it."

Suddenly his whole manner changed. Giving me a smile that was too quick to seem sincere, he clasped my hand. "Let's not let this little disagreement ruin the evening. What do you say?"

"Okay." But I was still upset by the anger I'd heard in his voice. *He's like a chameleon*, I thought, not liking him very much.

In the course of the meal, we talked about other hotels in the area.

"It's amazing that a town this size has so many hotels, but then, the beaches here are exceptional, very close to those in Sarasota," I smiled. "It makes for a very nice situation."

He frowned. "Yes, but you do realize, don't you, that as a long-time resident of Sabal, I've learned quite a bit about what this city needs and what it doesn't want. People like me, who take an interest in what is going on, will shape the future of Sabal, not you newcomers."

I held back a retort. A bullshitter, Rhonda had called him. I thought he was more like a pompous ass.

The waiter cleared our dishes.

Brock leaned toward me. "Let's not order dessert here. I've got something better in mind at my house. No need to worry. You're perfectly safe with me." At his wink, my stomach roiled. Were we going to have another evening of him overreaching the boundaries I set? I didn't think I could do it, not even for Rhonda and the hotel.

The maitre d' approached our table. "Mr. Goodwin, I'm sorry to disturb you, but there is an urgent phone call for your guest." He turned to me with an expression of regret. "Ms. Rutherford, if you'll come this way."

My thoughts on Liz, I hurried over to the small host stand and picked up the phone.

"Annie, it's Rhonda. Liz couldn't get hold of you on your cell, so she called here, crying. She wouldn't tell me what it's all about; just that she needed to speak to you right away. It's something she has to talk over with you alone. I knew you'd want to know."

My body turned to ice. Every "mother-nerve" in my body vibrated. I hung up and trotted back to Brock. "I'm sorry. I need to go home right away. My daughter Liz has some sort of emergency, and I don't want to call her from here."

His features hardened.

"I'm sorry, but it can't wait."

We left the restaurant and got settled in Brock's car. The silence in the car was deafening, but I vowed not to interrupt it. Brock was acting like a spoiled little boy. When at last he pulled in front of The Beach House, I breathed a sigh of relief.

"Good night. Again, I'm sorry. Thanks for dinner," I said, weak with relief the date was over.

He barely managed to say goodbye before speeding off.

I raced into the house, brushing past Rhonda in my haste to reach my phone. My fingers shook as I frantically punched in the number. I couldn't imagine what had caused my calm, cool, collected daughter to phone in tears. It wasn't like her.

Rhonda hung around the kitchen doorway as I waited for Liz to pick up.

"Liz? What's wrong, honey?" I asked when she finally answered.

"Mom?" She burst into tears. "It's everything. I got a C in biology and a D in history. Can you believe it? At this rate, I'll flunk out by June."

"What happened?" She was used to A's and B's.

"I forgot to hand in my history paper. I did it, but I missed class when we were supposed to hand it in. The teacher said she'd let me know if the grade can be changed after she has had time to read it."

"What about biology?"

"The professor agreed to let me do some extra credit work."

"Is that it?" I asked, still wondering at her behavior.

"I got my period and wouldn't you know, my face has broken out, and everyone but me seems to have a date Saturday night." The barely hidden wail in her voice told me there must be more.

"I'm sorry." I waited for more information.

"But that's not the worst of it, Mom. Dad called and told me I *had* to attend a baby shower for Kandie, whether I want to or not. I think I hate him, Mom, and I really, really hate her for all she's done to you." She started crying.

I wished I could float through the air and give her the hug she needed. "Listen, Liz, I know how upset you are, but I want you to try and put everything aside. Get a good night's sleep and call me tomorrow. I'm sure things will seem better then."

"Mom, I may hate *them*, but I really, really love *you*. You know?"

"Yeah, I know," I said softly and realized that no matter how much pain Robert had caused me, he'd also given me the person I loved most in the world. After reassuring Liz that things would turn out okay, I hung up and let out a long breath.

"Everything all right?" asked Rhonda. She gave me a worried look.

I filled her in on the conversation. "This whole divorce thing is harder on her than I thought. She's become so emotional about things. I've got to work hard to keep things on an even keel for a while."

"My Angie doesn't want anything to do with her father. I understand, but she won't even talk about it." Rhonda put an arm around my shoulder. "Liz is strong. She'll be all right."

"I know. It's just going to take time. But Robert and Kandie don't make it easy."

Rhonda sighed. "Too bad you cut short your evening with Brock. I'm sorry, I spoiled it."

I threw my arms around her and hugged her hard. "You have no idea how grateful I am."

At the end of each work day, I fell into the habit of surveying progress on the cottage. As much as Rhonda and I were getting along, I was becoming more and more eager to have my own space. I fretted when workmen failed to show up, rain kept work from being done, or lumber and other supplies weren't delivered on time. I'd all but given up hope of being able to move in when everything finally started to come together. Everything that is, except Robert's expected check—the first of the three payments he still owed me. So much for his cooperation!

Furious that Robert was in a position to continue to harass me in this manner, I called Syd Green.

Syd assured me he'd be in touch with Robert, but I was left to stew about it, growing more and more vexed. I was contemplating a trip to Boston to demand payment from him when Robert's certified check finally arrived.

Torn between elation and wanting to wring my ex's neck, I decided I needed someone to help me with my limited funds—someone different from Rhonda's financial advisor. Getting a business underway was one thing; keeping it going was another. I called the bank where I was doing business and asked for a recommendation.

The next day, I entered the office of the CPA the bank had suggested. A tall, thin man rose to greet me. He smiled and held out his hand. "William Grayson. 'Pleased to meet you, Ms. Rutherford." Thick gray hair swept back from craggy features. His smile crinkled the corners of his eyes and heightened their blue color. His handshake was firm and dry.

"Thank you for seeing me on such short notice," I said, taking a seat in one of the leather wingback chairs he offered.

He sat in a chair opposite me. "I'm always interested in seeing how I can help a new client. Why don't you tell me a bit about yourself and how you came to be in Sabal."

I launched into the story of my divorce, my meeting Rhonda, and our decision to open a small hotel. "It's more like an upscale bed and breakfast operation—very elegant, something hard to find."

He smiled. "You know, I've always thought it would be splendid to do something like that. But things never worked out that way. I opened this business, and soon after, my wife contracted and endured a long illness. She died two years ago. So here I am, doing the same thing after all these years."

I detected a note of sadness in his voice. "You don't think we're crazy?"

He chuckled. "No, but I want to hear exactly how you're going to make it work. There's been some talk in town about the project already."

"Rick Jamieson, a neighbor of mine in Boston, is a hospitality consultant and knows everything about the business. He agreed to do a quick-and-dirty feasibility study for us to determine if we were on track." I smiled, unable to hold back my excitement. "He feels we have a good opportunity to make a go of it by offering something unique. He thinks if we provide excellent service and control our costs, we'd have a special niche in this upscale market."

William nodded enthusiastically.

I warmed to his interest. "There's nothing else quite like it in Southwest Florida. Fortunately, Rhonda's house is well-suited to become a luxurious, small hotel. We don't have to do substantial work on the house."

"Rhonda owns the house?"

"Yes. I'm buying the small cottage on the property and renovating it to be my home. That's another reason I need your help."

William nodded thoughtfully. "We'll need to develop a strategy to make the most of your funds while keeping them secure."

At his willingness to help, hope swirled through me.

"You know, I've always admired that house," he said. "Before she got so sick, my wife and I used to drive by it now and then. That was before Rhonda DelMonte bought it and fixed it up." He spoke in a wistful voice, and I had the impression he was a lonely man.

"Would you like to see it? It would give you the opportunity to see the 'before' stage of the project." His face lit up. "I would, indeed. Yes, that would be most interesting."

When I got home, I told Rhonda about him. "There was something so sad about him. I hope you don't mind, but I've asked him to come by sometime to check the place out. He's fascinated by our plan. Apparently, he's always wanted to do something like this."

"He's welcome to come anytime." Rhonda clapped me on the back. "While you were gone, I spoke to Drew. He inspected the new dining room and the offices. They're almost done. And, Annie, he says when the girls arrive for their school break, Liz should have a very good idea of what her new home will look like."

I grinned. I couldn't wait for her to see it, and I'd missed her like crazy.

Over the next few days, Rhonda and I met with advertising people, hired a computer consultant, and interviewed several purveyors of food and wine.

We finally got permission from the city to extend the parking area and to put up signage for it, but the permit for the chickee hut was still outstanding. Partially satisfied, we made arrangements through Drew to get the work done on the parking lot.

I was looking forward to a quiet evening when the doorbell rang.

Checking my watch, I went to answer it.

In a white, button-down collared shirt and neatly pressed tan slacks, William Grayson stood in front of me.

"Hello, Ann. Am I interrupting anything?" He smiled shyly.

"Not at all," I said, pleased to see him. "Come in."

"Who's there?" Rhonda rushed into the foyer, wiping her hands on a kitchen towel. She stopped and stared at our guest.

"Rhonda, this is William Grayson."

Rhonda continued to gaze at him as if he were a hot fudge sundae. He *was* handsome in his own way. "Come in, come in," she gushed. "Annie has told me all about you. Aha! I know. I'll call you Will."

"Yes, but ..." he mumbled softly and gave me a helpless look.

I placed a hand on his arm. "Rhonda always finds a nickname for everyone. You'll get used to it."

He grinned and turned to Rhonda. "Why not Bill?"

Rhonda laughed. "That's easy. You stood there for the longest time, and I wondered 'Will he come in or not?' Get it?"

Looking pleased, he chuckled. "Okay, Will it is."

The two of them smiled at each other. Watching them, a warm feeling washed over me.

"Come in," said Rhonda. "Annie and I will give you a tour of the property."

We took him through the entire house—guest rooms, kitchen, the small formal dining room, and the larger, newly constructed one.

As we explained how it was all going to work, Will asked intelligent questions and listened carefully to everything we had to say. By the time we completed the tour, the sun was starting to go down.

Will smiled. "I'm impressed. It's a beautiful property, and, as you told me, Ann, it's well suited for what you're doing with it. I'm sure anyone would find pleasure in spending time here."

Happiness swept through me. His opinion was important to me.

"Would you like to stay for a drink?" Rhonda fluttered her eyelashes as she smiled at him. "We can sit on the lanai." She paused. "Unless you have someplace else to go?"

He shook his head. "Fridays I usually stay late at the office just so I don't have to go home to an empty house."

Rhonda clucked her tongue. "What an awful way to live. Go out by the pool with Annie, and I'll get some hors d'oeuvres and wine."

Will followed me outside and stood to look at the beach and the Gulf beyond it. "Gorgeous view. The house and its grounds are even more beautiful than I'd imagined."

"The first time I saw it, I couldn't believe just one person could live here. It's so elegant and regal. Amazing that Rhonda owns it all by herself."

"Yes. She's a very interesting woman," he commented,

smiling as he turned to watch Rhonda head our way.

"A wonderful person," I added enthusiastically. They were so cute together.

Rhonda carried a large tray with the wine, glasses, and a plate of appetizers. She set the tray down on the glass table and lifted the opened bottle of white wine.

"Please, allow me," said Will, coming to her side. Rhonda and I stood by while he poured three glasses of wine and handed them out. "Thanks for having me here."

"Nonsense," said Rhonda. "We're glad you came. It looks like you could use some good home cooking. Here, try one of these."

Will accepted one of the artichoke and cheese squares she offered, ate it quickly, and reached for another.

Rhonda beamed at him. "Nothing makes a cook happier than watching her food being eaten with enthusiasm."

"You should try Rhonda's sweet rolls some morning," I said to Will. "It's wonderful to lie in bed and smell them baking."

"Yes, I should like that." Will's cheeks turned pink as he and Rhonda stared at each other with obvious interest.

After finishing the appetizers and a second glass of wine, Will rose. "I'd better go home."

Rhonda jumped to her feet. "I'll walk you out."

I watched them go—one, tall, thin and elegant, the other, curvy and flamboyant. Why did I think they'd make such a wonderful pair?

Rhonda returned, her cheeks flushed, her eyes shining. "Isn't he the most handsome man? And so sweet! Annie, did you see how he just poured the wine for us? Like he'd always helped me?"

She sat in a chair and fanned her face with her hands. "I thought he was going to kiss me goodbye. We just stood there and stared at each other. The smile he gave me was almost like a kiss. Poor Will, all alone! Do you think he'll come back? I asked him to."

"Oh, yes. I'm sure he will." I'd noticed the way he'd gazed at her, almost adoringly, and knew he was attracted to her.

Rhonda's face glowed with happiness. "Do you believe in love at first sight?"

"Not for me, but maybe for you." I hugged her and hoped he wasn't like some other men I knew.

# CHAPTER EIGHT

The following day, I was surprised by a phone call from Rick Jamieson, the hospitality consultant who'd been so helpful to me.

"This is more a personal than a professional call," he said, after greeting me. "I'm sitting here in Boston, having my second cup of coffee in the sunroom, thinking about the project you and your partner are beginning. Jan and I ate at the country club last night, and seeing Robert there reminded me of something I intended to discuss with you."

I laid down the promotional material I'd been reviewing. Rick had been good enough to give me his professional opinion on The Beach House Hotel gratis. I wondered what more could be on his mind.

"You and Rhonda talk about The Beach House as a small hotel, but, really, what you're planning is nothing more than a fancy bed and breakfast operation. A friend of mine just returned from Sabal, and from what he told me, a small, full-service hotel makes more sense. Think about it. You're already planning breakfast and lunch and wine and hors d'oeuvres. Why not add dinner and make it more appealing for the upscale clients you hope to serve? The kitchen might need to be upgraded a bit, and your licensing requirements might change, but in the long run, it would serve you better. I'd like to see the two of you succeed, and what we're talking about is not much more work than what we've already discussed—additional staff, of course, but that's manageable. It's just food for thought, Ann. By the way, Robert was shocked to know we'd been in touch. I hope it won't cause a problem for you."

There was something in his tone of voice that led me to believe that Rick didn't like Robert any more than I did. "Thanks. I'll discuss this with Rhonda and see what her reaction is. With just thirty-two guest rooms, it shouldn't be too much of a problem, should it?"

Rick chuckled. "I'm not going to lie to you. The hospitality business is one of the toughest, but I think it's something you can handle."

My mind spun as I thanked him and hung up.

When I told Rhonda about the call, she became enthralled with the idea of a true hotel. Not even the Health Department's requirements for upgrading the kitchen facilities daunted her.

Over the next few days, she continued to talk about it with unbridled enthusiasm. I worried and pushed numbers. We'd have to keep it simple, starting out slow and easy, building into a full-scale operation with a chef and a larger staff than originally thought. I kept working the numbers.

Rhonda came into the office as I sat in despair. "What's the matter, Annie?"

"In order to keep to our business agreement, I'm going to need more working capital. The additional capital and operating expenses to move to a full-service operation are steep, Rhonda."

"Call Will. He'll help you." I couldn't help but smile. In a matter of days, Rhonda had fallen hard for him. In her mind, there wasn't anything he couldn't do.

She grabbed my shoulder. "Guess what, Annie! He's asked me on a date. We're going up to Sarasota to one of his favorite places for dinner." She clasped her hands to her cheeks. "Oh my God! What am I going to wear? Will you please help me choose something, Annie? Oooh! I'm so excited!"

She did a little dance and grinned at me. "I used to take dancing lessons, you know. Way back when at Tina's Tap Studio."

Chuckling, I rose and hugged her. "C'mon, let's go take a look at what you've got."

Rhonda's suite took up the top floor of one whole wing of the house. Her dressing area off the master bedroom was enormous. Two overstuffed chairs sat in front of a large window that overlooked a colorful side garden. A table and lamp between them provided the perfect place for reading and relaxing. Wooden closet doors painted a cream color to match the walls lined two of the four walls. Curious, I looked around.

"What?" said Rhonda, noting my frown.

"Where are the mirrors?"

She laughed and opened two narrow doors, exposing a large floor-to-ceiling mirror. "I only look at myself when I have to. Know what I mean?"

I nodded. Very few women, including me, liked what they saw reflected.

We pawed through the clothes in her closet and finally chose a fuchsia pink top and black silk palazzo pants. After the number of phone calls Rhonda and Will had exchanged in the past few days, I was certain he wouldn't care what she wore.

That afternoon, I called Will and explained the new financial situation to him.

"Why don't you give a friend of mine a call? John Hastings is vice-president of the Sabal Savings and Loan. I think he'd give you a fair hearing."

"Okay, I guess I have no choice. Thanks."

Depressed, I hung up, recalling each humiliating moment of the other bank interview. But I had no choice. Reluctantly, I made an appointment to meet with Will's contact.

Dressed in my subtle best and carrying a leather attaché case full of information, I appeared at the bank. I could use the cottage as collateral, along with my savings and future payments from Robert, but I worried they might not be enough.

John Hastings looked to be in his late forties and seemed friendly. My hopes grew as we shook hands.

Time passed as we discussed each detail of my proposal, making me feel hopeful. When we'd gone over everything, he sat back in his chair and shook his head. "I admire your tenacity, Ann, but the only way I could approve such a loan is with your partner's co-signature."

Discouraged, I gathered my papers and rose. "I'll get back to you. Thank you."

John stood and shook my hand. "I wish I didn't have so many rules to follow. If it's any comfort to you, I admire what you've done and are doing. Just give me the okay, and I'll put the loan documents together for you and your partner to sign."

Feeling unbearably trapped by all the decisions, I left his office. It was too late to back out of the hotel now.

Rhonda immediately agreed to co-sign the note. Seeing my despair, she patted me on the back. "Aw, honey. Don't be so down about it. We vowed to do anything to make this work. Co-signing your loan is just another one of those things."

I sighed, feeling as if I were about to become a slave—both mentally and physically—to Rhonda's generosity. *Robert, damn him, had better come through,* I thought, twisting my hands.

I was still in a funk, thinking my day couldn't get any worse when Brock Goodwin called.

"Hello, Ann." His voice was as silky as always. "They say the third time is the charm. What do you say I pick you up for dinner? I've got something special planned at my house."

A sour taste filled my mouth. "I'm sorry. I think it's better if we don't see each other. I'm not ready to date."

"Come now, Ann. Stop acting that way."

"But I ..."

"What? You're playing hard to get? Well, I'm warning you, I don't give up easily." His attempt at humor didn't hide his frustration.

I grew queasy. "Please don't call me again," I said as nicely and as firmly as I could. Trembling, hoping I hadn't made an enemy, I hung up the phone.


I stood inside the small Sabal airport awaiting Liz and Angie's arrival. The passengers deplaned, and I watched Liz stride across the tarmac as if she didn't have a care in the world. She saw me and waved gaily. With her blond-streaked hair, long, thin legs, and willowy body, she was attractive. More than that, she was a nice person. Young women today, I thought whimsically, have such bright futures in front of them. I hoped Liz would grab hold of the opportunities that awaited her and run with them clear up to the stars.

"Hi, Mom!" Liz grabbed me in a hug and, laughing, spun me around.

I hugged her back, loving the feel of her in my arms.

Angela stood aside, watching us. I opened my arms. She came into them and gave me an affectionate hug. "Where's Mom? She told me she couldn't come to the airport, that she had something important to do. She wouldn't tell me what."

I couldn't hold back. "Your mother is in love."

"Yes!" Angela shouted, pumping her fist in the air. "I knew something was going on! Tell me all about it."

I shook my head. "I can't. Your mother wants to tell you herself." Unwilling to disrupt Angela's studies, Rhonda had purposely kept her new romance from her.

Angela grinned. "Hurry! Let's get home! I can't wait to hear all about it."

Liz and I looked at each other and laughed. Angela sounded just like her mother.

We loaded the suitcases into my Honda, and the girls climbed in. Sitting in the front seat beside me, Liz turned to me with a devilish grin. "I talked to Dad before I flew down here. He asked all kinds of questions about what you're doing. I couldn't tell him much except you're restoring the cottage. He flipped out when he heard the news. When are you going to tell him about the hotel?"

"Rhonda and I sent out five thousand brochures this week," I answered crisply. "He can always go to our new website to learn more." My body burned with resentment at the thought of Robert's anger. *How dare he judge my actions!* He'd lost that right some time ago.

Liz chuckled. "Is he ever going to be surprised when he hears about the hotel! I'm so proud of you, Mom!"

I let go of my anger, determined not to let Robert destroy the time with my daughter.

At the house, the girls got settled in their rooms and came downstairs in their bathing suits ready for lunch and a swim. Rhonda joined us a short while later, her hair toned down in color and swept away from her face in a soft style that suited her. She looked, I thought fondly, like a woman in love.

"Hey, Angie!" she called. "Come here and give your mother a hug. I don't care if you're wet or not. It's been too long since I've held you in my arms."

Angela scrambled out of the pool and hurried into her mother's outstretched arms. "So tell me about this guy, Mom. Who is he?"

Liz came over to me. "I can hardly wait to see the cottage."

I smiled. "Put on your sandals and your shirt and let's walk over there right now. You'll love it. It'll be complete by the time school is out for the year."

Chatting about school, we walked across the side lawn and through the opening in the hedge. It felt good to have Liz by my side. The hurried phone calls we made to keep in touch weren't nearly enough for me.

The wallboard inside the cottage was up and almost ready to be painted. The wing that had been added was complete and looked as if it had been part of the house all along. Liz listened to me quietly as I told her about the finishing touches in the kitchen area and showed her which bedroom would be hers.

After we'd seen all of it, we headed back to The Beach House, arm in arm.

"Are you happy?" Liz asked me.

"Yes," I said, realizing I was truly happy, even as worry dogged me like a persistent bird of prey, flitting into my thoughts, pecking away at my contentment.

"What about Rhonda and Will?" She grinned. "Is she really in love?"

I smiled. "They clicked from the moment they met. He's a very nice man, a little on the shy side, definitely reserved. Rhonda has bowled him over with her outgoing personality, and he loves it."

"But what about the hotel? Will she stay with it?"

I paused. Liz was no fool. She knew this new love development with Rhonda would probably mean more work for me. "She and I made a pact. She won't let me down. No matter what it takes, I'll make this work. I've got too much invested in it to let Rhonda's diversion interfere with our success."

Liz nodded. "Good."

The days flew by. Liz and I made good use of the pool and enjoyed our time together and with Rhonda and Angela. It was a time of bonding for all of us.

Rhonda and Angela left us one evening to go with Will back to his favorite restaurant in Sarasota, so he could get to know Angela better. Liz and I saw them off and had a quiet dinner, just the two of us, chatting like friends. It was a wonderful evening—something I'd always remember.

Looking crestfallen, Rhonda came into the office the next morning and sank into a chair.

"How did the dinner go?" I asked.

"Not great. You should have seen Will! He was so sweet, asking Angie about her classes, telling her stories of Sabal before the developers took over, doing everything he could to be friendly."

"And?"

"Angela was polite and all, but there was something off with her the whole evening. I think her stand-offish behavior may have hurt Will's feelings."

I frowned. "That doesn't sound like Angela. What happened?"

"We talked after we got home. I think it all goes back to Sal leaving us. That was real hard on her, you know, going from being Daddy's little princess to having no word from him at all. It was devastating to her."

"So how did you leave it?"

Rhonda sighed. "Angela told me she needs time to get used to the idea of him and me together for real. She didn't know it was so serious. Bummer, huh?"

I nodded and thought of Liz trying to cope with Robert and Kandie.

A look of determination crossed Rhonda's face. "I can't let anyone, even my daughter, come between Will and me. He's everything I've ever wanted in a man. You know?" She got up and went into the kitchen.

Observing her slumped shoulders, I realized starting a new relationship wasn't going to be as easy for her as I'd thought.

Too soon it came time for the girls to leave. I tried to tell myself it was only a matter of months before I'd see Liz again, but it was hard for me to let her go back north closer to her father. Liz had confided that Robert was trying to convince her to live with him. She'd assured me she had no intention of staying with Robert and Kandie, but I knew Robert well enough to know he wouldn't give up easily.

At the airport, Rhonda and I watched the plane take off. She dabbed at her eyes with a tissue and slung an arm around my shoulder. "Guess it's time to go back to work, huh, Annie?"

"Yes, I guess," I replied, as sad as she to see the girls leave. But we'd set a lot of things in motion, and now we'd have to get down to the business of dealing with them.

With the brochures out to various businesses and potential clients telling them of our fall opening, we manned the office every day from nine to five o'clock. The new office set up behind the kitchen and adjacent to the newly completed dining room was plenty large enough to accommodate desks and equipment for both of us in separate cubicles. An empty secretarial desk sat by the door, poised for the time when we'd need administrative help.

I was gratified by letters and emails from some of the people who'd received brochures. Most extended congratulations; some promised to book a room during the winter season.

I was standing at the maids' closet one morning, folding the new towels we'd ordered when Rhonda rushed over to me. She waved a letter in the air.

"Listen to this, Annie. It's from a travel agent in New York City, someone named Brenda Bolinder. She wants to come down here to see the hotel. She has a special client who might be interested in booking a large number of rooms for about four weeks this summer for television production reasons. She'd like to spend some time here and check us out."

"Wonderful!" I said and then frowned as a thought occurred to me. "It's almost too good to be true. Do you think she's one of those people who just wants a free room?"

"Wow! I didn't think of that!" gasped Rhonda. "Let's call her and see if she's legit."

Concerned, I followed Rhonda downstairs to the office. I went to my computer and Googled Brenda's name and her company while Rhonda dialed her number.

Information about her company popped up on my screen. My pulse raced as I read about her and the special work she did. She was everything she claimed to be and more.

Rhonda's eyes grew bigger and bigger as she talked with Brenda. After she said goodbye, Rhonda grabbed me by the shoulders. "Guess what, Annie! Brenda Bolinder is A-okay! And you know that little television production thing she's talking about? It's filming portions of a soap opera right here in Sabal! Can you believe it? She couldn't tell me which show, but she said if they tape it here, it could mean marvelous advertising for The Beach House Hotel! She's coming down to look around."

Laughing like silly school girls, we hugged and danced up and down. This might be just the thing to get us off to a good start.

I was still glowing with triumph that afternoon when the phone rang. I answered it eagerly, pen in hand, ready for some more good news.

"Hello, Ann? This is Jack Henderson," said a familiar voice. "A friend sent Robert one of your brochures, and he's asked me to give you a call. As his lawyer, I told him I would. It seems that Robert feels you've deceived him. He had no idea when he made the financial settlement with you that you were going to do something like set up a hotel. Do you know how risky that is?"

Astonishment was quickly replaced by anger that flowed through me like red-hot lava. Too furious to utter a word, I remained silent.

Jack coughed and continued. "Well, in any case, he claims that by giving you the money to do this, he feels somewhat responsible should anything go wrong. He's reluctant to give you any more money, in other words, unless he can be assured that it's not being wasted."

I erupted. "How I spend the money which is rightfully mine should be of no concern to Robert."

"Now, Ann, he's concerned about Liz too," Jack said.

Ice replaced heat. "Liz is well provided for and always will be. I've been very circumspect in my business dealings. I would suggest that any other conversations be conducted with Syd Green, who is representing me. As a matter of fact, Syd and his wife, Marian, are due here next week to inspect the property. He'll be able to reassure you on this matter."

"The fact remains, Ann," Jack persisted, "that the hotel business is fraught with danger."

"We are well advised, which is more than I can say for Robert at the moment. Goodbye, Jack." I slammed down the phone. Tears of frustration blurred my vision. "Dammit! Why can't he leave me alone?"

"Why can't who leave you alone?" Rhonda asked, breezing into the office, loaded down with an armful of magazines and catalogs.

"That was Robert's lawyer. Robert is upset over how I am spending *my* money! He thinks the hotel business is too risky, and he's worried about Liz!"

"Liz, my ass!" Rhonda's nostrils flared. "He's worried you might succeed without him! That's what this is all about!"

"Well, partner, we're going to show him!" I'd die before I'd fail.

Rhonda sat down, facing me. "Look, hon, we've gone over the figures a hundred times. Will has looked at them. According to him, our financial projections seem reasonable and obtainable. It'll take us a while, but I think we've got a good chance of making it, especially if we stick to our guns and keep the place a high-class one like we've been told."

I let out a sigh. "You're right. I shouldn't let Robert rattle me so. Frankly, I have better business sense than he does."

"Then, have faith in yourself. Come on. We've got catalogs to go through. There are all kinds of soaps, shampoos, and other things to choose from."

Still seething inside, I accepted the few catalogs she handed me. Somehow I'd win at Robert's nasty game.

# CHAPTER NINE

Syd and Marian Green had requested an early visit to the hotel. They stood at the Sabal airport, blinking in the bright sunlight. My heart filled with joy to see them. Syd's legal support guiding me through the arrangements with Robert meant a great deal to me. And I knew Marian from the community mental-health fundraiser we'd worked on together. She was a nice, capable person who loved her husband and their three sons.

As they entered the small airport building, I greeted them both with hugs. "It's so good to see you!"

Syd grinned happily. "Marian was the one who suggested we come see 'Ann's project' as we call it."

Marian smiled. "It sounds wonderful."

I looped my arm through hers. "Rhonda and I are delighted to have you here. You can be our guinea pigs as we try out housekeeping routines and cook various meals for you."

Marian smiled. "We'll love it. Syd and I are ready for a break. Right, hon?"

He tugged at the collar of his shirt. "You bet. C'mon, let's find our bags and get out of these clothes and into something cooler."

As we waited for their luggage to appear on the conveyor belt, Marian asked softly, "Are you happy, Ann? You look wonderful."

I smiled and nodded. Over the past several days I'd reached a milestone. No matter what head games Robert played, I'd remain strong. The life I was building was worth any financial worries I might have because deep down I believed we'd succeed. Not easily, but well worth the challenge. It still amazed me that I, who'd always been so conservative, had thrown caution to the wind and moved to Florida into a business I was still learning. If, by some magic she knew, what in the world would my grandmother say to that?

We loaded bags into Rhonda's car, and I drove them to The Beach House.

"Oh, how lovely," Marian gushed as we pulled to a stop in the front circle.

"Welcome!" Rhonda cried, standing at the bottom of the front steps. I introduced Syd and Marian and stood back as Rhonda wrapped her arms around Marian and greeted Syd with a smile. "Annie and I have been waiting for you to get here!"

The three of them murmured greetings as Manny took the suitcases up the front stairs.

I led Syd and Marian inside and showed them to their room. "After you get settled, Rhonda and I will give you the grand tour of the property. We want you to see everything, so there's no doubt in your minds about the kind of hotel we're talking about." Marian was well-known in the higher social circles of Boston and would be able to send business our way.

Later, while Syd was trying out the new putting green in the front circle, Marian turned to Rhonda and me, her eyes shining. "Everything is gorgeous! I can already think of several couples who'd love to come for a stay. Be sure and give me more brochures before we leave."

Rhonda grinned. "Are you kidding? I'll get some now."

Marian and I looked at each other and smiled as Rhonda

hurried away.

"I like Rhonda," said Marian. "She has a very distinctive personality but makes one feel at home here."

"I think so too. It really is Rhonda's home, you know. She bought the original hotel and fixed it up."

"Ah, that's why it's so perfect for a small hotel," said Marian. Syd called to her, and she applauded his hole-in-one on the putting green.

That evening, we sat outside by the pool with drinks. Syd cleared his throat and looked thoughtfully from Rhonda to me. "From what you've shown us and told us, I think the two of you might be very successful here. I don't understand why Jack Henderson made such an issue of it the other day. I sent him a letter threatening to take them to court, but as you know, Ann, that kind of action does little for you and a lot for us lawyers. You might better sit tight."

"He's an asshole, and so is Robert," Rhonda said bluntly.

Surprise showed on Syd's face, but he nodded. "I think you're right, Rhonda. Yes, indeed I do."

I joined in the laughter that followed.

The doorbell rang, and Rhonda hurried to answer it. She returned a moment later with Will. After Rhonda introduced him, the five of us sat chatting comfortably as the sun went down.

Will told us stories of how Sabal used to be back in the '70s when it was a comparatively quiet little town. "It's amazing how it's grown. It's a tricky balance between the developers, the conservationists, and others who don't want any changes at all."

"But they'll love The Beach House Hotel!" said Rhonda. "I just know it."

"I'm sure they will." As Will smiled at her, I could almost see the electricity between them.

We went into the small dining room for dinner. Small individual vases filled with fresh flowers sat at each place. Printed menus lay atop the serving plates.

"Very nice," commented Marian, and I was glad we'd fussed.

After Consuela served the meal, the room grew quiet as we all dug in.

"Delicious," said Marian, taking her last bite of the rolled chicken breast stuffed with a fresh herb and mushroom mixture, topped with a light, lemony sauce. "Is this the type of thing you're planning to serve for hotel guests?"

Rhonda nodded. "I think so. We don't know how wide our menu choices will be, to begin with. We want to start slow and build up to it. We'll try to have chicken, fish, beef, and pasta available every night, but we're working on more items."

After dessert and a small cordial out on the lanai, Will announced he had to go home. Rhonda rose with him and gave Will a resounding smack on the lips before leading him away.

Marian caught my eye, and we smiled, pleased to see how happy they were together.


Syd and Marian left with promises to direct people to The Beach House Hotel. Though we wouldn't officially open until sometime in August, it had been good to see what kinks we'd need to work out in the dining room.

Rhonda thought she'd like to do a lot of the cooking, but it soon became apparent she could not be expected to cook every meal. After cooking breakfast, lunch, and dinner for two days straight, it had almost done her in. And while Consuela was content to work in the kitchen, she didn't want to handle service as well.

Progress continued on the cottage. It was just about complete. Outdoors, the kidney-shaped splash pool and spa were coated and tiled, awaiting the finish coating on the pool deck. The screening for the cage was stacked at the side of the house and would go up as soon as the pool contractors gave the word. The landscaping was underway, though the sod for the yard wouldn't be put down until the pool was complete.

Inside, the sparkling off-white walls and pale-gold carpeting awaited the added color of furniture and accessories. The living room stood empty save an old, light-blue Oriental rug that I'd brought from home. I'd hunted the sales at every furniture store along the west coast of Florida, looking for bargains to supplement the few pieces of better furniture that I'd brought with me and stored. The rest of the furniture I'd either sold or given away, as neither Robert nor Liz laid claim to it.

I stood by myself in the growing dusk, looking out through the French doors to the pool area and the beach beyond it. The fading sky was lit by the setting sun and cast a warm golden glow to the interior walls. I stared in awe at the place I could now call home. The small house was as gorgeous as I'd imagined. Maybe, more so. I felt a peace and contentment here already.

"Annie?" Rhonda's voice echoed in the empty house. "Where are you?"

"Right here! Come on in." I took a look at her face and froze. "What's the matter?"

Looking as if she was about to cry, Rhonda lowered herself down on the carpet and leaned against the wall. "I just got a call from Brock Goodwin. He returned from a trip to the Far East over the weekend. He wanted me to know that last night the Gold Coast Neighborhood Association voted against the chickee hut and now they're going to fight us on the whole hotel concept. They don't like the idea of a commercial enterprise in the middle of their high-class neighborhood. There'll be a hearing in the next couple of weeks."

My legs grew weak. I collapsed on the floor next to her.

Tears swam in Rhonda's eyes. "Annie? What are we going to do? Brock sounded pleased about the whole thing. I bet the bastard is behind it, but I don't know why."

My mind spun. It didn't make sense. Surely he wouldn't do this because I didn't want to date him. There had to be something more to it.

I patted Rhonda's arm. "We'll make it work out. I'm not sure how, but we will. In the meantime, the only thing we can do is move forward with all our plans. We already have most of the permits in place. That's why I don't understand Brock's taking this approach."

Rhonda remained silent. I'd never seen her so discouraged.

I took a look around at what was to be my beautiful new home and prayed I'd be able to move in, after all.

Later that week, Liz called to tell me she and Angela had signed up to be counselors at a summer camp for underprivileged children in New Hampshire. "You don't mind my not spending the whole summer down there with you, do you?" she asked. "When school ends, we'll come home for a few days to get ready for camp, and then we'll have to leave. Angela especially wants to do the camp thing because she's leaning toward social work."

I hid my disappointment. "No, I don't mind. It sounds like it might be fun."

Liz let out an audible breath of relief. "Thanks, Mom. Dad

was mad when I told him. I think he wanted me to spend the summer with them. Not that I would."

I remained quiet, thankful she hadn't chosen to stay with Robert and Kandie.

"You're sure it's okay, Mom?"

"Yes, I'll be busy with the hotel so it's nice to know you'll be busy too. Send me the information so I can see what the camp is like."

We chatted a while longer, and I hung up. My baby had grown up, and I was truly on my own. Having her become so independent was bitter-sweet.

The school year ended, and Liz arranged to come home. When I watched her descend the stairway from the plane, my heart squeezed with love for her. One year of college had given her a new air of confidence. It scared me to realize in many ways she wasn't mine anymore.

She gave me a hug, more woman to woman than mother and child, and I marveled at how grown up she'd become.

"Angela couldn't make it. She's flying down tomorrow."

"Rhonda was disappointed, but she understands."

As I drove Liz to The Beach House, my excitement rose. She would finally see her new home. The house represented so many things to me—security, independence, even survival.

I pulled through the gates of the hotel and took a driveway off to the right to the cottage.

Liz looked over at me and grinned. Her eyes widened when I pulled into the two-car garage. "It's ours? Truly ours?"

We got out of the car, and I took her hand. "I want you to see it as if you were a visitor." I led her to the front door and swung it open. I held my breath as I waited for her response.

Liz let out a gasp that rose to a squeal. "It's beautiful!" She darted through the living room and peered through the French doors leading to the lanai. "A pool! I didn't know we were going to have a pool!"

The sound of water cascading from the spa into the small pool was musical as I opened the doors to show her. It had been a bit of an extravagance, but one I felt was warranted in such a lovely setting. In case, God forbid, I was ever forced to sell the house.

Liz turned in circles, taking in all the details with a huge grin on her face. "What does my room look like? Is it the way I wanted?"

"Let's go see."

We walked to her bedroom, and I opened the door with a flourish.

The pale-yellow walls and the blue floral quilt on the queen bed were exactly what she'd ordered. Liz clapped her hands with delight. "This is great! Mom, the whole place is beautiful! I'm so proud of you!"

I grinned. It was beautiful, and small was just fine with me. I'd be too busy with the hotel to worry about a larger house of my own. I was lucky, so lucky, to have this.

The time with Liz was precious. We selected a sleeping bag and other camping gear for her to take to New Hampshire, saw a movie, and spent as much time together as my schedule allowed. In too few days, she and Angie left for their summer adventure. It almost seemed as if they hadn't been home at all.

I went back to dealing with the problems I'd held at bay during her short visit.

Syd Green had been forced to make another call to Robert's lawyer. He phoned me with an update. This time, the excuse for Robert's not paying was because he'd had to fund the pension plan for his company and was short on cash.

My hands knotted helplessly as Syd gave me a blow-by-blow description of his conversation with the lawyer. It seemed so wrong that Robert was holding me back from moving on with my life while he was thriving in his new one.

I hung up the phone with a promise from Syd that he'd stay on top of it. He was as angry as I was about Robert's constantly backing away from his promises. Though Robert was being fined for late payments, it didn't help me. I needed the money now.

My situation wasn't the only difficult one facing us. Rhonda and I agonized over the threat of the neighborhood group's going against us and decided to proceed with our plans. As Will advised, with permits in place, their objections shouldn't be allowed to derail us. And we had some time to think of a plan before their next meeting.

The reservations book was still embarrassingly empty. I racked my brain, trying to come up with ideas of how we could attract people. We wanted a "soft opening"—when people could come and quietly test the property before we officially opened—but the blank pages of reservation listings taunted me.

"What are we going to do, Annie?" Rhonda held up the blank print-outs of the reservations program. "We've got to pull more people in."

"Why don't we call Brenda and ask her for a list of other travel agents? We'll invite them down for a free, one-night stay. We've got to get 'heads in beds,' as they say."

Panic kept us busy. We called Brenda, and Rhonda met with a writer for the *Sabal Daily News*. He agreed to do a big spread on us. He also agreed to attend our first scheduled

Breakfast at The Beach House Hotel in August. Well aware the short trip from the east coast of Florida to Sabal represented a big change in lifestyle, we placed ads in the Miami papers.

We soon discovered there is nothing like freebies to attract travel agents and corporate planners. Calls began to come in.

Will came to dinner one night and did a magnificent job of trying to boost our drooping spirits. I could see how much he cared and loved him for it. To give Rhonda and Will some time alone, as soon as dinner was over, I excused myself.

"Wait! Where are you going?" Rhonda asked me, waving me back into the room.

"It's late, and I'm exhausted." I was puzzled by the panicky tone in Rhonda's voice. "I've been up since six o'clock this morning. I'm going home."

Will rose. "I'd better be going, too."

I waited for Rhonda to tell him to stay, but she didn't.

Will walked out with me. "Is everything O.K.?" I asked him.

He shrugged. "I guess so."

I let it go, but something wasn't right. They'd been hanging all over each other before dinner and not only had Rhonda failed to ask him to stay, she wasn't even walking him to the front door. Curious as I was, I decided to wait for Rhonda to talk to me about it.

Over the course of the next few days, we worked to build our staff. We hired Consuela's cousin Rosita to be head of housekeeping. She'd had a lot of experience working for the Royal Hotel. We hired her sister Ana as a maid. She would also act as a waitress when called upon. For the time being,

Consuela, Rhonda, and I would handle the kitchen.

A notice from the Gold Coast Neighborhood Association arrived in the mail, requesting our presence at a meeting to be held at the end of the week. Disheartened, I went into the office and handed it to Rhonda. "You'd better look at this."

Rhonda read it, crumbled it and threw it down on the floor. "Brock Goodwin and the other condo-commando types can never let go, can they?"

I nodded, saying nothing, but words flew in my mind—words that would make my grandmother wince.

Later, I worked in the kitchen with Rhonda, icing the sweet rolls that were one of her signature items. We were stockpiling them in the freezer in anticipation of the time we'd need them for guests.

I cleared my throat and asked the question that had been haunting me. "Rhonda, is something wrong between you and Will? He hasn't been around."

With a pained expression, Rhonda set down her spreader. "Will is the nicest man I've ever met. I'm afraid if things go too far, he'll be turned off. I don't have a figure like yours, Annie. Why do you think I wear these caftans all the time? He'll take a look at the real me and take off as fast as he can."

I blinked in surprise. When I'd first met Rhonda, I thought she was big, brash, and garish. Now, I saw a sweet face, bright blond hair, and an aura of kindness surrounding her. "Will realizes you're not petite and I'm sure he doesn't care a bit. Have you seen the way he looks at you?"

Rhonda hung her head. "Toward the end, I could tell Sal was turned off by me. He'd been going out with all those young girls, and there's no way I could ever compare to that..."

"Whoa! Wait a minute! This isn't about Will. This is about Sal. Are you going to let an old memory ruin something new and wonderful?"

Rhonda gave me a look of misery. "I'd be so disappointed if I lost him ..."

"Then don't." I put my arm around her. "Let things just happen. It'll work out. You'll see. You're wonderful just the way you are."

Rhonda's eyes glistened. "Do you suppose Will thinks so?"

"I *know* so."

"Okay. I'm going to give him a call. Wish me luck!"

I smiled at the slight swagger in her step as she strode out of the room, more like the Rhonda I knew.

Sorting through the mail was something I enjoyed doing. On this day, one particular piece caught my eye. When I read the all-too-familiar handwriting, my fingers turned cold. The envelope slid from my hand. Drawing a deep breath, I picked it up and opened it.

Moments later, my pulse pounding, I raced into the kitchen and slapped the letter down on the counter where Rhonda was working. "Look at this! Robert and Kandie want to bring little Robbie here for a long weekend in late July! How am I going to handle that?"

"Sonuvabitch," Rhonda murmured. "How are you going to handle it? Like you've done everything else, Annie. With style and grace."

My stomach knotted like a pretzel. I sank into a chair. "What if we can't get Brock and the neighborhood group to stop fighting the hotel? And Robert finds out we've failed?" At the thought, my throat thickened.

"It's that Brock Goodwin! I could kill 'im!" Rhonda sank onto a kitchen chair across the table from me. The flour on the tip of her nose was no distraction.

"He told me he doesn't give up easily." I drew myself up, ready to take on anyone who got in our way. "This is one battle he's not going to win." I couldn't; I wouldn't let Robert be a witness to my failure.

I left the kitchen and hurried along the sidewalk to Dorothy Stern's apartment, scarcely noticing the beautiful flowers lining the building's front walk.

Dorothy greeted me at the door of her apartment, her eyes full of questions. "My! You're all flushed from the heat, my dear. Come inside. I've made some nice, cold iced tea."

I sat on the couch in her living room and faced Dorothy. "Rhonda mentioned you were excited about our hotel opening. I guess that makes you the only friend we'll have at the hearing tonight."

"What do you mean? All my friends read the newspaper article. They can't wait to join me for Breakfast at The Beach House Hotel! It sounds perfect."

My jaw dropped. "But I thought everyone in the neighborhood was against the idea of the hotel. Brock said ..."

"Stop!" Dorothy's eyes bulged with fury. "I've been part of this neighborhood since long before Brock Goodwin arrived in Sabal. He may think he runs this neighborhood group, but he doesn't. You'd better tell me the whole story, Annie. I've got a feeling I know exactly what's going on here, and I'm not so old I can't smell a rat."

I smiled.

By the time I left, Dorothy and I had agreed on a plan.

# CHAPTER TEN

An excited buzz filled the crowded clubhouse of one of the condominiums in the neighborhood. I sat in a metal folding chair, nervously twisting a sapphire ring around and around my finger, wondering how it was that Rhonda had appointed me a spokesperson for the hotel. She knew most of the people. I didn't.

Glancing around at these strangers, I tried to guess who might support us. My pulse jumped nervously when Brock strode into the room, surrounded by a group of men. My gaze followed them as they walked to the front and sat at the long table positioned there.

Sitting next to me, Rhonda leaned over and said in a stage whisper, "There he is. The bastard."

"Please, Rhonda," I murmured as glances were cast our way.

Will took hold of Rhonda's hand, and Dorothy Stern gave her a look of disapproval.

"All right," Rhonda whispered. "You know I can't hold my tongue. That's why you've got to handle this for us, Annie."

Brock stood. Quiet descended as he introduced himself and the other members of the board. I studied him, wondering what had made him the way he was—his smooth, polished exterior hid a ruthlessness that rose from inside him when he didn't get his way. He cleared his throat. "We've come here today to discuss The Beach House Hotel. Most of us feel this neighborhood doesn't need a commercial enterprise in our midst. We plan to appeal to the city to rescind any permits for the hotel. Everyone knows what can happen if we allow a hotel in our quiet neighborhood. There will be noise, traffic, and who knows what kind of people roaming the streets." His voice droned on and on.

I watched several people in the audience nod their heads in agreement, and my heart sank. Stirring in my seat restlessly, I silently rehearsed what I wanted to say.

When I was finally allowed to speak, I rose on wobbly legs, walked to the front of the room, and stood by the microphone that had been set up in front of the board's table. The sea of faces that gazed up at me blurred as I focused on Rhonda's smile, drawing encouragement from her.

"You've heard all the reasons why The Beach House Hotel should not be allowed to open." My voice quivered, and I took a breath. "I'd like to tell you why those same reasons are cause for a place like our hotel to exist."

I swallowed nervously and then laid out my case, describing the layout, the function, and the future clientele of the hotel. "Our hotel is self-contained within high walls, giving our guests privacy and appearing no different from what you've seen since it was restored."

I heard Brock whispering to the man beside him and took a calming breath. "Local residents will have a place for guests to stay conveniently close by. They'll also be able to hold small, private meetings and host intimate, tasteful parties."

A few people nodded thoughtfully.

Brock rose and moved to the microphone, forcing me to step aside. "Some of you may think Ms. Rutherford's position is sound, but I say, consider the source." He turned to me. "How long have you lived in Sabal, Ann?"

My cheeks grew hot. "Since right after the winter holidays."

"And why did you come to Sabal?" Brock asked, knowing the answer.

I swallowed my anger, though I wanted to wipe the sneer off his face with a baseball bat. "I came to Sabal because Rhonda DelMonte, whom most of you know, asked me to join her in this venture."

Titters of laughter broke out among the crowd. Brock was smiling broadly now. "There we have it, folks, straight from the horse's mouth. Here is a woman who doesn't give a hoot about the neighborhood. All she cares about is this venture of hers. We all have had experience with developers and interlopers like this before ..."

A scraping noise stopped his speech. Will rose to his feet.

Dorothy Stern pushed him back in his seat and marched forward on short, stocky legs, spots of red on her cheeks. "Will the chair recognize me?" She waved sheaves of papers up in the air. "Before we go any further with this discussion, I'd like to make something perfectly clear. I'm one of the oldest residents of this neighborhood, having arrived long before Mr. Goodwin did. I wouldn't say he was still in diapers when I started visiting Sabal, but, then again, I may be wrong."

Laughter filled the room.

"I'm also a member of the board of the Gold Coast Neighborhood Association, though I chose to sit with my friends. The board has had very few meetings since Brock Goodwin became its president because he chooses to run the board like a dictatorship. I'm here tonight to make sure he doesn't. When I heard of his opposition to The Beach House Hotel, I did a little survey of my own. I have here before me a petition with the names of over 100 people who live nearby and actively support the hotel. Those of us who've lived here for some time can well remember what an eyesore The Beach

House was before Rhonda DelMonte bought it and restored it. We can think of no better way to ensure the fact that it remains a focal point of our neighborhood as it's always been."

Brock's face darkened with fury. "You had no right to do that ..."

Dorothy looked up at Brock through her thick glasses and appeared to grow a foot in stature. "I would suggest, Mr. President of the Gold Coast Neighborhood Association, that in the future you not let personal concerns interfere with your duties."

She sat down to loud applause. Rhonda clapped Dorothy on the back. I wanted to hug her as I took a seat nearby.

After a few more people spoke, a motion was made for the Gold Coast Neighborhood Association to officially support The Beach House Hotel. It was seconded, and Brock was forced to take a vote on the item. The issue was quickly resolved in our favor.

"Yes!" Rhonda shook her fist in the air and gave me a high five.

I leaped up out of my chair. Without the weight of worry that had kept me sleepless, I felt as if I could fly. Dorothy hugged me. I hugged her back as Brock stormed out of the room.

Will and Dorothy spent some time greeting people in the audience and then joined Rhonda and me. We returned to The Beach House to discuss the meeting and devise a few plans to forestall any other attempts to put us out of business.

Sitting in the living room sipping coffee, Will confided that he'd heard through the grapevine that Brock was having financial troubles and had been forced to add a second mortgage to his house.

"Even so, he shouldn't have tried to mess with us," groused Rhonda. "Good thing we went ahead with our plans. Right, Annie?"

I nodded. We were due to receive our first guests—travel agents and their friends—in a few days.

Rhonda and I did a final inspection of the guest rooms with Rosita and Ana. Short and stocky, Rosita was a bundle of energy. Her dark eyes sparkled, and her lips always seemed to have a hint of a smile. Ana was taller and thinner and much more serious. They'd spent a couple of days getting all the rooms ready with fresh sheets, towels, blankets, and bathroom supplies.

We checked closets and bureau drawers for dust and debris. Bathtubs, sinks, and cabinets were inspected as well. Bedspreads were rolled back to make sure there were triple sheeting and lightweight blankets. I even looked under the skirts of the beds to check for dust balls, while Rhonda went over the inventory sheets she'd designed with Rosita and Ana.

Rhonda and I roamed restlessly through the house, waiting for the arrival of our first guests—Mr. and Mrs. Martin Weatherbee from Connecticut. They were due to arrive from the airport in Ft. Myers, but the Weatherbees wouldn't be our only guests. Will had agreed to come and spend the night so the Weatherbees wouldn't feel so alone. He'd also agreed to critique the stay for us, letting us know if he found any problems.

The sound of a car pulling into the driveway had me racing to the office. "Rhonda, they're here! C'mon!"

We hurried to the front of the house and descended the front steps to greet our guests. My pulse raced with excitement as we watched them get out of their rental car.

"Welcome to The Beach House Hotel," Rhonda said, beaming at them.

"Yes. We hope your stay will be pleasant," I added. "Leave your bags. Manny will get them for you."

We ushered them up the front steps, into the hotel, and gave them a quick tour of the facilities.

"It looks okay," said Mr. Weatherbee, with little enthusiasm.

His wife said nothing, and my heart plummeted. They didn't seem the least bit impressed. After showing them to their room, Rhonda and I met in the office.

"They didn't even crack a smile," groused Rhonda. "Maybe Will can lighten them up."

Too nervous to sit still, I went into the kitchen for a glass of water. Standing there, looking out toward the pool, I noticed Mrs. Weatherbee strolling around the lanai, studying everything.

I joined her outside. "Is there anything we can do for you? If you care to swim, the pool should be pleasant."

She shook her head. "No swimming for me. I just wanted to take a look at your landscaping. Tropical plants are so interesting."

"Yes, they are. Please let me know if I can be of any help."

"Thank you. My husband and I won't be staying here for dinner. As soon as he's ready, we're leaving to look at other places."

Disappointment cut through me. They didn't even want to eat here. I returned to the office and picked up a brochure. Had it been misleading?

Will arrived as scheduled. Because Rhonda was on the phone, I showed him to his room. The Weatherbees were coming down the stairs as we went up.

"Nice evening," commented Will. "And this is a beautiful place. Don't you agree?"

"Should be for the price we're paying. Good thing it's just for one night," grumped Mr. Weatherbee. His wife gave me an apologetic smile.

My stomach churned as I watched them leave the hotel.

At breakfast the next day, I surreptitiously kept an eye on the Weatherbees. They were quiet and subdued, eating every bit of the bacon, eggs, and potatoes Consuela placed in front of them. Politely, they asked for seconds on the sweet rolls, along with another cup of coffee. They finished their meal and went upstairs.

I crossed over to the small reception desk we'd placed in the front entry and took a seat behind it. I did some paperwork to kill time until the Weatherbees were due to check out. Hopefully, I'd learn why we didn't measure up.

Mr. Weatherbee came downstairs and approached me, his expression stern as always.

My mouth dry, I braced myself for his complaints.

"Is it possible for us to stay another night? My wife and I have decided of all the places we've seen, we like this hotel best. It's small but classy."

I blinked in surprise and forced myself to speak calmly, though I wanted to dance across the foyer floor. "I'm sure we can accommodate you."

Happiness whirled inside me as I made the change on the computer. The Beach House Hotel was working its magic after all.

The next guests to arrive were due that afternoon. From upstate New York, the two couples were friends who'd known each other for years and were anxious to take advantage of our pre-opening rate. They arrived shortly before four o'clock and immediately filled the house with their presence, going from room to room, talking and joking with each other, bringing the place alive.

At cocktail time, I helped pour drinks and noticed the Weatherbees had been included in all the activity. The six guests sat together in the living room, sipping drinks and chatting with one another . I let out a sigh of relief. In a small place like ours, it was important for each guest to feel welcomed.

On the day the group from upstate New York was to leave, they asked for a late checkout. We gave it to them, happy they were having so much fun. After they finally left, Rhonda and I went upstairs to see how Rosita was doing cleaning their rooms.

I peeked into the room where one of the couples had stayed. The bedclothes were scattered on the floor, closet doors were thrown open, and table tops were cleared of everything—magazines, the basket of fruit brought to each room each day, and even the plate that had held the cookies the night before.

"What happened?" asked Rhonda, walking into the room behind me.

"It looks like they've taken a lot of our things with them." I went over to the closet. The lightweight terry robes we'd hung there for our guests' use were gone, along with the multi-colored golf umbrella with our name on it.

"Shit! They've even taken all the items from inside here!" Rhonda cried from the bathroom. "Those frickin' thieves!"

Stunned, I looked around at the chaos. The stolen goods added up to quite a lot of money. We couldn't let them get away with it.

"You know something? The robes and umbrellas with our name and logo on them are really attractive. Maybe we should offer them for sale. It would be good PR, and it might help avoid times like this."

"You're right, Annie." A mischievous smile lit Rhonda's face. "These people can be our first customers—whether they like it or not!"

I laughed. We might have to learn about the hotel business the hard way, but no matter what, the two of us would succeed or die trying.

# CHAPTER ELEVEN

Rhonda and I descended the steps together to greet Brenda Bolinder's limousine. She exited the car and glanced around with a smile on her face. Tall, she carried herself with a regal grace as she strode toward us. Her luxuriant red hair was pulled back in a refined, braided twist. Huge, but tasteful emeralds sparkled at her ears and on her fingers, matching the green linen suit she wore.

I rushed forward to greet her. "Welcome! Rhonda and I are so happy you're here. We hope you love our hotel."

Rhonda shook her hand. "After you get settled in your room, we'll give you a complete tour of the property. "

Brenda nodded. "Thank you. I need to see all of it."

While Rhonda answered a phone call, I showed Brenda to her room. "Take your time. When you're ready, we'll be downstairs."

She smiled. "It won't take me long to get into something more comfortable."

Rhonda's face was aglow when I met her in the office. "That Brenda! What a class act! I'm dying to know who her client is. They gotta be big. Did you check out those jewels of hers?"

I nodded. Brenda wasn't your normal travel agent.

We walked Brenda through the downstairs rooms, showed her all the facilities, and described the services we could provide to her group.

"I love it so far," she said. "I can't believe this was all yours, Rhonda. It's perfect for what you're doing, and I think it might work for my client. The living room especially has a lot of features we could use. The woodworking, the trim, the high ceilings are all I imagined them to be from the pictures in the brochure. Can you show me the grounds?"

Like a proud child showing off a new toy, Rhonda took Brenda's hand and tugged her outside. We showed her the pool area, took her to the tennis court, shuffleboard court, and the horseshoe pits by the garage. Then we walked her to the putting green in the front circle and finally led her to my house. As we sat on my lanai, sipping cold drinks, we chatted comfortably. Brenda appeared to be well-traveled and knowledgeable about running a hotel.

"You have a lovely place here." Brenda indicated the grounds with a wave of her hand. "I need to take a look around in the early morning light to be sure, but, so far, I think it might do nicely. Now, let me tell you a bit about my client. Are you familiar with the afternoon soap opera, *The Sins of the Children?*"

Rhonda's eyes rounded. "Holy crap! You've got to be kidding!"

"I've never seen it," I admitted.

"Well, it's one of the hottest shows going," said Brenda. "The producers planned a whole series of episodes to take place in a tropical setting. I was hired to find the right location, and this seems like the perfect place to me."

Rhonda and I exchanged looks of awe.

I leaned forward. "How long will they want to stay?"

"I'd have to reconfirm it, but from what I've been told, it would be for about four weeks—from early to mid-August until sometime after Labor Day. The major stars would stay here. They'd need to use space inside the hotel for shots of some interior scenes, as well."

My pulse raced. I was already adding numbers in my

head. "How many people are we talking about?"

Brenda hesitated. "I imagine between the stars, the director, the producers, and others, they'd take up the whole hotel. Some of the crew can stay somewhere else, but the stars need to have a luxurious setting. They get tired of large, commercial hotels and want privacy, which is why I thought your property might work. We'd want to be sure no screaming fans would be hanging around. With the space around the house and the high walls surrounding the lawns, the property appears secure, I should think."

"Oh, yes." Rhonda bobbed her head eagerly. "That shouldn't be a problem. It's one of the reasons I originally bought the place."

Brenda smiled and leaned back in her chair. "Tomorrow morning, I'll go on the beach, and then I'll check out other areas of the town." She checked her watch. "As a matter of fact, a friend should be picking me up soon. I'd better go back to the hotel."

"I'll walk you over," said Rhonda, rising.

Brenda waved her back to her seat. "Don't bother. I know my way, and I'm sure the two of you have lots to talk about."

She left, and Rhonda gazed at me, wide-eyed. "Oh my God, Annie! Do you realize what this means? A television show filmed right here?"

"It could be the beginning of something wonderful." My voice shook with possibility.

Rhonda gave me a playful punch on the arm. "'Told ya. Everything is going to work out just fine. See? It's all falling into place."

A shiver crossed my shoulders. I hoped she was right. This was BIG.

###

I was placing a vase of fresh flowers on each of the tables in the pool area the next morning when Brenda rushed up.

"I've just come from the beach." She frowned. "I had no idea that filming here could become such a problem. A neighbor of yours explained it to me. I'm awfully sorry, but if we can't be assured of having adequate access to the beach, this whole project will have to move somewhere else."

I almost dropped the vase from my hands. A terrible certainty filled me. "Are you by any chance talking about a man named Brock Goodwin?"

"Why yes! That was his name. He runs the Gold Coast Neighborhood Association. He told me he doesn't think people in the neighborhood would like having the beach restricted. I must say, he wasn't very nice after he found out what I was doing here. In fact, he came right out and told me I could just plain forget it!"

I set down the vase before I threw it. Forcing myself to remain calm, I said, "I believe there's been a gross misunderstanding. There will be no problem with filming on the beach. We'll take care of it."

"I hope so," said Brenda. "I was so pleased with everything else."

She left me, and I raced into the office, as angry as I'd ever been, to give Rhonda the news.

Rhonda pounded her desk with a fist. "That jackass isn't going to ruin this opportunity for us! Don't worry, Annie, I'll take care of him." There was a dangerous edge to her voice.

I eyed her suspiciously. "What are you going to do?"

"I'm calling all the board members of the Gold Coast Neighborhood Association now before Brock can get to them. I'm going to ask them to impeach Brock. This whole thing of being president has gone to his head."

Rhonda and I both set to work on the calls.

Before leaving, Brenda met with us in the office.

"I understand your situation," she said, "but I can't wait too long for your assurance that everything is all right. My client will insist on it. I'm sure you realize this is an opportunity of a lifetime for any hotel."

"We'll be back to you as soon as possible. Believe me; we want your client here. We promise to do an excellent job for them. "

"Yes," said Rhonda. "We want you here, not anywhere else."

"We'll see how it works out," said Brenda. "I can't make any promises."

After seeing her off, Rhonda and I returned to our office. Slumping in her chair, Rhonda said, "What are we going to do, Annie?"

Determination hardened every bone of my body. "We're going to get the issue resolved and go ahead with all our plans. No one is going to stop us!"

Rhonda grinned at me. "I like it when you get all fired up, Annie."

I returned her smile, but I knew it would take more than being fired up, so to speak, to solve our problems.

That afternoon, we hurried to Rhonda's private wing of the house to watch *The Sins of the Children*. An image of a tall, broad-shouldered man with strong, well-defined features appeared on the screen.

"Oooh. Vaughn Sanders," gushed Rhonda.

I had to admit, with his dark, tumbling curls and snappy, intelligent, brown eyes, he was handsome. A real hottie, as Liz had once told me on our first plane ride to Sabal.

"Isn't he gorgeous?" Rhonda's voice turned breathy. "And just think, Annie! He might stay right here with us this summer!"

"He's just an actor," I said, even as my eyes focused on his sensuous, full lips.

# CHAPTER TWELVE

Days flew by. We continued to maintain a low profile on summer bookings until we had the issue of the soap opera filming settled. Brock was on another of his overseas trips. I hoped he'd stay away so we could get the approval without more interference from him. And that wasn't my only worry.

No matter how much I might wish otherwise, Robert and Kandie's visit approached relentlessly. I dreaded it. He still owed me money. And it seemed like such a mean trick for him to come now, while we were still testing things out. It was meaner still for him to bring Kandie and the baby. But, then, Robert wouldn't see it that way. He'd see his visit as a means of protecting his "investment" or some such bull. I was having none of it.

On schedule, Robert and Kandie's rental car pulled up to the front of the house. Rhonda and I stood at the top of the stairs, waiting to greet them. Rhonda gave me an encouraging wink.

"You can do it, Annie."

I drew a deep breath. Though a part of me was itching to slap a certain someone's face, I'd do my best to act the cheerful hostess.

Kandie got out of the car, and I blinked with surprise. Her blue jeans looked as if the stretch in them was about to fray with a figure gone awry. Her hair streaked with red highlights turned orange was pulled into two ponytails that made her look twelve. A feeling of sweet revenge curled itself around me. *What had Robert ever seen in her?*

I didn't look at the baby in her arms, but bypassed him and his mother, and walked over to where Robert stood on the driver's side of the car, stretching lazily. Rhonda trotted at my heels.

"Hello, Robert," I said coolly. "Welcome to The Beach House Hotel. I'd like you to meet my partner, Rhonda DelMonte."

Rhonda and Robert eyed each other warily, and I prayed Rhonda would restrain herself. Her fingers were tightening into fists, and a fiery gleam had entered her eyes. She extended her hand to him.

Ignoring Rhonda's gesture, he turned in a circle. "Looks like you two have got quite a place."

Dots of red appeared on Rhonda's cheeks, and I knew she was not only angry but hurt by Robert's action. She laid a hand on my arm. "Here comes Manny. I'll go see if he needs any help."

Furious, I faced Robert. "If you're going to be rude to my partner, you can leave right now, Robert. We don't need your business."

His eyes widened in surprise, and then he glared at me. "Don't lecture me, Ann. You can't imagine the hellish trip I've had to get here."

The baby wailed, catching his attention.

The timing was perfect, I thought with satisfaction. Robert wanted another child; well, he had one. Maybe, two, I thought, as Kandie whined about being tired.

While Manny and Robert collected the luggage, Rhonda and I ushered Kandie and the baby inside.

"Oh, this is beautiful!" Kandie cooed. "From what Robert told me, I didn't expect anything like this!"

"And just what did Robert tell you?" I asked, deceptively

calm, though my jaw clenched and unclenched with anger.

Kandie shrugged her shoulders. "I don't know. He just said that you were wasting his money ..."

"Now, sweetheart," said Robert, joining us. "You know I didn't say that."

"Oh, yes, you did, Robert! I know what I heard!" Kandie retorted in a high, baby-like voice. Her lips formed a pout as she glared at him.

Fascinated, I watched their byplay. *How could I ever have loved this jerk?* I asked myself, feeling better by the moment.

"Ah, here's Consuela," said Rhonda. "She'll show you to your room. We set up a crib for the baby." She hesitated, and I knew the effort it was taking. "Welcome to The Beach House Hotel."

"Yes," I added, forcing a pleasant tone to my words. "We hope you have a pleasant stay!" If that didn't merit an acting award, I'd be surprised. I was relieved when they left the living room. It was not going to be an easy time, but, somehow I'd get through it.

After they disappeared up the stairway, Rhonda shook her head. "What an asshole!"

My lips thinned. "Ya think?" I couldn't agree more.

Even though two other rooms were booked for the weekend, we'd given the staff strict orders to dog Robert and Kandie, filling their every need with prompt, polite service. Formal, rather than familiar, was the way we'd decided to handle them. I'd warned Rhonda ahead of time that I intended to stay out of sight, either working in the office at the hotel or working in my small office at home. Now, having met Robert, she understood.

Robert came back downstairs. "We need to warm up this bottle of milk." He thrust a baby bottle at Rhonda. "Here. You take care of it."

Rhonda stared at him. "You really are as big an ass as Annie said."

Robert's eyes bulged. Before he could erupt, I signaled to Rosita. She came right over to us.

"Will you please help Mr. Rutherford warm this bottle?"

She nodded, and I turned to Robert. "You'd better go along with her to make sure it's done exactly like Kandie wants."

The look he gave me could have withered a tree.


I was working in my office at the cottage when I heard a knock at my front door. When I saw Robert peering through the side panel of glass, my heart fell.

He waved me outside. "I want to talk to you."

I shook my head and turned away. I had no intention of speaking with him.

His voice rose. "You can keep avoiding me and keep me out of the house, Ann, but you can't prevent me from looking around. I've already seen what a classy place it is. It must have cost a pretty penny." His voice carried toward the main house.

I let out a disgusted sigh. I didn't want the other guests to hear us, and the Robert I knew wouldn't give up. He'd push, push, push, until he got his own way. Seething, I opened the door, feeling like a prisoner in my own home.

"What do you want to talk to me about, Robert? Surely, it isn't about the house."

"I want to set you straight on something. I've done a lot of consulting to businesses about personnel problems, as you very well know. So, I think it's fair to tell you that I don't like what I see."

I studied his superior smile, realizing he was about to hurt me. Seeing him through different eyes, I gasped out loud. How often had I seen that look on his face during our years together? All the things I'd done and endured to make him happy paraded before me in my mind. I clenched my fists until my nails dug into my palms. At all costs, I wouldn't allow him to get the better of me. Not this time, not ever again.

Oblivious to my feelings, Robert continued, sure of himself. "You've got a beautiful hotel. I admit it. We've had good service, so I have no problems there. But I do have a problem with your partner, Ann. She's not right for you." He let out a sound of disgust. "Look at her! All gold and glitz, entirely inappropriate for a classy operation like this. She looks like she came in off the streets! Image is important, and she doesn't fit it."

I was so incensed I could hardly choke out a reply. "Are you aware the house and the property are hers? She's the one who renovated it. Why, Rhonda DelMonte is one of the kindest, most loving, and generous people I've ever met." I shook my head. "Ah, you wouldn't understand ..." *What's the use*, I thought, there was no point in trying to talk to him.

I turned to go back inside the house.

"Hey! Wait a minute! I get it! You two are lovers." He laughed spitefully.

I whipped around, facing the vicious glint in his eyes. "Sorry, Robert, you're fishing in the wrong pond. Rhonda and I like men, Robert, real men. Something you wouldn't know anything about!"

I went inside and slammed the door in his startled, angry face. Adrenaline continued to pump through me, then ebbed away, leaving my legs like rubber. I gritted my teeth, thinking of Robert's maliciousness. *Now I understand why people murder their spouses,* I thought spitefully and then quickly corrected myself. *Ex*-spouses.

Only later, after Robert had left Sabal, did I begin to wonder about my role in the verbal exchange we'd shared. A nagging doubt ate at me. Why were Robert and Brock so eager to control me? Was there something wrong with me that I attracted men who wanted to abuse and hurt me like that? Would I ever meet a decent man? An awful thought occurred to me. Maybe that's what life was all about—men and women tearing at each other. If that was the case, I'd never get involved again. I was independent now. I didn't need a man. I could stand on my own two feet. And, God knew, I had a business to run.

I grabbed a cup of coffee from the hotel kitchen and was settling at my desk when Dorothy phoned us. "Ann? The Neighborhood Association has called an emergency meeting for this afternoon. They're going to discuss your filming request. As usual, some people are opposed to it. I think you'd better come to it. Brock Goodwin is back in town."

I let out a long sigh. "Thanks for letting us know, Dorothy." I hung up the phone wondering why, no matter what we did, someone wanted to undermine us.

Rhonda came into the office, and I shared the news.

She drew a deep breath. "You have to represent us again, Annie. Those swanky people aren't gonna listen to me. It's up to you."

I prayed I'd know the right words to say to save our business.

Dreading another confrontation with Brock, I reluctantly returned to the condominium clubhouse for the Gold Coast

Neighborhood Association meeting. Brock reminded me of Robert—someone who had to have his own way to prove his power—sometimes, for no other reason.

Will and Rhonda took seats on either side of me, like guard dogs protecting me. Dorothy sat at the table in front of the assembled group. She looked very small next to some of the other board members sitting beside her.

Brock entered the room as if he owned the place, his three sycophants in tow.

The meeting started with the usual items of business. When it came time for me to discuss the hotel, I rose and went to the front of the room. My knees shook, but I stood straight.

"I understand some of you are concerned about the filming that might take place on the beach in front of The Beach House Hotel. We've been told filming there can be done with little or no inconvenience to the neighbors. We understand the beach itself is public, and we'll make sure no one is denied access to it. This is a professional company, well acquainted with the need to be flexible. We ask you to be just as flexible." I paused, letting my gaze sweep over each face in the room. "This could be a very big thing for Sabal. Companies like this spend money. Businesses can get the exposure they might not get otherwise. "

"You mean *your* business," sneered Brock.

I shook my head. "I mean every business. Our community is small. We can help one another."

Clapping broke out among the members of the audience as I took my seat.

"Good job, Annie!" said Rhonda in a stage whisper. "You did good. Now let Will finish the job." She looked at Will with adoring eyes as he rose and walked to the front of the room.

Will cleared his throat. "I'm William Grayson, a CPA, and financial consultant. I've had a business here in Sabal for many years. In fact, I see a lot of familiar faces in the audience. With all due respect to the chairman, I believe he does not see the big picture. Filming a show in the neighborhood, under carefully agreed-upon restrictions, is a huge plus not only for the neighborhood but for Sabal itself. Sabal has a reputation of being a beautiful, high-end destination. The Beach House Hotel exemplifies all of that and more. Don't let the naysayers destroy what could be a very good thing for everyone involved."

Amid more applause, Will sat down.

Brock jumped to his feet. "This is just the beginning of a burgeoning problem for the peace and quiet of the neighborhood. Neither Ann Rutherford nor Rhonda DelMonte cares about Sabal or our neighborhood community. All they care about is money. We must put a stop to their constant, infringing requests, or we'll lose all the value of our property."

Dorothy jumped to her feet. "We've heard many people speak about what is really a simple matter. Filming is scheduled to take place over a short period of time and in the off-season. Allowing this gives the small business people of Sabal the opportunity for outstanding publicity. I, for one, am tired of always being in conflict with our president, who, I believe, has overstepped his role. In fact, I'd like to ask Mr. Goodwin to step down from that position and give the rest of us on the board a voice."

I held my breath.

Brock's face registered incredulity; then anger colored his cheeks a deep red. He turned on his heel and walked out of the room without a backward glance.

"May we have a vote?" Dorothy asked, raising her hand.

"Mr. Vice President, will you ask for a vote?"

A vote was taken, and we won handily. But I knew that wouldn't be the end of Brock Goodwin's opposition. As he'd warned me, he wasn't one to give up easily.

Excited, racing each other, Rhonda and I hurried back to The Beach House Hotel to call Brenda Bolinder.

Rhonda dialed the number, and we waited impatiently for Brenda to pick up. "Good news!" Rhonda said as soon as Brenda said hello. "We've got approval to do the filming here at The Beach House Hotel. We thought you'd want to know. We can't wait to have you here."

"Oh! I'm sorry. I was going to call you. Unsure as I was about The Beach House Hotel, I set something up in the Virgin Islands." Over the speaker phone, she sounded genuinely disappointed.

My heart plummeted.

"But ... but you can't," wailed Rhonda. "We want you *here!*"

"Mmm, let me get back to you," she replied. "Actually, it would be cheaper for them to come to Florida. I'll talk to the powers-that-be once more and call you back."

Nausea struck me as Rhonda hung up the phone.

Rhonda swiped a fist in the air. "I'm tellin' ya, Annie, if Brock Goodwin has screwed this up for us, I'll make his life miserable!"

For the next two days, we did our duties with little attention to them. If we missed out on the opportunity to host *The Sins of the Children*, we'd be off to a painfully slow start.

Brenda finally called while Rhonda was out doing errands. "Good news, Ann! The producers of the show have decided to use The Beach House Hotel after all. They'll take all the rooms from the middle of August through Labor Day.

I'll confirm dates and times in an email."

Tears of relief stung my eyes. "Wonderful! As soon as you confirm, we'll fax an agreement to you for your signature."

"That'll be fine," said Brenda. "You also need to be aware they have some personal requests, as well. I don't remember if you have a private limousine available to guests, but they'll require at least two. And perhaps you can help us arrange to lease some vans for their equipment. I'll send you a list of other special needs. They've agreed to pay for any of these additional services. That's one good thing about the entertainment business. They usually have allowances for costs like this in their budgets."

I quickly agreed to handle all requests, and we said goodbye. As soon as I hung up, I punched in Rhonda's cell number. She picked up right away.

"We've got it! *The Sins of the Children* is coming here!"

"I knew it!" she cried.

I laughed. "Hurry back. We need to get to work." In addition to preparing for the soap opera people, we'd decided to open The Beach House Hotel for a public Sunday breakfast—the first of many, we hoped.


On a glorious Sunday morning, Rhonda and I circulated among the guests in the dining room. They were digging into their breakfast with enthusiasm. I listened to them rave about the food, the house, and the grounds, and the tension that had built into a mild headache evaporated in a cloud of optimism. A reporter from the *Sabal Daily News* arrived with a photographer, and several of the county commissioners appeared along with some other movers and shakers from the city who'd been invited to our special event.

The happy sounds of the guests filled me with

satisfaction. I'd always loved entertaining at home. This was even better. The staff seemed to enjoy it too.

Rhonda and I took turns greeting people or giving them tours of the property.

As she was about to leave, Dorothy Stern came up to us. "Wonderful meal! You two are going to do very well." She sighed. "Watching you flit around, you girls make me envious. I used to love working. The mere idea of sitting and doing nothing makes me feel so old. You wouldn't need any extra help, would you?"

Rhonda and I exchanged glances. We'd already decided we'd need a part-time office worker, at least temporarily.

Rhonda smiled at me and placed a hand on Dorothy's shoulder. "How would you like to come and work for us in the office a couple of days a week? Annie and I were talking about needing someone the other day. We never have any free time."

Dorothy's eyes rounded, appearing even larger behind her thick lenses. "Why, I'd love to do that, sweetie. It's hard to go from owning your own business to doing nothing. I'd do a really good job for you. Honest!"

"We know that, honey," said Rhonda. "That's why we're asking you."

She left, and I gave Rhonda a high five.

With the success of our first Breakfast at The Beach House Hotel event, we moved forward, preparing for the arrival of the soap opera cast and crew. Ironically, after stumbling through an empty house on the Fourth of July, we started to receive requests for rooms over Labor Day weekend.

"I'm sorry," I told Dolores Johnson, our latest caller. "The hotel is completely booked. The soap opera, *The Sins of the Children*, is being filmed here during that time. Is there another time you'd like to come?" I waited for her response with bated breath.

"*The Sins of the Children*? Really? But that's so exciting! You mean Vaughn Sanders is going to be there?"

"Yes, he and all the others will be staying here for a couple of weeks."

"Oh my God! I'm green with envy. Wait'll my friends hear about this! Let me see, how about Veteran's Day weekend? Do you have space then?"

My smile grew even bigger as she gave me specific dates. I quickly entered them. "Okay, you're all set. We're looking forward to having you here."

"Thank you so much." She hesitated. "Do you think it would be possible to stay in the same room as the one Vaughn has? I don't want my husband to know, but it would be thrilling. Absolutely thrilling."

I held back a laugh. "I'll make a note of it."

Still chuckling, I told Rhonda about the conversation.

Rhonda jabbed a finger at me. "I told you, Annie! He's a real hottie! All the women love him." She blushed. "He's almost as cute as Will."

I laughed. They both were cute, but I had no real interest in either of them or any other man.

Working together, Rhonda and I addressed the special requests for the cast and crew. We came up with special menu items to satisfy certain stars, hired limo drivers, leased a couple of vans, and worked with the police department and a private security company to protect the privacy of the stars.

As happy as I was with the progress we were making in the hotel, money problems stalked me at home. Robert had taunted me when he'd left, saying he didn't know whether he'd send a check or not. I'd informed Syd about his threat, but a check hadn't arrived, and now I couldn't reach Robert.

# CHAPTER THIRTEEN

The television crew came two days ahead of the stars. Rhonda and I stood by in awe as vans filled with equipment filed through the gates of the hotel.

We tagged along as the cameramen, producer, and director walked through the entire house, deciding which rooms would best serve their purposes. Their enthusiasm added a sense of excitement to the process. Seeing the beauty and flexibility of the house through their eyes, my hopes for the hotel rose.

The house sparkled with their presence. Theirs was a jovial crew, with a lot of teasing as they went about their work or took breaks by the pool.

On the day the stars were due to arrive, Rhonda and I waited anxiously at the top of the stairs for the first of the limousines. Manny had called us from the van stationed at the airport to give us a heads up.

Even as I told myself they were just ordinary people with unusual jobs, I couldn't help feeling nervous. The first limo pulled in. I wiped my hands on my linen slacks and turned to Rhonda with a grin.

Rhonda's arms flapped for balance as she hurried down the steps in a gold caftan and strappy sandals. Sharing her excitement, I quickly followed.

Susannah Scoville, the actress who played the lead in the show, stepped out of the first limousine. She greeted us with a nod of her head and indicated the man standing quietly behind her. "My husband, Philip Gardner."

I shook hands with him, warming to his unassuming manner and easy smile. A little boy, about four, jumped out of the car, narrowly missing my feet.

"And who are you?" I asked, cheerfully.

"Garrett." He stuck his tongue out at me.

His parents smiled indulgently at him.

Shaking my head, I moved on to the next limo.

A man reached into the backseat of the second limo and straightened, briefcase in hand. I immediately recognized Vaughn Sanders as the tall, handsome and distinguished mayor from the television program. He turned and looked at me and broke into a dazzling smile.

I felt a jolt of pleasure and introduced myself. He held out his hand, and I took it, feeling very small next to his bulk. "Rhonda and I are pleased to have you here."

"Really?" His eyes shone with humor. "I'd think it would be a nuisance to have all of this mess here." He gave me a crooked smile. "But I, for one, am grateful to be able to leave the city for a while."

The momentary silence between us was interrupted by shouts from Garrett Gardner. He ran up the front steps of the hotel, pursuing a neighbor's adventuresome cat.

His father stood at the bottom of the stairs. "Garrett! Come back here! If you don't, I'll have to count to ten!"

Vaughn rolled his eyes at me.

"He's as bad as I thought?"

Vaughn nodded. "I had to put up with him all the way from New York."

I laughed at his woeful expression, and he grinned at me. My breath caught as his brown eyes continued to gaze into mine, reaching deep down inside me. I turned away, relieved to find Manny standing nearby to collect Vaughn's luggage.

Vaughn followed Manny into the house. His lean

muscular body moved easily. I watched him go, surprised by my strong reaction to him. As everyone constantly told me, he was one hot guy.

Once we'd shown everyone to their rooms, Rhonda met me in the office.

She elbowed me. "I saw the way Vaughn was staring at you. What was that all about?"

I shrugged, still shaken by the energy between us and what it might mean. "I think he was just being friendly."

She gave me one of her smart-ass grins. "He sure is a hunk."

I couldn't help the way my lips curved. I thought so too.


The first day of filming took place in the living room. From the sidelines, I watched them shoot a few scenes and was surprised by the tedium involved in the process. It was a "hurry-up-and-wait" kind of thing. One mistake in one person's lines or bad lighting meant reshooting the whole thing. Vaughn, I noticed, was very professional, delivering his lines without flubbing. Susannah, I decided, was a darker-haired version of Kandie—messing up her lines and pouting when she had to redo the scene.

"It's a lot different from what I thought it'd be," said Rhonda, joining me later in the office. "If I had to work with her, I'd have to choke Susannah. As it is, I'm ready to choke that little boy of hers. Do you know what he did now? He threw his father's robe and all the poolside towels into the swimming pool. I don't know why his father didn't take him aside and give him a good scolding. He didn't, though." Her brown eyes flashed. "If that sort of thing keeps up, I just may do it myself. Rosita doesn't need any extra work to do. She's busy enough as it is."

Rhonda and I joined the crew and cast for lunch in the new dining area. We'd set up a buffet of hearty cold salads, fresh bread, and fresh fruit. The camera men had no inhibitions about going back for seconds and thirds, and when Consuela brought out a tray of brownies still warm from the oven, they dug in with abandon. The cast, I noticed, ate small amounts of low-calorie food, no doubt concerned about the effect of an extra pound or two on camera.

Vaughn carried a plate over to the table where I sat with Rhonda. "Okay if I sit here?"

"Of course." Rhonda flashed him a big smile and patted the chair next to her.

He settled in his seat and turned to us. "What did you ladies think of the filming? I saw you watching from the sidelines this morning."

"Pretty boring," said Rhonda. "It seems like you have to do things over and over again."

"It's too bad you can't be sure everyone knows their lines," I added.

Vaughn nodded. "It's too bad you can't choose who you work with and, therefore, who you're going to be spending most of your time with."

Garrett Gardner chose that moment to race over to Vaughn, grab his arm, and swing on it like a monkey. "I wanna get up on your lap."

Vaughn grimaced. "Sorry, pal. I'm eating my lunch. Go find your father."

"No!" Garrett shouted. "I want you!"

"Garrett! Leave poor, old Mr. Sanders alone," Susannah called from her seat. "He doesn't like pesky little boys."

We waited for her to come over to get him. When she didn't, Rhonda rose and took Garrett's hand.

"C'mon! I'll take you over to your mother." She marched

him to Susannah's side and then went into the kitchen, leaving me alone with Vaughn.

I was curious about him. He seemed so nice. "Tell me a bit about yourself. Do you have a family?"

He nodded. "I have a daughter who works in D.C. for a lobbyist. Her older brother lives in San Francisco and works with computers."

"You're alone?"

Sadness flicked in his eyes. "My wife died three years ago."

"I'm sorry. I know what it's like to be left on your own. My husband and I are divorced, and my daughter, Liz, just completed her first year at Boston University."

He finished a bite of salad. "I keep busy with the show, of course, and when I can, I go to my summer place on Long Island. There's always something going on there."

We continued to make small talk. I was surprised by how down-to-earth he was. We chatted for a while longer, and then I excused myself to go back to work.

During the next few days, it became a habit for Vaughn and me to sit together for lunch. I learned Vaughn was an avid reader, and he liked to dabble with painting whenever possible. He confided he'd brought his painting supplies with him and hoped to be able to find some free time to capture the colors in the flowers and the Gulf waters.

One morning, I slipped on a pair of shorts and a T-shirt, eager for some relaxing time on the beach. Pleasing everyone at the hotel, catering to their requests, was exhausting.

I stepped out onto the sand and inhaled the salty air as the sun was rising. The sky held pink hues of early morning light, adding a rosy touch of brightness to the dancing water of the Gulf. I saw Vaughn standing by the water's edge in the distance, painting supplies in hand, and hurried to join him.

He turned to me and smiled. "You're up early!"

I smiled. "I'm always up early. In this business, we have to get up before the guests. I saw you out here and decided to come say hello."

"I'm glad you did." He held out his hand to me.

I took it, liking the feel of his strong fingers curled around mine.

"Stand here with me, just like this, and imagine we're the only two people in the world." He spoke softly. "Let the peace wrap around you. Isn't it marvelous? Just the sound of the waves and the calls of the birds to let us know we're not all alone in the universe."

I closed my eyes, feeling the promise of a warm day on my cheeks as I lifted my face up to the sky. Vaughn's hand helped to steady me as I continued to keep my eyes closed so I could take in the sounds. When I opened my eyes, Vaughn's steady gaze was on me.

"I guess I got carried away," I murmured, feeling heat creep up to my cheeks.

He smiled and trailed a finger down the side of my face. "It was nice to watch you. You're beautiful, you know."

Even as a rush of happiness filled me, warnings rang in my head. I removed my hand from his and stood before him, overwhelmed with confusing emotions. "Look, I'm not interested ..."

"Oh! I've said something to make you uncomfortable. I was just commenting on how lovely you look, nothing more than that."

My cheeks now flamed with embarrassment. I wished a giant wave would rush on shore and carry me away. "I'm sorry, I didn't mean, oh damn! I'm ..." I stumbled over words.

Vaughn tilted my chin up, forcing me to look into his eyes.

"I loved my wife deeply, Ann. The love we shared was very rare. I don't expect ever to find that again. Not in this lifetime. And I don't try. I'm happy and content just the way I am."

I froze. In the one program of *The Sins of the Children* I'd watched with Rhonda, Vaughn had said those same words about his fictional wife. Was he reciting them to me now for his own purpose? Or were the tears that had seemed so maudlin on the show tears of loss over his real wife? I stood there, not sure what was real and what wasn't.

I checked my watch. "Guess I'd better run. It's getting late."

"I'm sorry, Ann." He gave me a long look that confused me even more.

I took off, uncertain what all of it had meant.

For the next few days, I found myself on an emotional roller coaster. Now that I knew Vaughn had no real interest in pursuing a relationship with anyone else, I conversely found him more attractive than ever.

I watched Vaughn act out a love scene with a tall, young redhead, purportedly one of his many women on the show. A pang of envy shot through me as I watched his sensuous, full lips come to rest on the actress's welcoming smile. And when Vaughn wrapped his strong arms around the girl, I filled with a longing so sharp that I had to turn away. Disgusted with myself, I headed back to the office, tripping over my feet in my haste to get away.

At my desk, I held my head in my hands, wondering what was wrong with me. It had been a while since I'd been with a man, but that, I told myself sternly, was no reason to act like a star-struck teenager.

Vaughn continued to seek me out. Each time I met up with him, I felt drawn to him in a way I couldn't explain, even to myself.

Just as we'd settled into a comfortable routine with the soap opera people, the director informed Rhonda and me the show was likely to wrap early. At lunch, Vaughn confirmed it. He told me he, along with some others, had decided to stay a few extra days, filling their time slot.

I was pleased to hear it. It was nice to have money coming in.

As we finished our lunch together, Vaughn said, "My daughter Nell is coming down tomorrow to join me. Is that a problem?"

"Not at all," I answered, anxious to meet her. Just mentioning her name, his face had lit up.

I stood by the front door, awaiting Nell Sanders' arrival. Manny pulled into the front driveway, and I started down the front stairs to greet her. My breath caught when Nell stepped out of the van. She looked uncannily like Liz. Her lighter hair color, height, and fuller body altered the perception to a degree, but her blue eyes accented a strikingly similar facial bone structure.

She approached me, and I introduced myself. "Your father is in the middle of filming right now. He asked me to show you around and get you settled."

"Lovely place," Nell murmured, looking up at the façade of The Beach House Hotel. "I'm ready for a break from the antics of Washington. I have a good feeling Sabal is exactly what I need."

As we entered the reception area in the front hall, we heard the director announcing an end to the day's shooting.

Nell smiled. "What do you know? Wonders never cease."

Vaughn came bounding over to us. "Nell! I thought I

heard your voice!" He pulled his daughter into a strong embrace. "Welcome to Sabal! I'm glad you're here. Come up and see the views from the balcony. It's gorgeous here! Hurry! Then we can go down to the beach!"

He was too distracted by his daughter even to acknowledge my presence. Watching him all but carry his daughter up the stairs in his enthusiasm, I felt achingly alone.

I went back to the kitchen. Rhonda was kneading dough for the next day's sweet rolls. Feeling blue, I plunked myself down in a chair at the kitchen table. I was happy Rhonda and Will were seeing each other and certainly didn't want to rush into anything, but sometimes I felt so, so ... single.

"How's Vaughn's daughter?" Rhonda asked.

"It's the strangest thing. She and Liz look a lot alike. And you should see Vaughn with her. He really loves her."

Rhonda frowned at me. "What's the matter? You seem a little down."

"It's nothing. Lonely, I guess."

Rhonda gave me a little punch in the arm. "Hey! You've got Will and me, kiddo! And the girls will be here tomorrow."

"I know." My eyes filled with gratitude. Without them, I didn't know what I'd do.

# CHAPTER FOURTEEN

As the girls exited the plane, Rhonda and I glanced at one other with pride. They looked healthy, happy, and tanned from their summer camp experience.

A sigh of contentment escaped me as I hugged Liz. It felt so good to have her with me.

We gathered their belongings and headed to The Beach House Hotel. On the way, the car filled with their chatter—music to my ears.

Filming had stopped for the day when we drove through the gates of the hotel. The putting green was hosting three people. Four other men were tossing horseshoes on the side lawn. The pleasant ping of tennis balls being hit could be heard from behind the hedge as we parked by the garage, next to Manny's car.

"Where are the stars of the show?" Angela asked, opening the car door. "Susannah Scoville is great! She's not only pretty; she's smart. I've always liked her."

Rhonda and I glanced at each other and burst out laughing.

Angela frowned. "What's so funny?"

"You'll see," said Rhonda.

"Hey! What's that little boy doing?" Liz pointed to the front of the house.

Garrett Gardner was crawling under a hibiscus bush, laughing wildly as his father chased him. Colorful blossoms fell to the ground as the boy pushed his way into the plantings, breaking branches as he went.

"What a brat," murmured Rhonda.

Shrieks suddenly filled the air.

"Ow! Ow! Ow!" Garrett scrambled out from beneath the bushes, brushing wildly at his legs.

I knew exactly what had happened and ran toward him. Taking hold of his arm, I swiped at his legs.

"Stop! What are you doing to him?" Scowling, Garrett's father stood aside, looking as if he was about to hit me.

"It's fire ants. And they hurt!" I swept the last of them away as Rhonda joined us.

Garrett's father lifted him in his arms and turned on me. "You expect your guests to put up with this kind of thing? What kind of place is this?"

Rhonda's expression changed from concern to one of growing fury.

"Don't ..." I murmured and stood back as Rhonda faced Philip Gardner with narrowed eyes.

"You listen to me!" she said. "That boy has no business crawling in the bushes! He's ruined some of the landscaping. He had no business throwing all the towels in the pool, and he has no business annoying everyone around him. If you'd discipline him, he might not act that way. Don't tell me how to run my hotel when you don't even know how to control a four-year-old!"

A hush fell among the onlookers who'd gathered around us.

Susannah Scoville hurried over and stood beside her husband. She patted Garrett's cheek. "There! There! It's all right. That lady is just mean."

Silent for once, Garrett stared wide-eyed at Rhonda.

Susannah glared at Rhonda. "You just don't like kids. Honestly, I've never met so many people who absolutely hate kids."

I held my breath.

Rhonda stared at her defiantly, hands on her ample hips. "I love kids, but I don't like *brats!*"

Susannah stamped her foot like a spoiled child herself and took Garrett in her arms. "Come, Philip. We're leaving. I'm through with all my scenes except one, and that can be filmed in New York."

Garrett started to pound his mother on the chest. "Put me down! Put me down! I wanna stay!"

"Stop that!" Susannah grabbed his hands. "We're leaving whether you want to or not!"

"That," said Rhonda in round tones, "is the first sensible thing I've heard you say."

Susannah stomped up the stairs into the hotel, her husband at her heels.

I drew a breath and waited for a reaction from our guests. At the sound of nervous tittering behind me, I turned to find Liz and Angela staring at Rhonda, their mouths open.

One of the cameramen who'd been watching the whole scene from the putting green started to clap. "Way to go, Rhonda Baby!"

The other onlookers joined in, and soon the sound of applause filled the front yard.

A grim expression on his face, Roger Sloan, the producer of the show, made his way through the crowd that had gathered around us.

I braced myself for bad news.

"Look, I'm sorry I was rude to one of your stars," Rhonda said contritely. "We've appreciated your business. I shouldn't have blown my cool like that."

"You shouldn't have had to." Roger placed a hand on Rhonda's shoulder. "Don't worry about it. Susannah's right. She doesn't have to stay. Most of the rest of us, however, intend to remain a couple of the extra days we booked. We want to enjoy a relaxing break before heading back north. In fact, my wife is flying down here tonight."

A look of relief smoothed Rhonda's face.

"We'll arrange for a limo to pick her up, if you'd like," I said, anxious to smooth things over. "And as long as you and so many others are staying, we'd like you to be our guests at a special picnic supper tomorrow, to celebrate your success in filming here at The Beach House Hotel."

Rhonda's eyebrows rose until they were hidden by the blond curls cascading over her forehead. I prayed she'd play along with me.

"Excellent," said the producer. "You're on!"

Liz and Angela followed us into the hotel and went off to Angela's room. Alone in the office, Rhonda faced me. "So what's this about a picnic? Where'd that come from?"

"I didn't want their final image of the hotel to be of an unhappy guest storming out of here. A nice picnic under the stars should make a better lasting impression on them, don't you think?"

"Oh, yeah. Great idea!" Rhonda gave me a broad smile. "You're good for me, Annie. I need your nice, proper manners to balance my temper."

I laughed. I couldn't help it. "We need each other, and you know it!"

"Ya know, Annie, as long as we're doing this picnic thing, we should invite the people on the neighborhood board, to thank them for their support."

"I think so too." It was a good political move. And if I remembered what Dorothy had told me, Brock would be away on another of his business trips.

###

A breeze off the water helped cool the air as the party got underway. I surveyed the scene. We'd played up the tropical theme with flowers everywhere. Glowing lanterns placed strategically shone like fallen stars. Tables covered with crisp, sea-green tablecloths held dishes and platters of assorted food items, garnished with fresh fruit and colorful flowers, adding to the theme. A keg of imported beer sat in one corner of the lanai, where Will stood chatting with some of the crew members. A number of our other guests gathered by the small bar set up at the other end of the pool deck.

Dorothy Stern came bustling over to me. "This party is wonderful! Let's hope Mr. President of the Gold Coast Neighborhood Association doesn't join us. I think he's back home."

I turned anxious eyes to the doorway.

Dorothy tugged on my arm for attention. "There's Vaughn." She fanned the air with her hand. "He's so handsome I swear, even at my age, he takes my breath away. And he's the nicest young man!"

I smiled at the pretty blush that colored her cheeks. "Have you met his daughter? She's talking to Angela. She's nice, too."

Dorothy hurried away, and I was relieved to stop talking to her about Vaughn. Like it or not, I'd become attracted to him. The thought of his leaving the hotel made me sad.

"Nice party," said a voice behind me, and I turned to face Vaughn's tall figure.

"Thanks." I smelled his distinctive aftershave lotion and inhaled it, storing the aroma of it in my memory for the lonely time ahead.

"I heard about Rhonda's shouting match with Susannah yesterday," he said. "Good for her. She did what the rest of us have wanted to do all along."

Liz came rushing over to me, interrupting us. "Mom! I've been talking to Nell Sanders. She's invited Angela and me to visit her in Washington so we can see what a lobbyist does. Isn't that cool?"

"Yes." I gave her a quick hug. I'd never been able to keep up with Liz's ever-changing plans. "Have you officially met Nell's father?"

Liz shook her head and held out her hand, looking up at Vaughn with uninhibited delight.

Smiling, Vaughn took hold of Liz's hand. "I've enjoyed getting to know your mother."

"Cool," said Liz, giving us both long looks before she was called away.

Vaughn's gaze bore into me. "You must have been surprised when you met Nell."

"You mean at how much Liz and Nell look alike?" I nodded. "Yes, I was. I must admit it has made me very curious."

"Nell takes after my wife. Some say she has my personality. I don't know about that, but she definitely has the look of her mother." The pride on his face was telling, and I realized he still loved his wife.

At the sound of a commotion, I looked up to see Brock Goodwin standing by the door taking in the scene. My heart fell. We'd sent him an invitation for political reasons and only because we thought he'd be out of town.

His eyes met mine. He waved and came right over to me, making it impossible for me to avoid him. Though I'd grown to detest the man, I stood my ground, resolved to be as pleasant as possible.

Ignoring Vaughn, Brock said, "I see you and Rhonda have outdone yourselves catering to the stars. I saw your email earlier and wasn't going to come, but the mayor called and asked me to represent him. How could I refuse?"

I gritted my teeth and reminded myself of my duties as hostess. "Vaughn, this is Rhonda's neighbor—Brock Goodwin. Brock, Vaughn Sanders."

Brock cocked an eyebrow and leaned toward me. "My dear, I'm *your* neighbor too."

For a horrifying moment, I thought Brock was going to kiss me. I quickly stepped back.

Vaughn glanced from Brock to me with interest.

Unwilling to spend another moment with Brock, I left the two of them sizing up each other.

"Some picnic!" The producer, Roger Sloan, approached me with a smile, compelling me to take my focus off Vaughn and Brock. A tall, svelte blond hovered at Roger's side.

"I was telling my wife, Darlene, that this would be a wonderful spot for us to visit for long weekends in the winter. I don't have time for extended vacations—four-day weekend trips are better for me. Darlene told me the flight down here was a breeze."

My spirits lifted. "Call us anytime. We'll be sure to squeeze you in."

"You have a wonderful place," Darlene said, glancing around. "I'm in the fashion business, and I know several people who'd love to come here. The only thing is they'd want to be assured of privacy because they're well-known— names anyone would recognize."

My pulse quickened. Offering a small, private location was one of the things that Rick Jamieson, our hospitality consultant, had said made us unique.

"I'm sure that privacy wouldn't be a problem. It's worked out pretty well these past weeks, don't you think, Roger?"

He nodded. "Very much so. I think what Darlene is trying to say is that the other guests, not just the staff, would have to be asked to respect the privacy of those around them."

"I see. No problem." But I wasn't exactly sure how that would work.

Brock approached. Before I could hurry away from him, he caught up with me, placed a hand on my shoulder, and pulled me to a stop. "So, Ann, what do you have going on with Vaughn? He warned me not to cause any trouble at this party. What's up with him?"

"I have no idea why he would say something like that unless you purposely baited him. What did you say to him?"

Brock smirked. "Just that you and I are dating."

Dismay knotted my stomach. "Why would you say something like that? It's not true."

"Everything all right, Ann?"

At the sight of Vaughn striding toward me, I fought the urge to run to him. "Brock is just leaving."

Brock's eyes widened. "Don't keep avoiding me, Ann. It's not good for business." He glanced at Vaughn and threaded his way through the crowd toward the living room doors.

I watched him carefully to make sure he actually was leaving. When I turned to face Vaughn, he was talking to Roger Sloan. Not wanting to interrupt, I went to check on Manny. My mind spun at Vaughn's concern for me. What did it mean?

The next morning, Rhonda and I sipped coffees in the office. I told her about Roger and Darlene's comments regarding privacy for our guests.

"What do you think they meant by that?" I asked.

Rhonda grinned. "It could be the people they know would want to bring special guests, not necessarily their wives or girlfriends or boyfriends."

I could feel my eyes widen. "Oh my God! You don't mean we're going to run a high-class whorehouse, do you?"

Rhonda laughed. "Of course not, honey. I wouldn't want to do that! But I've read that sometimes high-powered people need a place to go where they know the maids aren't going to sell a story to a scandal sheet, and other guests aren't going to stare at them. I once heard about a place in Wales like that. Famous people go there knowing no one is going to talk about them if they don't wear makeup or their toupées or whatever. Their privacy is guaranteed."

"Oh, I think we can do that," I said, mollified by Rhonda's revelation. "In fact, when we have the new brochures printed up, why don't we add a blurb that says privacy and discretion are a special part of your visit, or something similar."

"Good idea." Rhonda rose to her feet. "See you a little later. I'm going to help Angela pack the car with the girls' things while you see how we're going to get all these people to the airport this afternoon. Just think, by tonight we'll be all by ourselves again. It's going to seem mighty quiet around here."

"Too quiet." I was disappointed I wouldn't have more time with Liz and sorry that the television people, especially Vaughn, would no longer be around. His smile and the way we talked so easily would be sorely missed. The tension of wondering when I'd meet up with him during the day had added anticipation to each of my activities.

Later, Rhonda and I waved goodbye as the girls pulled out of my driveway in the little white BMW. They were driving to Boston, so Angela could have her car at school. As I watched them disappear down the driveway, my eyes misted over. Where had the years gone?

Tears rolled unabashedly down Rhonda's cheeks. "Seems like yesterday Angela was a baby, taking her first steps. Now, she's off on her own. I'm getting old, standing here crying like a baby myself."

I gave her a sympathetic squeeze, wiped my eyes, and blew my nose.

At the hotel, the scene was of organized chaos. Manny and Paul were piling luggage into the van while the crew and stars of the show stood about, waiting for the limousines to arrive.

Vaughn came over to me. "Thanks for everything. It was a great way to film these segments. You have a beautiful place here, Ann. Good luck!"

His dark eyes bore into mine. My pulse sprinted. Once more, I had the feeling that he was able to see deep inside me where I hid my feelings. He lifted my hand and smiled at me, a little sadly. "I meant what I said about you on the beach that day. You're beautiful, and I don't mean just the way you look. I wish ..."

"Hey, Vaughn, come here." Roger waved him over.

Vaughn left me, and Nell approached, smiling. "I'm trying to talk Dad into coming down here for Thanksgiving. We'll see. He can be very stubborn, and for some reason, he's resisting me on this." She gave me a knowing look. "I think you scare him, Ann."

"Me?" Surprised, I glanced at Vaughn, now chatting amiably with Manny.

"He told me how attracted he is to you. Yet he still misses my mother. I told him it's time for him to move on," she said softly, glancing at him. "We'll see if he does."

A warmth that had nothing to do with the heat of the day burned inside me. I hadn't imagined the attraction, after all. I blurted out, "I understand. I like him a lot, Nell." Feeling like a school girl with a crush, I added, "Actually, more than a lot."

Nell smiled and gave me a kiss on the cheek, then walked over to one of the limousines waiting in the front circle.

I watched Nell and Vaughn settle in the backseat of the limo. The memory of Vaughn's hand curled around mine on the beach that special early morning filled my mind. He'd made me feel spiritually one with him. I'd never felt that way with anyone else—certainly not with Robert. Looking back now, I realized Robert and I had been more business partners than anything else.

After the last of the vehicles left, I was suddenly overcome with ambivalent feelings. I was so attracted to Vaughn it almost hurt. But realistically, Vaughn Sanders, the actor, would be difficult to live with. His schedule, the fact that women threw themselves at him, and his dedication to his craft would be problematic.

Rhonda came over to me. "The staff is busy cleaning the rooms. Will called and asked me to lunch. You don't mind if I go, do you, Annie?"

I shook my head. "Of course not. Go and enjoy yourself!"

*Time for a dose of reality*, I told myself, as Rhonda went into the hotel to get ready for her date, and I returned to the office to check the financials from the soap's visit.

That night, as I restlessly switched from one evening television show to another, I tried to relax. But every male character on the screen morphed into a broad-shouldered man with dark tumbling curls and eyes that challenged me. I finally switched off the TV and stumbled into bed, determined to put Vaughn Sanders behind me. No matter what Nell said, I knew Vaughn was not ready for a new relationship. And with him in New York and me in Florida, there was no chance of it going any further.

I was just about to turn out my light when the phone rang.

"Annie! I saw a light on in your room and had to call you! The most wonderful thing has happened. Will has asked me to marry him! We think we're going to get married around

Christmas! Will you be in my wedding party?"

All grumpiness left me. "Oh, Rhonda! Of course! I'd love to!"

"I didn't think this would ever happen to me!" Rhonda gushed. "I'm so happy I can't stand it! Wait'll I tell you what he did! He put a diamond ring in my water glass. It was so adorable."

My heart surged with joy for her. Eager to hear all the delicious details, I curled up under the covers on my bed, the phone to my ear.


Our days fell into a new routine. When Rhonda was not on duty at the hotel, she spent her nights with Will. After catering to demands from guests, purveyors, and advisors all day, his home in another section of town was, she said, a welcome retreat for her. Lately, my free time was spent in front of my sewing machine working on window treatments for the house. As much as I didn't enjoy it, I figured I was saving a whole lot of money by doing this myself. Whenever I felt self-pity about to overwhelm me, I reminded myself I was much better off independent and lonely than in a marriage that was a failure.

Rhonda approached me one day. "Annie, I've watched you for weeks now. You're not doing anything for fun. Don't you think you should? You can't stay here and work all the time."

I sighed. "It seems like such a chore to get out. It's hard to meet people in town when I'm so involved with work. I feel like we can't leave the hotel. We never know when we'll be needed around here."

Rhonda nodded. "It's tough on both of us. Maybe it's time to hire more help—at least during the season. The New York crowd is starting to come through with reservations.

February, March, and April are pretty well booked. We're gonna need some breaks, or we'll go crazy." She gave me a pat on the back. "In the meantime, you're going to a Halloween party with Will and me Saturday night. And, Annie, I won't take no for an answer. I'll have Dorothy come and stay here so we can both go. She'll love it."

I wasn't crazy about the idea, but once Rhonda made up her mind about something, there was no use arguing with her.

By Saturday, I was glad I'd accepted Rhonda's invitation. The week had been trying.

To top it off, late that morning, Robert finally returned my phone calls.

"What is it, Ann?" he snapped. "You're spoiling my weekend."

"Your check is past due, Robert. You signed a legal document agreeing to pay on a certain schedule. I need the money, Robert. It's mine."

"C'mon, Ann. I'm not stupid. In one of her magazines, Kandie read all about *The Sins of the Children* being filmed at The Beach House Hotel. You don't need the money. I do."

I clenched my teeth together so I wouldn't scream.

"You there, Ann?"

"One week, Robert. If the check isn't here, I'll be forced to turn it over to Syd."

"You ... you ..."

Burning with resentment, I slammed down the phone. He thought our having the soap opera group here for a couple of weeks meant we were wildly successful and had no worries. But I knew better. Rhonda and I had been warned time and time again the hotel business was one good cycle followed by a not-so-good one or worse. A turn-down in the economy, rising gas prices, iffy weather, and the ever-present threat of hurricanes could ruin our goals.

I dressed for the party and gazed into the mirror. The black robe of the witch's costume concealed my body. Green paint covered my face. The pointed hat atop a gray wig hid my own natural color. No one, I thought gleefully, would recognize me.

Will and Rhonda came to the door to pick me up. I waved a long-handled broom at them and emitted a nasty laugh.

"That's great, Annie!" Rhonda wore a red cape and hood that almost covered her wild, blond hair. "How do you like Little Miss Red Riding Hood?"

I chuckled. "I do." With Will's diamond ring on her finger, Rhonda's self-image had been transformed into a lovely, young thing. *Good love is magic*, I thought wistfully.

At the party, I strolled among guests I didn't know, feeling secure hidden behind my costume. A group of costumed men stood talking at the bar. Hearing a familiar voice among them, I took cover behind a nearby pillar.

"It makes me mad, I tell you, to think that a beautiful neighborhood like ours has a commercial enterprise like a hotel in the middle of it," I heard Brock Goodwin say.

"Come now, Brock," said another masculine voice. "The Beach House Hotel isn't just any little hotel. It's a first-class establishment. And, you must admit, it looks a lot better now than it did a few years ago. Rhonda keeps it in meticulous condition—something the former owners couldn't afford to do."

"Say, Brock," another voice added with a sly tone. "Why are you so upset? I thought you had a thing going with Rhonda's partner."

"She's a looker, all right," said someone else in the group.

"Yeah? Well, looks can be deceiving," growled Brock. "Trust me. I know. She's nothing but a cock tease."

"I'd like to give her a whirl, just the same," one of the group members added.

Feeling queasy, I leaned against the marble column. Why couldn't Brock just accept I didn't want to go out with him? And why the bad stuff about the hotel? Was he one of those guys whose ego dictated badmouthing everything and everybody who'd ever rejected him?

From his place near Rhonda, an elderly gentleman dressed like a pirate, edged over to me.

"My wife and I wish all the success in the world to you and Rhonda. I understand you're going to be receiving some pretty important guests. My contact in Washington tells me a senator from Iowa is coming down this winter to stay at your place."

I turned to him with a smile. "Actually, we have quite a few famous people making reservations with us. But, of course, I can't mention any names. Our guests trust us to be discreet."

His eyes twinkled. "I like that. My wife and I have been talking about coming over for one of your Sunday breakfasts for some time now."

"Breakfast is Rhonda's specialty. Come anytime. We'd love to have you."

He shuffled away, and my earlier worries about Brock's remarks eased. Sabal was filled with interesting people who would, I'm sure, see Brock for the shallow, egotistical, selfish man he was. But in the meantime, what other nasty things would he try to pull?

# CHAPTER FIFTEEN

We remained busy, learning more and more about unexpected situations with guests in the house. But as busy as we were, my thoughts drifted to Vaughn. I relived that day on the beach with him over and over in my mind. I even imagined him calling to tell me how much he missed me. Worse, just to see him, I'd taken to sneaking into the hotel library when his show came on television. Foolish of me, but I couldn't stop. Rhonda sweetly pretended not to notice.

As I was researching on-line advertising campaigns, the phone rang. Hoping for another reservation, I eagerly picked it up and chirped, "The Beach House Hotel!"

"Hello ... This is Rhonda's husband, Sal DelMonte. Where's Rhonda?"

My breath caught with surprise. "I'm sorry, but she's not here at the moment."

"It's really important. I gotta talk to her. Tell her I'll call back at six, and tell her she'd better be there."

Before I could protest, he hung up the phone.

*Rhonda's husband?* I didn't think so.

Rhonda came into the office a little later, and I gave her the message.

She frowned. "I wonder what he wants. He never calls unless he wants something. And what is this business about being my husband? He *was* my husband. He damn well isn't now!"

Rhonda went ahead and changed her plans to meet Will

so she'd be available to receive Sal's phone call.

At six o'clock that evening, the phone in the office rang.

I got up and left the office to give Rhonda privacy. When I returned, Rhonda was sitting in her desk chair staring blankly into space, her face unusually pale.

My pulse sprinted. "What's wrong? Are you all right?"

Tears filled Rhonda's eyes. "You're not going to believe this. Sal's dying of cancer. They've told him it's a matter of weeks. He's scared and wants to come home."

I frowned. "Come home? This isn't his home anymore. You told me he hasn't been in touch with Angela or you for a long time now."

Rhonda nodded sadly. "The sonuvabitch didn't even call Angela on her last two birthdays."

"So, what did you tell him?" I asked gently. She looked pale.

Rhonda let out a deep sigh. "I told him I'd think about it." She held up a hand. "I know what you're thinking, but Sal and I go back a long way. He's going to call me tomorrow."

"Tomorrow?" I thought of all the problems to be worked out in a situation like this.

Rhonda bit her lip. "He didn't say so, but I betcha he's out of money. I don't know for sure, but I suspect he got into drugs in Miami. He called me one time when he was high."

"Are you sure he's not dying of AIDS?"

"Oh, I hadn't thought of that. But I've got a choice to make, and I'm not sure what I'm going to do."

A little while later, Rhonda came to me. "Will's real unhappy with the news. Now I really don't know what I'm going to do."

"What did Will say?"

"He told me Sal should be with hospice. After all the years of taking care of his sick wife, he knows that even with nurses doing most of the work, it's a tremendous drain on energy and money."

Her eyes filled. "He asked me what it would do to our wedding plans. I told him it shouldn't make a difference, but you know Will. He's old-fashioned. He said it would place him in an awkward situation to be planning a wedding while my ex-husband was living with me, and dying. If Sal comes back, Will wants to postpone the wedding."

Rhonda buried her head in her hands. My heart went out to her. I understood her goodness, but I was worried what it would do to everyone if she took him in here at the hotel.


Sal DelMonte arrived "home" to die on a gray day. I stood with Rhonda at the base of the steps, ready to greet him. I'd known he was short in stature, but when he emerged from the taxi that delivered him to The Beach House Hotel, he seemed shrunken to a child-like size. His body was emaciated and his face pale.

He acknowledged me with a nod and turned to Rhonda. "You look good, Rhonda. Uh ... real ... uh ... healthy."

Rhonda let out a snort. "When haven't I ever been big and healthy, Sal?"

He held up his hands. "I meant it as a compliment. Honest."

I left them and went back to the office to write up an ad for extra staff. I had no illusions about the time commitment Rhonda had made in promising to help Sal.

She returned to the office, and I handed her the ad copy. "What do you think?"

Rhonda glanced over it. "Fine. We're going to need somebody because it's going to be a rough few weeks with Sal. He looks awful, Annie. Absolutely awful. You should have seen him after he climbed the stairs. He's so weak. And he was a guy that was always on the go. It used to make me tired sometimes, just watching him."

"It's sad, I'm sure." I took her hand. "No word from Angela, yet?"

Rhonda shook her head. "I want to give her a chance to think about my letter before calling me. She might not understand why I'm doing this. After all, he's hurt her terribly."

Sal's first day at The Beach House Hotel indicated what a poor patient he was going to be. He called Rhonda on the intercom several times requesting in a whining voice for her to come and help him unpack, to bring him a glass of homemade lemonade, to bake him his favorite cookies, and on and on.

I made myself remain silent each time Rhonda ran out of the office to take care of his needs. No doubt about it, we'd need extra help.

Telephone calls came in, responding to the ad I'd placed on the internet and in the newspaper. Over the next couple of days, I eagerly screened callers and started a list of possible candidates. I soon narrowed the list down to two. Rhonda agreed with my choices.

Preparing for the two interviews, I reviewed the notes I'd made on Tim McFarland. He was young, currently working at a hotel in Sabal as a bellman, and had attended the hotel program at the University of Massachusetts for two-and-a-half years. He seemed promising. I checked my watch. He was due in my office in ten minutes.

At the appropriate time, Consuela ushered a tall, well-built young man into my office. He smiled at me when I rose and offered my hand, then shook it firmly.

"Let me guess," I said. "Football. Right?"

He laughed. "My freshman year. After that, I gave it up. I didn't want to miss out on the good times at my fraternity."

I liked his honesty. "Sit down, Tim. Let me tell you a bit about The Beach House Hotel and what we need around here."

Tim listened carefully as I told him how the business got started, how it was shaping up, and the type of clientele the hotel was attracting. "We need someone who's willing to work erratic hours, sometimes very long hours, performing an assortment of tasks. And someone who understands the importance of being discreet. No talking to anyone else about guests who might come and go. What do you think?"

He nodded. "I'm the man for the job. It sounds perfect."

I studied him closely as we talked about his schooling and his future. I liked his energy, and when he told me he'd already heard about The Beach House Hotel and wanted to work in a classy place like this, he won me over.

"I'll check your references and get back to you," I said as I walked him to the front door.

The middle-aged man who arrived for the second interview couldn't hold a candle to Tim's enthusiasm and willingness to take on any job we wanted him to do.

Later, I gave Rhonda a short version of the interviews, and she agreed that as long as his references checked out, Tim was our guy. I made follow-up calls and was pleased to learn the other hotel was sorry to lose him.

Tim started immediately as our Assistant Manager, and I couldn't have been happier. Thanksgiving was approaching, and business was picking up. It was due, in some measure, to the cold, wet weather up north. I found myself racing to catch the national weather reports, cheering inwardly when lousy weather prompted more phone calls.

As busy as I was handling as much as I could by myself while Rhonda dealt with Sal, I continued thinking of Vaughn. Nell had wanted to return to The Beach House Hotel with her father for Thanksgiving, but we'd heard nothing. Soon the last room was booked for the holiday with no word from either Vaughn or Nell. I hid my disappointment behind the excitement about being fully booked and counted the days until Liz came home.

I was in the kitchen with Rhonda and Consuela when Liz called.

"Guess what? Nell Sanders called me a moment ago. She's invited Angela and me to visit her in Washington over Thanksgiving weekend. She was going to be alone for the holiday and remembered we wanted to come to D.C. and decided to give us a call. Cool, huh?"

"Nice of her." I tried not to let my disappointment spoil Liz's pleasure. "She's not going to spend Thanksgiving with her father?"

"Nope. He's going to see a close friend in London—a woman he's known for a long time. You won't be too disappointed if I don't come down there for the holiday, will you? You said you were going to have a full house, and I thought you'd be busy ..."

"No, honey, that's fine." My voice turned hollow at the thought of Vaughn with another woman. "This is the time when you should take advantage of opportunities like this. Go and have a good time."

I hung up the phone, overcome by the emptiness inside me.


Thanksgiving Day was clear and cool. Puffy white clouds

raced across the bright blue skies, urged on by the cold front to the north. The pool deck, filled with guests soaking up the sun's rays for most of the morning, emptied in the afternoon as they disappeared to their rooms to prepare for our traditional meal.

I stood at the sliding doors in the living room watching the Gulf. My mouth watered as I inhaled the aroma of roasting turkeys drifting from the kitchen. Outside, waves caressed the sand with foamy fingers. It was hard for me to believe that one year ago, I'd just met Rhonda. So much had happened since then.

The new dining area was abuzz with happy conversations as old friends of Rhonda's gathered with some of our guests before the Thanksgiving meal. At one end of the room, Tim was acting as the bartender. Sal remained seated at one of the tables by the entrance, greeting their old friends as if he were still Rhonda's husband. Giving me a worried look, Rhonda hovered by the doorway, waiting for Will.

When he appeared, Rhonda threw herself into his arms. Will's pleasure at seeing her dissipated when his gaze came to rest on Sal.

Rhonda grabbed Will's hand and pulled him toward the table where Sal was sitting. "Will, meet my *ex*-husband, Sal DelMonte. Sal, this is my *fiancé,* Will Grayson."

They nodded at each other and shook hands, but it was obvious neither man was comfortable.

"Come have a drink." Rhonda hurried Will away from Sal.

I was seated at the table closest to the door, with Sal, Dorothy Stern, and Father Hennessey. During the meal, Dorothy, who'd imbibed more than two glasses of wine, said in a loud whisper, "It's a shame, isn't it, Father, that Rhonda and Will had to postpone their wedding. I hope it doesn't affect their plans permanently."

A gloating expression covered Sal's face, and, surprised, I realized how pleased Sal was with himself.

I glared at him.

"What? Why are you looking at me like that?" Sal asked.

"We'll talk about it later." I wanted to wring his scrawny neck.

Sal picked at his meal with no evident enthusiasm and finally pushed his chair back. "I'm tired. I think I'll go upstairs for a nap. Rhonda! Rhonda! Come here."

Rhonda started to rise from her chair. When I noticed Sal's smile of satisfaction, I jumped to my feet. "Never mind, Rhonda. I'll take care of it. You stay here with our guests."

I grasped Sal's elbow and helped him rise. "Rhonda can help me," he whined, "not you ..."

"Yes, me," I said into his ear. "You and I need to have a little talk. And there's no better time than now when Rhonda is occupied with our guests."

Upstairs, gathering words in my mind, I helped Sal up onto his bed, fluffed his pillow, and spread a light cotton blanket over him.

"So, what did ya wanna talk about?" He crossed his arms like a defiant schoolboy, leaned back against the pillow, and glowered at me.

I cleared my throat. "I've been watching you. You actually seem pleased Rhonda and Will had to put off their wedding because of your arrival. You've been nothing but a whining pest since you came here, and if you think I'm going to let you interfere with Rhonda's happiness, you're wrong! I don't know a more deserving person than Rhonda! She's warm and kind and loving!"

Sal gave me a startled look but remained quiet.

I couldn't stop myself from saying more. "You made your choice to leave her. Now that you've come back, you seem to think you can have her at your beck and call, night and day. That's not fair, and you know it! You've already made her change her wedding plans. What more do you want?" Breathing hard, I stopped, shocked by my outburst.

A smile spread across Sal's face. "Ya know what, girlie! I like your style! You're a real street fighter."

My jaw dropped as Sal continued. "Yep! I was mighty worried when I first met you—too pretty by a long shot. All style and no substance, I thought, but you proved me wrong. That's good. Now leave me alone. I'm tired."

I left the room enormously pleased. Never in my whole life would I have dreamed of being called a street fighter and liking it.

Late that afternoon, Liz called to wish me a happy holiday. When I realized she was calling from a house Vaughn had visited, fresh longing filled me. Pushing away memories of Vaughn, I chatted with Liz, forcing gaiety.

That night, in my bed, feeling all alone in the world, I cried myself to sleep.


My confrontation with Sal was the beginning of an unlikely camaraderie between us. We quickly became fast friends. Perhaps, as Rhonda's doctor had confirmed, it was because the time he had left to him was so limited.

I spent some time with him every day so Rhonda wouldn't feel she had to be with him as much. We either sat on the balcony of his room watching shore birds or reading, or when he felt stronger, we debated issues ranging from politics to business. I discovered that though he was an unpolished man, he was bright and quick-witted. We both enjoyed our free-wheeling, good-natured arguments.

In too short a time, however, caught up in a race against

the cancer that threatened him, Sal grew much weaker. It was a contest no one could stop, and everyone knew the winner.

Rhonda called hospice in, and she and I took shifts helping to take care of Sal. I wondered if he would live long enough for Angela to see him. She'd resigned herself to the idea of meeting with him at her Christmas break.

Mid-December approached in a flurry of activity as we prepared for our first holiday season. The bookings were good, with Senator Snyder, the jovial representative from Iowa, leading off the holiday season in style.

He arrived from Washington, booming hello in a voice that made me wonder if he realized he was in Florida and not in his home state. His many requests turned the hotel upside down. The fax machine seemed to whir endlessly while Rhonda and I worked to turn the library into a small, secure meeting room.

When Senator Snyder's well-known opponent on the Senate Foreign Relations Committee arrived under wraps, I began to understand the secrecy that cloaked his visit. A hush-hush meeting in the hotel was scheduled for the next day, away from the curious eyes and long noses of the press.

Over the next few days, and in between meetings, the senator and his wife were able to enjoy the pool area without being pestered by the other guests, thanks to the privacy policy we'd established.

With the senator's visit, the idea was confirmed that The Beach House Hotel was a special location where the powerful could feel at ease and meet their peers to either relax or conduct business in private.

The Snyders left with the promise that not only would they return, they'd also spread the word among the other members of Congress and their families.

After the limousine carrying them pulled out of the circular driveway, Rhonda gave me a high five. "We're on our way, kid! We're gonna be bigger and better than we ever imagined! You watch and see."

I laughed. Things were taking on an entirely different shape. The thought both exhilarated and frightened me. If we wanted to handle more than one small group at once, we'd have to redo some of the downstairs rooms into meeting rooms. And if we were going to serve upscale, private dinners worthy of world figures, the formal dining room needed some attention.

That evening, I relieved the evening hospice nurse on duty so I could spend some time with Sal. I had something to discuss with him, something that had been bothering me for days.

"How are you doing, Sal?" I asked softly, clasping his cold hand in mine.

"I'm doing fine for a little wop who's dying," he mumbled. "How about you?"

"Good. Senator Snyder and his wife had a wonderful time here. They promised to tell all their friends about us. Things like that will help our business grow."

"You girls will do all right." Sal squeezed my hand slightly.

"Can I ask you something personal, Sal? Rhonda once told me her father forced you to marry her so you could become part of the family butcher business. Is that true?"

Sal's eyes rounded. "Forced me? No! Why would she say that?"

"She told me she overheard you talking with her father one day, and that's how she knows. She seemed really sad, talking about it."

"But that ain't true!" Sal struggled to sit up. "I didn't care what her father said. Rhonda and me, we were together already, just like I wanted."

Surprised, I stared at him. "Maybe you should tell her that while you can."

It was his turn to be surprised. "Why? It's water over the dam."

I didn't know whether to laugh or cry. "Sal, you dummy! It would mean the world to Rhonda."

His brow creased. "You think it would make a big difference?"

"It would be a wonderful farewell gift," I said quietly, fighting tears.

That night, I heard a knock on my front door and went to see who it was. Rhonda peered at me through the side window.

I hurried to let her in. "What's the matter? You've been crying. Is everything all right?

Rhonda nodded. "I've just had the most wonderful talk with Sal. You'll never guess, Annie, but he says nobody forced him into marrying me, that he loved me all along. Why didn't he ever tell me that? I could kill him for not telling me!" She let out a shaky laugh. "Oh, well, at least we're ending up friends. And you know what else he said? He hopes Will and I will be real happy."

I gave Rhonda an affectionate hug, "Sal's a lot nicer than I first thought. I'll miss him when the time comes."

Tears filled Rhonda's eyes. "I like him a lot better now than I have in years." She blew her nose on a tissue with a loud, honking sound. "He asked me to call Angela. He wants her to come home now." She looked at me with round, sad eyes. "Oh, Annie, I don't think he's going to wait until Christmas, after all."

My heart was heavy as I made my way to Sal's room the next morning. We'd shared so much in the past weeks.

Sal appeared to be sleeping soundly when I approached his bed. His breathing was shallow, and his complexion had turned to gray. I lifted his hand and found it colder than usual.

"That you, girlie?" he whispered, his eyes fluttering open.

"Yes. I just wanted to say 'thank you' for talking to Rhonda. It was a nice thing to do."

"Not bad, huh? Is Angela coming?"

I heard the desperation in his voice and blinked back tears. "She's on her way. Hold on."

It was difficult to see him struggling to cling to life until his daughter could say goodbye. I left him sleeping deeply. I'd come to love the little bantam fighter and could understand why Rhonda had too. I smiled, understanding how important it was for him to leave this life in a place like The Beach House Hotel, which matched his love of nice things.

While Rhonda picked up Angela at the airport, I sat with Sal. Rhonda had told me earlier that, faced with the thought she might not have the chance to make amends with her father, Angela was now frantic to get back home.

I heard footsteps on the stairs and rose. Angela stood in the doorway, staring at her father. Her face registered shock.

"Is he ... is he gone?" she asked tearfully.

I shook my head. "He's sleeping. Come over here. It's all right. Take his hand and talk to him."

Rhonda appeared at the door, and though my heart was breaking, I gave her my best smile. "I'm just leaving."

Before I could reach the doorway, I heard Angela say, "Daddy? Daddy? I love you, Daddy! It's me, Angela. I'm here."

I gently shut the door behind me. *Let the healing begin,* I prayed, and swallowed my own tears—tears that burned my throat as they slid past the lump that lingered there.

# CHAPTER SIXTEEN

The day after the small, private funeral for Sal, Rhonda drove Angela to the airport so she could attend the last of her classes and prepare for exams.

The pace of business at the hotel kept the rest of us focused forward instead of lingering on the sadness of Sal's death. Dealing with all kinds of people became a fascinating and sometimes tiresome task. Some of our guests were easy to please; others were not. And each had a story to tell.

Wilkins Jones, a free-lance writer, called wanting to do an article on the hotel for the holiday travel section of the *New York Times*.

Rhonda and I greeted him as he got out of a rental car. I was surprised by his appearance. He was not the sophisticated man I'd thought he'd be. His suit was rumpled, and he appeared oblivious to the brown stain on his white shirt where his belly extended. The young, tall, blond, curvaceous woman at his side wiggled and giggled and batted her eyes at him in a very unspouse-like fashion. Hands on his hips, he ignored her as he surveyed the façade of the hotel.

"Senator Snyder wasn't kidding when he told me about your place. It's beautiful! Let's see inside." He turned to Rhonda. "I hope you have your special cinnamon rolls on the menu for tomorrow. I've heard all about Breakfast at The Beach House Hotel."

Rhonda's face flushed with pleasure. "Don't worry, Mr. Jones. They'll be warm from the oven whenever you want them." The popularity of the sweet rolls had already prompted a New York publisher to request the recipe for a new cookbook they were doing.

"This is definitely my kind of place," Wilkins Jones said enthusiastically. He bounded up the front stairs on feet surprisingly light for his girth. Trying to keep pace with him, the blonde teetered dangerously on four-inch heels. I glanced at Rhonda. We waited until they were well inside before letting out our laughter.

That afternoon, Wilkins Jones' companion lay out beside the pool, wearing the smallest bikini I'd ever seen. Every male eye around the pool remained glued to her figure. In contrast, the overweight writer was a sight of another kind in his Speedo suit. I shook my head, surprised he didn't seem the least bit embarrassed to be seen like that.

Some time later, Wilkins called the office, urgently requesting homemade cookies be brought to his room. I put together a plate of them and carried them upstairs. Before I could knock on the door, it opened. Wilkins, wrapped in one of the hotel's thick terry robes, beamed at me. "Ah! Just what I wanted."

"Who's there?" came a feminine voice from another room.

"Nobody!" Wilkins placed a warning finger on his lips. "I don't want her to see me snacking. You know how these young people are—they never eat!"

I grinned and turned away.

Not long afterward, a loud shriek came from upstairs. My heart pounded with alarm. I dropped my paperwork at the reception desk in the front hall and dashed up the stairway.

The blonde was standing at the door of Wilkins' room with just a towel wrapped around her. Her face had drained of color. Her eyes rolled in her head like those of a spooked horse.

I grabbed her by the shoulders. "What is it?"

The blonde pointed into the room. "There. In there."

I hurried into the room and stopped short. A very rotund, very naked Wilkins Jones lay sprawled across the king-size bed, his large, white buttocks exposed.

I gasped as I took in his stillness, his blue-tinged lips. "Call 911!" I screamed to the girl, who, I now realized, had been sharing the space with him moments ago. I lifted Wilkins' hand, searching for a pulse. Then, I tried for a pulse at the neck. Nothing. "We've got to try CPR!"

"I will!" gasped the distraught girl. "You talk to the people on the phone!"

Rhonda and Tim hurried into the room.

"What's wrong?" Rhonda cried and staggered back when she took in the sight. "Oh, my God! Annie! Is he ... is he dead?"

The blonde stepped away from Wilkins' body and shook her head. It's...It's... not... working."

"Keep everyone away," I said to Tim, waiting for the 911 operator to pick up.

Tim went out, closed the door behind him, and directed the few other mid-week guests away from the room.

My voice shook as I gave the 911 operator the details. "I'm pretty sure he's dead," I ended, feeling sick to my stomach.

"Help is on the way," she said. "Stay on the phone with me until I know they're there."

"Better get dressed," I whispered to the blonde. "They'll be here any minute."

At the sound of an ambulance pulling in, I told the operator they'd arrived and hung up. Waiting for the EMTs to appear, I stood with Rhonda, staring at our very dead guest.

Rhonda cupped her cheeks with shaking hands. "What

are we going to do?"

Still reeling from the shock, I could only shake my head. I'd never imagined something like this.

Tim led the EMTs to the room. They worked in tandem, checking every possibility, trying to bring him back. But it was too late.

Later, after the police and coroner had done their work, I helped the distraught blonde pack her things. When she requested a ride to the airport, Tim left with her.

Rhonda made arrangements with Wilkins' wife to have the body taken away and prepared for a flight home. I gathered his belongings and packed Wilkins' suitcase, then stepped aside so the room could be cleaned.

Later, shaken by all that had happened, I sat with Rhonda in the office feeling numb.

Rhonda gave me a worried look. "Annie, we've gotta keep it quiet about the way he died— in bed with a young floozie. You know?"

I nodded. It was all part of our vow of discretion. I could only imagine what the press would do with news like this.

It didn't take long for a news reporter to call the hotel, requesting information about Wilkins Jones. He was more well-known than I'd suspected. The questions came at me like rapid gunfire. How exactly had Wilkins died? When? What had we talked about? My hands grew sweaty as I answered as truthfully as I could while being discreet.

The next morning, Rhonda waved me over to her desk and held up the morning paper. "Listen to this. 'Mr. Wilkins Jones, a free-lance writer, well-known for his interesting travel articles, died peacefully in his sleep yesterday afternoon while vacationing in Florida at The Beach House Hotel.'" She beamed at me. "Good job, Annie. We even get some publicity out of it."

I let out a breath of relief and wondered how in the world I'd ever been talked into this zany business. Dealing with people from all walks of life made things interesting, but it was a never-ending roller-coaster ride.

Responses to the invitations to our first annual Christmas Open House rolled in. Everyone, it seemed, wanted to see where *The Sins of the Children* was filmed. We'd invited people from the neighborhood, members of various hotel associations, and the movers-and-shakers of the community.

On the appointed day, Rhonda and I stood side-by-side greeting guests at the front door. Rhonda wore black slacks and a bright red Christmas sweater adorned with fluffy, furred angels. To complement the red of Rhonda's sweater, I'd chosen to wear an emerald green long skirt and matching top. Tim's burgundy sport coat kept the holiday theme going as he ushered guests through the house, giving them a tour of the property.

The huge Christmas tree in the entry hall sparkled with glass balls of every color. Clear glass icicles hung from the branches, absorbing the colors around them. The scent of pine permeated the air, adding a nice holiday touch.

Consuela, Rosita, and Ana circulated among the guests, carrying trays of food whose tantalizing aromas filled every room. We'd hired two bartenders to work the bar we'd set up in the living room.

Rhonda and I meandered among the guests, welcoming them. I noticed Will and Dorothy and some of the other people from the neighborhood talking together and knew from their happy expressions they were enjoying themselves. Pleasure filled me. Hosting a party like this was something I enjoyed. Setting up and running the hotel had become my life, and I was proud of all Rhonda and I were accomplishing.

After the last guest left, I kicked off my gold sandals, collapsed on a couch, and massaged my tired feet. "What do you think? Did we pull it off?"

Rhonda sat beside me, grinning. "They loved us! I think we're going to fill in some of the blank spaces for the season."

"Great." January, February, March, and April were the high season months in Sabal. If the hotel was going to do well for the year, those months had to be solidly booked.

"Annie? I'm proud of all we've done. Aren't you?"

I smiled. "Sure am." It had taken a lot of luck to bring us to this point, but we'd worked our tails off too.


The girls arrived home for Christmas grumbling about their exams and anxious to laze in the sun. At the airport, I hugged Liz close to me, happy she'd be with me for the holidays. A gleam on Liz's wrist caught my eye. "What's this?"

She held out her arm. "My Christmas present from Dad and Kandie. Cool, huh?"

"A Rolex? That's a little extravagant, don't you think?"

Liz shrugged. "I don't know. I like it. Besides, Dad's doing great. He and Kandie are going to build a big house. They showed me the plans. It's going to be beautiful. They even have a room for me."

My heart thumped wildly. Robert clearly had not given up on the idea of having Liz move in with him. Worry knotted my stomach. I wondered how much I should say to Liz. Surely she could see Robert for what he was and not be taken in by his gifts.

It was so like Robert to play the game this way. He knew

perfectly well I couldn't compete in a game of one-upmanship. How could I? At the same time he was buying expensive gifts for our daughter and building fancy houses, he was withholding his last payment to me. I couldn't let him get away with it.

According to our signed agreement, I was to be paid the third and last payment by the middle of December. And I was counting on it. We were trying to finalize our budget for next year. Money was coming in, but money was going out at an even faster clip because we were continuing to upgrade the facilities to accommodate our upscale guests.

I waited until Liz was at the hotel with Angela before I called Robert. "Where is the money you owe me?" I asked him. Though I wanted to scream at the top of my lungs, I fought to keep my voice from becoming shrill.

He snorted into the phone. "What are you carrying on for? I saw the article in the *New York Times* about your hotel and how wonderful it is and how anybody who is anybody wants to go there. So, what's your problem? You're doing well. Give me a break. I'll pay you when I can."

My body turned fiery hot. I struggled to keep my voice from wavering, though I was so angry I was afraid I'd cry. "Our deal was signed, sealed and delivered almost a year ago. I'm counting on that money for my own use. I'm not going to give up what is mine so you can give our daughter a Rolex watch and build a brand new house!"

"Oh, so that's it! Liz told you about the house, huh?" His voice grew triumphant. "Well, it's going to be a beauty. Better than anything you and I ever had."

Oh, how I hated him, listening to him boast, each word a stab to my heart and self-esteem.

"Yeah," he continued. "I figured the boy would need the room, especially with another baby on the way."

"Kandie's pregnant again?"

"Not exactly. But we've decided to go ahead and try for another one. It probably won't take long. If I have to educate one more, it might as well be two."

Reeling from the vicious intent of his words, I drew a deep breath. He knew my vulnerabilities, how I'd yearned for more children. Tears, hot with pain and indignation, sprung to my eyes and washed down my cheeks. I was grateful he couldn't see them and wouldn't know he could still wound me so.

Using every ounce of self-control, I said, "I'm not waiting any longer for what you owe me, Robert. Syd Green will call Jack Henderson today."

"You really are something. Know that?" Robert snarled. "I just made a payment before Thanksgiving. It's Christmas, for Chrissake!"

"And business is business," I responded firmly. "A deal is a deal. It wouldn't come to this if you'd paid the second payment on time, as we'd agreed. You're the one who set up the payment schedule. I didn't. Now, you have to live with it."

"What a bitch!" he sputtered, his voice rising dangerously.

Heart pounding, I hung up the phone. I hated confrontation, but in the past year, I'd learned that if I didn't stick up for my rights, Robert would try to manipulate me out of them. I couldn't let that happen. The more I'd given in to him, the more he'd taken. I wouldn't allow him another opportunity.

Willing myself to let go of my anger, I sat in my kitchen trying to calm myself. It was, after all, the Christmas season.

Later, I walked by the lanai at the hotel. At the sound of giggling, I stopped. Liz and Angela were huddled together at the shallow end of the pool.

"What's up?"

"Somebody named Tim." Liz nudged Angela.

"Oh! So you've finally met him. He's doing a great job for us."

"He's awfully cute." Liz rolled her eyes playfully. "Angie thinks so, too."

A flush brightened Angela's face.

"Well, girls, for whatever it's worth, I think he's a hottie too."

The girls burst out laughing.

# CHAPTER SEVENTEEN

Christmas rolled into New Year's Eve in what seemed the blink of an eye. I'd hoped to hear something from either Vaughn or Nell, but though I'd sent a Christmas card to Nell, thanking her for the time she gave to Liz over Thanksgiving, I'd received nothing in return from her. And Vaughn? I couldn't even watch the show anymore.

*Men!* I thought with disgust. They were either like Robert or Brock—too demanding and insisting on things their way, or like Vaughn—too good to be true. What I had once thought was a real connection between Vaughn and me was, I realized, my seeking something substantial. How foolish.

Liz entered the office at the hotel. "'Bye, Mom. Angela and I are off to South Beach. Sure you don't mind my leaving you alone for a couple of days?"

Touched by her concern, I smiled at her. "Have a fun-filled weekend. I know how excited you are to meet your friends from school for New Year's Eve. But, Liz, please be careful."

"Thanks!" Liz gave me a hug and left.

I went back to checking financial reports, pleased by the business we'd done over Christmas. We'd been able to attract locals for our special holiday meals along with our usual Sunday breakfast bunch.

At the end of the afternoon, I was sitting in the office checking receipts when I heard the door open.

"You've gotta see this, Rhonda!" I cried, delighted by the numbers.

"Hello, Ann. It's good to see you again," said a melodious voice I knew well.

I swiveled around and let out a gasp. Shock and pleasure swept through me.

Vaughn Sanders' gaze settled on me. He gave me a crooked smile that set my heart to pounding.

"What a wonderful surprise!" I managed to say.

He stood there like the ghost of my dreams and held out his arms to me.

I hesitated for only a moment. Joy lifted me out of the chair and into his embrace.

He let out a satisfied chuckle and held me close. "I decided to surprise you. Nell thought it was a good idea. I'd like to take you to dinner tonight if you can get away. I see how busy you've become."

I wanted to pinch myself to make sure it wasn't one of my dreams come to life. *What did this mean? What did he want from me?* I fought to think clearly. There was no question of business as usual.

"Dinner with you would be wonderful," I said. "I've got the perfect place in mind."

I led Vaughn to the kitchen, where Rhonda was working with Consuela. "I'm going to take the rest of the day off."

"You bet you are!" Rhonda threw her arms around Vaughn. "Boy! Are we glad to see you! You have no idea how much Annie ..."

I shot her a warning look that stopped her cold. I still didn't know what Vaughn's visit meant for me.

"How long are you staying?" I asked him. "And where?" I'd seen no evidence of luggage.

Vaughn smiled. "I've got reservations for two nights right here. Under an assumed name."

Rhonda elbowed him. "You sure are a sneaky one!"

He laughed. "In my business, you sometimes have to be."

I smiled, but self-doubts lurked inside me. Was this just a little vacation break for him—a dinner date that filled the hours away from New York or maybe London?

"What do you say we make it seven o'clock? That'll give me time to get settled," said Vaughn.

I walked him to the lobby. "That'll be fine. I'll make the reservations. They know me, so a last minute request shouldn't be a problem."

As I left him, my emotions flew in many directions at once. No matter how much I wanted—no, needed—to know his purpose, I decided to simply let the evening evolve. I didn't want to appear over-anxious or assume anything beyond what it was—a dinner date.

Heading over to the Palm Island Club, I sat alongside Vaughn on the motor launch listening to the sound of the boat slice through the water. The happy tattoo of my heartbeat rose above the noise of the motor. "He's here! He's here!" seemed to be the cry of the gulls swooping above us in the cool air. I turned to Vaughn with a smile, wondering if he knew how deeply happy I was to see him.

His expression brightened, and he reached for my hand. At the dock, he handed me out of the boat, and we walked up a path to the rustic main building of the complex on Palm Island, a short boat ride from the mainland.

We entered the restaurant. The hostess took my name and led us to a small table sitting by itself in a corner of the dining area. Holding my chair, she murmured, "It should be nice and private here, Ms. Rutherford."

She turned to Vaughn. "Have a good dinner, Mr. Sanders. We're pleased to have you here. I never miss the show."

Surprised, I looked at Vaughn, and we laughed.

"I guess there's no getting away from being a well-known mayor on television," I said with amusement as the hostess walked away.

"Yes, especially in a place where the sins of the children cause so much trouble." He shook his head. "People take their soap operas seriously."

Throughout the meal, I listened eagerly to Vaughn tell me what had happened since I'd last seen him. He amused me with stories of the trade, making me feel a part of his world. "The Christmas show was a blast, with everyone dressed up, fake snow and all."

"How was your Christmas? Were you with Nell?"

"She and I had a nice day together. My son stayed in San Francisco for Christmas day, but we were together earlier when he came to New York for the Christmas show."

"And your Thanksgiving?" He hadn't mentioned the trip to London.

"Very nice, thanks."

Vaughn took my hand and gave it a squeeze. "It's so good to see you again."

My pulse sprinted. Gazing into his eyes, I felt he was every bit as sweet as I'd remembered him during the empty months without him.

Later, on the return trip to the mainland, I settled in the boat beside Vaughn and held his hand, filled with the need to touch him. A cool winter breeze ruffled my hair as the boat skimmed the water's surface like a bird about to take flight.

Vaughn leaned over and pushed strands of my hair away from my face. Smiling at me, his eyes crinkled at their corners as he gave my hand a squeeze. "You look lovely."

A young, attractive woman on the boat edged her way over to us. "Vaughn Sanders! I thought that was you!" She grinned at him and pushed her way in beside him.

He acknowledged her with a bob of his head and his lips curved into the smile he'd just given me.

My self-confidence turned to dust. Vaughn had elected not to come to Sabal for Thanksgiving and had visited his lady friend in London instead. Now he was flirting with the woman sitting next to him. Vaughn could have his choice of any woman. Why would he choose me? For him, this was nothing more than a dinner date. The blood drained from my face as realization struck me. *Oh, my God! I'm going to be hurt all over again!*

I tried to remain composed as we disembarked, got into my car, and drove back to my house.

Getting out of the car, Vaughn smiled at me. "Shall we go for a walk along the beach?"

"All right," I answered hesitantly, not sure I could bear to stand beside him in the moonlight while my shattered dreams were strewn about on the sand.

Vaughn took my hand, and we walked down to the water's edge. "You've become awfully quiet. Is everything all right?"

Not trusting myself to speak, I could only nod my head. I was afraid the tears I felt inside would start to spill over. I scolded myself for being such a romantic fool.

Vaughn tilted my face upward and with an innate tenderness gently wiped the moisture from the corner of my eye. "Come here," he whispered, drawing me up against him and enfolding me in his warm embrace.

I rested my head on Vaughn's broad chest. The size of him made me feel protected. Leaning against him, I heard the wild racing of his heart.

"Ann, I don't know where this will lead us, but I want to take the first, faltering steps," he murmured. "Will you help me along the way?" He leaned down and kissed my lips, burning them with the fire of promise.

I gave into it for a moment and then forced myself to step back. "What about the woman in London?"

His eyes widened, and then he chuckled. "She's an old family friend whom I've always been able to trust to set me straight. At ninety, she's still amazingly aware. She's known me for years." He stroked my cheek. "Worried, were you?"

As I absorbed his startling information, I gave him a shaky smile. "Just hold my hand and stand here with me for a moment without saying a word." I had to see if my memory of the two of us standing together was real.

We stood side by side beneath the clear, star-scattered sky. The waves gently lapped against the shore, a soothing sound in the silence. I looked up. The belt of Orion's constellation blinked like a friend's hello. A deep, satisfying bliss filled me. I closed my eyes and whispered "Thank you" to the heavens above.

When I opened my eyes, Vaughn was smiling down at me as if he too felt the special bond we had. His lips brushed mine, and I stretched on tiptoes to invite him in.

After returning to my house, Vaughn and I went outside and lay side-by-side on lounge chairs holding hands. The sweet perfume of nearby tropical flowers surrounded us, and silvery moonlight allowed us to see each other in stark relief, accenting our features. I thought I'd never tire of looking at him beside me.

"I promised myself I wouldn't rush into anything," Vaughn murmured. "Quick, easy relationships that don't last are just a matter of course in my business. I see it all the time and, believe me, I have offers all the time. One of the things I loved most about Ellen was that she made me realize that all the adoration and flirtation was just a part of the business I'm in—a very fake part, at that. She kept my feet on the ground when I first started on the show and jerked me back down to earth whenever I started to think I was worth all that attention."

As I listened to him talk about his wife, I became more and more concerned. How could I ever measure up to a woman whose memory burned so bright? I rolled onto my back and gazed up at the twinkling stars, thinking what a wonderful man Vaughn was. There was an honesty to him, a humbleness that Robert had never possessed. Fame hadn't created a monster, I realized, but a happy, satisfied human being.

"Penny for your thoughts." Vaughn rubbed his thumb up and down the palm of my hand before bringing it to his lips.

I turned to him, smiling. "I like you, Vaughn Sanders. I really, really do."

His eyes sparkled with mischief. "Do you think it could be more than that?"

I laughed. "Definitely."

Pulse sprinting, I took his hand, and we went inside.

In the master bedroom, I turned down the bedding. Vaughn removed his shirt, exposing his manly chest sprinkled with hair. I removed my dress and paused, shy about exposing all of me to him.

He removed his trousers, allowing me to see how ready he was. At my hesitation, Vaughn came over to me.

"Here. Let me help you."

Unhooking my bra, he cupped my breasts. "Beautiful," he murmured and leaned down to kiss their tips. At his warm, moist touch, I held back a moan.

We lay down on the bed, beside one another. He smiled and kissed me, and I tasted the after-dinner mint he'd eaten. His kisses grew more urgent and, with a groan, he removed my panties. I turned to him, as eager to explore as he.

Inhaling his spicy aroma, I stroked him, marveling at his manly shape.

His hands moved with a gentle sureness as he learned the curves of me. As his fingers found my sensitive core, I couldn't hold back a sigh of pleasure. I wanted him so much.

"Ready?" he whispered in my ear.

My body hummed with need. I pulled him closer. "Yes. Hurry."

He mounted me, and with a sense of joy I opened up to him.

Later, sated, we snuggled up to each other. Vaughn had talked about taking it slow, but what we'd had wasn't slow at all, but the most exciting lovemaking I'd known.

Soft sleeping sounds came from him.

I rolled onto my back and stared up at the ceiling. He was everything I wanted in a lover. But I'd learned a painful lesson by giving up my independence for a man. Vaughn was right. We needed to go slowly.

# CHAPTER EIGHTEEN

I rose and tiptoed around my room, dressing silently. I couldn't help staring at Vaughn lying on his back, snoring softly. The silky dark curls on his head spread across the pillow like a promise of further playtime. It took all my willpower not to wake him by running my fingers through those locks of hair.

I walked over to the hotel, still feeling the workout Vaughn's lovemaking had given me.

When I entered the hotel kitchen, Rhonda looked up from the stove. "Well?"

I snatched a piece of bacon from the counter, looked at her, and grinned. "He's a wonderful man, truly wonderful. I like him a lot."

"*Like* him?" Rhonda squealed, her eyes round. "You *like* him?"

"Yes, he's very nice." I struggled to keep the teasing going, and turned to leave, well aware Rhonda was dying for every detail.

Rhonda flew at me, the sleeves of her black-edged orange kimono flapping like the wings of a Baltimore Oriole. "Wait a minute, Annie! Ya gotta talk to me! I wanna know all about it!"

I burst out laughing. "C'mon! Let's go into the office."

Sitting at my desk, I looked up at my dearest friend, eagerly perched on the edge of it. "Okay, I'd say he's about the most perfect man I've ever met. At least, that's what I think now. But both of us want to spend a lot of time getting to know each other before we even consider the next step. We both agree it's best to do that."

"Damn! That sounds so practical." Rhonda crossed her arms. "Far too practical when I see that glow of happiness on your face! When I know what I want, it's hard for me to hold back."

"You're telling me?" We both laughed. There was no holding Rhonda back for anything. "Seriously, there are a lot of things Vaughn and I need to take into consideration. You should have seen all the people staring at him last night. Everyone seems to know who he is. It can't be easy living like that. I love my life right now, living and working here with you. We've made a commitment to each other to have this hotel running well. I just wish there was a way for Vaughn to be a part of it, down here, with me."

Rhonda nodded. "I see your point. Will already has a life here. With Vaughn, it's different. But, Annie, keep that glow. Will ya?"

She left me, and as much as I hated having to be so cautious, I knew I was right. While Vaughn was the man of my dreams, I didn't see how we could blend our lives.

Vaughn stopped into my office a short while later. I couldn't help the breathiness of my hello. He was just as gorgeous in the morning as he'd been in my arms in the moonlight. He closed the office door behind him and smiled at me. At the desire I saw in his eyes, my pulse pounded.

He drew me to him. "You're bewitching me! I dreamed of you."

All but purring, I smiled and rested my head on his chest.

Rhonda knocked and entered. "Hey! The two of you look great together, just great. Sorry to disturb you, but the Murrays are wondering when they can come back for a longer stay. I told them I'd have to check the system. I knew you were working on it."

I became all business as I turned to the computer. "Let's see, the Murrays are leaving today. What about the week after Easter? I think there might be some time then."

Rhonda and I huddled, looking over several possibilities, trying to fill in the blanks on our system.

"See you later." Vaughn slipped out the door as Rhonda and I continued to talk.

When I caught up with him later by the pool, Vaughn looked up from the book he was reading. "Business all taken care of?"

"The Murray request, yes; the rest of it, no. I have some things I have to handle, and then I'll be free. Sorry."

"I see. Well, I'd better go back to my book." I was surprised by the hint of irritation in his voice.

"Okay. See you later." No one, not even Vaughn, was going to interfere with what I had to do to survive. He was used to a lot of attention, but if we were together, there would be plenty of times I wouldn't be able to give it to him.

Number one on my list of things to do was to call my lawyer. Robert's check had not arrived, and my personal bills were piling up. Fuming, I crossed the lawn to my house. The hotel was doing well for a start-up, but Rhonda and I were not taking much money out of it yet. We couldn't. We had to use funds to convert the library to a meeting room and embellish the small dining room for private dinners.

Inside my office, I punched in the numbers for Syd.

He picked up right away and listened to me. "Sorry I haven't been able to get back to you, but I had a hard time reaching Robert's lawyer," he said. "We finally talked this morning, and he advised me things are not going all that well with Robert's business. In light of that, he's requested additional time to pay off this last piece of the debt."

"And what did you say?" My heart stopped and then raced with apprehension. I stood and looked out my office window, hoping the swaying palm trees would help calm the fear that gripped my body with suffocating fingers.

"I told him that, according to the agreement Robert had established, you were entitled to the money and needed it now. "

I felt a glimmer of hope.

"Jack Henderson all but snorted at that remark." Syd sounded apologetic. "He said his client had been under undue pressure to come to an agreement, that he hadn't thought it through, and as his former wife who, quote, took him to the cleaners, unquote, you should just be patient and wait for it."

My voice turned to ice, even as my body heated up. "Did you mention the fact that Robert and Kandie are building an enormous house, giving extravagant gifts, and generally spending money like crazy?"

"Indeed, I did. I told him we were well aware of Robert's plans to build a large, expensive house, and under the circumstances, we did not feel that a lack of money was causing this change in attitude."

"And what did Jack say?" My heart was pounding so hard, the room grew fuzzy.

Syd cleared his throat. "These are his words, not mine. He said that you had become a selfish, hard woman and that after all Robert has done for you throughout the years, you should be willing to allow him to make this payment sometime in the next year or two."

His words stabbed me. I took an unsteady breath. What I'd asked for had been more than fair; Robert had agreed. I willed myself to stay calm and to be strong enough to fight Robert's latest betrayal. I brought my agitated pacing to a stop. I had to convince Syd he was working for me.

"Let's look at this from a different point of view. If I were a man and the sole provider of my family, what would you advise?"

"Well, but you're not the sole provider."

Amazement mixed with fresh anger. "But I am! Robert hasn't paid for any of Liz's expenses since the divorce. I pay for everything for myself and Liz, except for Liz's education, which is being taken care of by the fund we set up with the proceeds from the sale of the house. Robert is carrying her on his health insurance policy at no extra added cost to himself." I took a deep breath. "My old Honda is starting to give me trouble. I'll hang onto it for as long as I can. In the meantime, The Beach House Hotel is like a hungry child demanding to be fed."

"You're right, Ann. I'm afraid if we don't persist, you'll never get the money. Robert hasn't been trustworthy. Let me continue conversations with Jack and call you back when we have a resolution."

Nauseous, I hung up the phone. What would I do without the money I was owed? Frantic, I went back to work on year-end figures for the bank. I'd just finished punching some numbers into an Excel spreadsheet when I heard my name being called.

I jumped up from my chair and went to the front door. All thoughts of numbers disappeared. Vaughn grinned at me, wearing a T-shirt over his swimsuit and sandals on his feet. A towel was draped around his shoulders but couldn't hide their breadth. He looked ... delicious.

"Can you come out and play?" His eyes sparkled with good humor.

"Sure can," I answered, setting aside problems for the moment. While Vaughn was here, Rhonda and Tim had agreed to handle the hotel on their own as much as possible. "You want to go for a swim?"

"I was hoping you'd say that. I came over here, thinking we'd have more privacy in your pool. Do you mind?"

"That's fine! Let me change, and I'll join you. Why don't you go on outside?"

His brown eyes bore into mine. "Is that what you really want?" His voice turned husky. "I could help you change, you know."

Happily playing his game, I grinned at him. "It would take twice as long ..."

"Oh, I could make it quick," he retorted.

I laughed. "No way. I'll hurry and meet you outside."

In my room, I hastily pulled on the green bikini Rhonda had chosen for me on my first visit. I stood a moment at my window, observing Vaughn swim the length of the pool and back again. His muscular arms moved steadily through the water. For a man who was in his mid-forties, he was in very good health. His waist was still trim and his stomach taut. Television doesn't do him justice, I thought, as he turned onto his back to do the backstroke. My body grew liquid as my gaze lingered on him. He was my dream come true.

I went outside and walked over to the steps of the pool to test the temperature with my big toe.

"Better hurry!" Vaughn teased. Skimming his hand across the water, he grinned like a naughty schoolboy.

I shrank back. "Don't you dare splash me! I have to go in one step at a time!"

His hand skimmed the water again, and this time, I was drenched with cold water.

"Ohh!" I gasped. "You're going to be sorry!" I dove into the water right at him, catching him off guard, and came up out of the water with a triumphant cry.

He surfaced near me, and I scrambled for the steps.

"Now you've done it!" he cried, laughing, his hair hanging down in front of his eyes like a shaggy dog. He headed toward me with outstretched arms.

I hurried away from him as fast as I could. I'd just reached the steps when Vaughn grabbed me from behind with a cry of victory.

"No!" I shrieked, jerking away from him, and stared in shock at the sight of my bathing suit top in his hands, leaving my breasts exposed. I heard a strange clicking noise, and then a flashing light blinded me.

My head jerked up. "Who's there?"

A man was aiming a camera at us from the cover of the bushes, taking a whole series of pictures, one after the other.

"Hey! Stop! What are you doing here?" I called out.

Vaughn raced up the pool steps. "The bastard! He must have found out where I was staying. You wait here! I'll try to catch him!"

He took off at a dead run, out through the screen cage door and into the thick bushes surrounding my pool. Mortified, I watched him go. The private part of me shuddered at the idea of a picture of me, half-naked in a pool with Vaughn Sanders.

Vaughn returned moments later, breathing heavily.

"Did you find him?" My voice shook. "Who is he?"

Vaughn raked his fingers through his hair and let out a sigh. "His name is Geno Ferraro. He hounds certain people in show business. I'm one of them. I've tried to get him to stop, but as long as he doesn't break any laws, there's not much I can do. He's never threatened any harm to my family or me . He just turns up at the most inopportune times."

"Like now." My heart sank to my stomach.

"Aw, honey, I'm sorry." Vaughn gave me an encouraging

pat on the back. "There's not a whole lot we can do. I'll call my agent and ask him to get in touch with Geno. But I'm pretty sure he won't be able to convince him to hold onto the picture. The scandal sheets love stuff like this. It's dollars in his pocket."

"But what about me? And The Beach House Hotel? People will have the wrong impression. This is a respectable place that ensures privacy! That picture could ruin everything." Shock froze my tears. Something like this could destroy what Rhonda and I had worked so hard to accomplish. If this caused an uproar, what could I ever do to make it up to her? My heart missed a beat. What could I say to my friends back home in Boston?

Vaughn put an arm around me. "Hey, listen. I'm sorry it happened. I had no idea the guy was anywhere around here. If this should make the papers, the best we can do is to tough it out without making any comment. Most people know that any story the tabloids concoct about stars is mostly trash— full of lies and innuendos."

"But they'll still look at it and read it." My lips quivered. "I'd better get dressed. I have to tell Rhonda what happened. I owe her that, at least."

"Look, Ann ..." Vaughn began.

I stopped him. "I'm too upset to talk about it anymore. I need time to think. And I need to get dressed."

Vaughn stayed in the kitchen while I changed my clothes, and then he walked me over to The Beach House Hotel. I remained a half-step ahead of him as if I could disassociate myself from the photographs by staying away from him now. Foolish, but my whole thought process was in overdrive.

He went up to his room while I headed into the office. Rhonda looked up from her desk, took a second look, got up and closed the office door with a firm click.

"What's the matter, Annie? You look awful." She pulled a chair out. "Here, you'd better sit down."

My throat thick, I lowered myself onto the edge of the chair, wondering where to begin. "Something terrible has happened," I got out. "I think I've ruined The Beach House Hotel's reputation!"

Rhonda's face turned ashen as I told her the story.

When I finished, she leaned back in her chair and let out a sigh. "It can't be that bad. I bet it doesn't even hit the papers. Don't worry, Annie, it'll be all right."

But even then, I knew it wouldn't be.

# CHAPTER NINETEEN

None of us had any idea what an instant sensation the picture would cause when it hit the New York papers and then the internet. The camera had caught me with my hands covering my nipples, but there was no mistaking the fact that I was cavorting half-naked in the pool with the handsome, well-known, sexy, soap opera star named Vaughn Sanders.

Neither Vaughn nor I realized that catching him with a woman for the first time after his wife's death would be such big news, but apparently, it was a huge coup for Geno. The news spread fast. Every time I looked at the picture of us, my stomach whirled with humiliation. I was glad my grandmother wasn't around to see it. If she were alive, it would destroy her. I couldn't believe that some of the most famous movie stars had to live under this kind of duress all the time. My last day with Vaughn was nothing like I'd once imagined. As much as I wanted to go back to the way we were, I couldn't.

I invited Will and Rhonda to dinner at my house, thinking that would make things easier for Vaughn and me. I tried to have a good time, but I couldn't get over the feeling I'd been raped by the press.

Rhonda cornered me in the kitchen. "Annie, you've got to get over this," she whispered. "Don't let it ruin your time with Vaughn. That would be crazy!"

"You don't understand," I told her. "I'm absolutely humiliated. You forget that I'm a very private person. Look what's happened to me because I was with him. I didn't realize that becoming the laughing stock of the nation would be part of the bargain. We were in the privacy of my own home!"

She wrapped her arms around me. "Oh, Annie. I'm so sorry. I really am."

Vaughn waited until after Rhonda and Will left and then took me in his arms. "Let's just forget about what happened."

Emotionally frazzled, I stepped away from him. "I'm trying to, but right now, I can't."

He shook his head, and a long sigh came out of him. "Well, then, I'm going back to the hotel."

Helpless to hide my feelings, I watched him leave, and then I dragged myself to bed.

I was startled out of a restless sleep by the ringing of the phone. Gasping with fright, I lifted the receiver, wondering if something had happened to Liz. "Hello?"

The sounds of partying in the background almost overrode the mocking voice on the phone. "Well, Ann, you proved my point. I was right all along. The picture of you proved it!"

My blood ran cold. "Who is this?"

A low laugh was the only reply before the caller hung up.

My skin felt as if ants were crawling all over it. I collapsed against the pillows and fought to calm my beating heart. An image of Brock Goodwin came to mind. I sat up, sure I was right. Tears of frustration rolled down my cheeks. No doubt he would now use this against Rhonda and me and the hotel.

I awoke with a headache, and, groggy and grumpy, made my way into the shower. Damn Brock! Of all the people who would make fun of me, I minded him most. Dressed for the day, I went into the kitchen to make coffee. Extra strong, I decided, grinding the beans from Starbucks.

I'd just taken a sip of coffee when the phone rang again. Private caller. Wary, I picked it up.

"Ann, it's Robert. And I'm not calling to wish you a Happy New Year! I'm calling to tell you I don't want Liz staying with you anymore. I've become the laughing stock of Boston. Your half-naked picture plastered in the newspaper and on the internet was faxed and emailed to me from all over the country with remarks I won't even repeat! There's no way I want my daughter down there with you while you're doing God knows what in the pool with some pansy soap opera star named Vaughn!"

"It wasn't anything like that," I protested. "I know what it looks like, but ..."

"May I speak to Liz? "Robert said, interrupting me. "She's not answering her cell."

"Liz isn't here." My voice was as tight and controlled as I could make it. "She and Angela and a group of friends went over to South Beach to spend the rest of the holiday there."

"South Beach?" shrieked Robert. "That place is full of all kinds of weird stuff. Why did you let her go there, for Chrissake? What's the matter with you, Ann?"

Anger stiffened me. "Stop it, Robert! Nothing is the matter with me. I'm doing well—living life and loving it! So back the hell off! It's not your concern anymore. When Liz returns from her trip, I'll tell her you called. Goodbye!"

My hands shook as I clicked off the call. Thank God, Syd had emailed me to say a cashier's check from Robert had been sent. I was certain in his present state of mind, Robert would have tried to use the photo of me as the latest excuse for not paying. No doubt he'd now use it as an excuse to renew his campaign to have Liz live with him. My stomach knotted at the thought. No man would ever have control over my life again.

I'd no sooner sat at the kitchen table than someone knocked at the front door. I peered through the side glass. At the sight of Vaughn, my heart leaped treacherously. I opened the door but held back when he bent to kiss me. I was so uncertain about where this relationship should be in my life.

Vaughn gave me a puzzled look. "How are you feeling?"

I shrugged, not wanting to drag him into my argument with Robert. "C'mon in. I've got fresh coffee on."

"Are you feeling different about things today?" His dark eyes probed mine.

I shook my head. "I had an anonymous phone call during the night. I think I know who made it, but it wasn't very pleasant."

He took my hands. "And?"

"I've just had a very angry phone call from Robert. He's convinced I'm living a hedonistic life of sin and not running a hotel. He says I'm a bad influence on Liz." My lips quivered. "He's going to try to keep her from staying with me."

Vaughn frowned. "Are you sure it isn't just talking on his part?"

I tried to swallow the lump in my throat. "Robert's been trying to draw her away from me ever since she went away to school. He knows she's the only child I have. I don't want to lose her. I'll fight him if I have to."

Vaughn drew me closer and stared down at me. "Are you willing to fight for our relationship, Ann?"

Confused, I looked away. *Time*, I thought frantically; *I need time to sort things out.*

Vaughn sighed. "Well, that says it all. Ann, look at me."

The misery I felt was reflected in his eyes. "Tell me you don't feel something special when we're together. Tell me you want to walk away from this beginning and end it forever."

I stepped back. "You don't understand. I'm a very private person. I can't go about my life wondering who's going to pop out of the bushes next. I love this hotel. Rhonda and I have worked so hard to make it a success; I can't let it be destroyed. You have to help me," I sobbed. "I don't know what to do. If this hotel fails, it will be my fault. Don't you see? I've let my emotions ruin my business."

Vaughn's mouth straightened into a thin, angry line. His dark eyes snapped with resentment, but he remained silent.

"Vaughn, I don't know what I mean. I'm too upset. Please don't ask me to be reasonable. Not now."

He stiffened, and I knew I'd hurt him. "I have to leave soon. I'd better go back to the hotel to get ready. Goodbye, Ann." I could hear the pain in his voice, but I felt helpless to do anything about it.

He turned on his heel and left me standing in the kitchen, immobilized by my conflicting feelings. Vaughn was the best man I'd ever met. But would the cost of loving him ruin all I'd worked for?

I sank into a kitchen chair, let out a wail, and sobbed.

At the time Liz was due back from South Beach, I left the hotel and walked over to my house to await her return. I thought a nice lunch together would help give me some perspective on my situation. As I was setting the table, Liz walked into our house, threw down her purse on the kitchen counter, and stormed into her room.

I followed her anxiously. "What's wrong? Did you have a good time in South Beach? Is it as much fun as they say?"

She turned to me with narrowed eyes. "Not as much fun, apparently, as playing naked in the swimming pool with Vaughn Sanders. Mom! How could you? You've embarrassed me in front of all my friends!"

She was about to slam the door in my face, but I stopped her. "You're not the only one who's upset. Your father called this morning. He was furious. He feels I'm not a good example for you and that you shouldn't be allowed to live with me. He was even more upset when I told him you'd gone to South Beach with your friends. He doesn't like the idea of you being there where all sorts of weird things happen, according to him."

"That's ridiculous!" cried Liz. "I'm sick of hearing that kind of stuff from him. Some of the kids are talking about spending the summer in D.C., and I told them I'd go with them. That way, I'll be on my own, and nobody will have to worry about where I live."

Wishing things were different, feeling more uncertain about the future than ever, I watched my daughter struggle with her emotions. Everything I'd thought was in place had been blown apart.

"Take some time alone to think things over," I said and left her to take a seat at the kitchen table. Sitting there, trembling at the thought of all I might lose, I decided my only recourse was to continue to work as hard as I could to keep the hotel afloat.

Disheartened, I said goodbye to Liz and went over to the hotel. In the office, I set to work on financial data for the year-end review with the auditors. The numbers, unlike the rest of my life, fell into order, requesting little from me in return.

Just before dark, Liz stuck her head into the office. "Can we talk?"

"Sure, sweetheart. What is it?" She looked as if she'd been crying.

She took a seat opposite me. "Mom? I called Dad and

straightened him out on a few things."

Surprised, I sat up straighter. "You did?"

She nodded. "I told him I have rights, too, and that it's time for me to be more independent. I told him I wouldn't be coming to live with him, that all Kandie was interested in was a live-in babysitter." She smiled. "I said I was over-qualified for that job. And ... I told him to stop bugging you."

"I bet he didn't like that." I studied the look of satisfaction on Liz's face. There was a resoluteness there I hadn't seen before.

"Yeah, Dad wasn't happy with me, at all." She gave me that impish grin of hers. "And wait until you hear this! I told him he should be proud of all you'd accomplished. The picture was cool from that point of view. You're dealing with well-known people who've come to love the hotel. Besides, you didn't look so bad. You know, for a woman your age. That's how I've decided to handle this whole situation with my friends. I'm just going to say my mom's pretty cool. I'm going on the offensive, not the defensive."

Struggling to hold back tears, I rose to my feet and hugged her hard. "I love you, Liz, and I'm proud you're mine."

"Love you, too," she murmured, and I let out a sigh of relief. No matter how much either Robert or I wanted to keep Liz a child, she was an independent woman who would have a life of her own.

# CHAPTER TWENTY

Liz's departure for school was especially hard for me. I felt so adrift, so vulnerable. I hadn't heard from Vaughn, and I was too unsure of myself and what I wanted from him to call him.

Standing beside me at the airport, aware of my insecurity, Rhonda said, "Hang in there, Annie. We're in this together, and it's gonna be a ride."

I did my best to smile. Rhonda was the best friend I'd ever had. Together, we waved at the airplane taking our girls away. The holidays had been traumatic for all of us.

Life at the hotel moved forward. As Syd had promised, Robert's last check arrived. I studied it with a feeling of relief. I never wanted to have to ask Robert for another thing. My tie to him, except through Liz, was over. He'd turned into a man I didn't know, understand, or like.

My thoughts flitted to the other men I'd let into my life recently. I'd once imagined Brock would be different from Robert but soon found out his ego was even larger than Robert's. Vaughn, who had every right to be egotistical, was humble and easy to get along with— until the photo episode. Then, he didn't understand the hotel was more than a business to me. It was my life—everything that represented the best of my abilities.

I couldn't stop a long sigh from escaping. I might be learning a lot about the hotel business, but I was, apparently, ignorant when it came to men.

### #

One evening in late January, Rhonda came over to my house and took a seat in my kitchen. She looked glum.

"What am I going to do, Annie? I've always thought a spring wedding was nice, but when I mentioned it to Will, he said no. After forcing him to change our original date because of Sal, I'm afraid to push him." She twisted the diamond ring on her finger and looked up at me with sad eyes. "Maybe it'll never happen. Maybe he's changed his mind."

My heart went out to her. "Oh, hon, I don't think so. He sees how hectic things are and is probably wanting to wait until you have time to plan the wedding properly. He's very considerate that way." I hoped I was right. He'd break her heart if plans didn't go forward.

"Ya think that's it? Okay, maybe June would be a good time for a wedding." She accepted the glass of wine I offered her. "It's pretty weird when you're working too hard to get married."

"I know." But we *were* busy with guests coming and going, especially now with a lot of cold weather up north. It was both exhilarating and exhausting.

"Here's to us!" I said, lifting my glass to Rhonda.

"And to my wedding in June," said Rhonda, smiling at me.

One morning, I was working alone in the office when the phone rang. I eagerly picked it up.

"How are you, Ann?" said Harry Morton, an old neighbor of mine. "Ruth and I were reading about The Beach House Hotel in a travel magazine. We'd like to come down for a few days. Can you give us a room?"

I hesitated. This was the eighth person in my old

neighborhood to call in the last two weeks. Boston was in the throes of battling a bitter cold front from Canada, and people were desperate to get out of town.

"Hold on and let me check our reservations schedule." I popped it up on the computer. "Harry? I have one room a week from now, for two nights. That would be Tuesday and Wednesday nights only. The rest of the time, we're booked. If you want those rooms, it's $450 a night, $900 total. We'd need a deposit of $450 to hold the room."

"Whoa! Wait a minute, sweetheart! It's Harry and Ruth you're talking to. After all the years we've known you, we thought you'd give us a room for a much better price than that."

I bit my tongue. This was nothing new. Every acquaintance in the world now talked to me as if we were best friends. And Harry Morton was no friend of mine. One night after Robert left me, he came to the house to assure me that he was available if I got too lonely. I understood at the time that he'd had too much to drink, but I'd never felt the same about him again. I tried to push aside my personal feelings, to keep things on a pleasant, business-like basis.

"You know I can't give rooms away, Harry," I said, cajoling him. "It wouldn't be fair to my business partner. I'm sure you understand. After all, you can't give free accounting services to the neighborhood any more than I can give free rooms to them."

"Yeah, okay. I can see that. Well, I guess for that price, Ruth better come up with a different idea—something cheaper. So, how are things going? Really? Anything I can do for you?"

I shuddered at his suggestive tone. "No, Harry. Say hello to Ruth for me. I've got to run."

I hung up the phone, thinking about my life. Outside of

work, I was lonely. I longed for male company but would do nothing to harm the reputation of the hotel. I knew very well that some of our guests were attracted to me, but I didn't want to be considered part of the package. And though I'd found some of them appealing, I decided to play it straight, stay by myself. But, being with men, overhearing them talk, and flirting with them occasionally, I missed Vaughn so much it was a constant ache.

Rhonda walked into the office and handed me the daily newspaper. Her cheeks were flushed with anger. "Read this. That bastard Brock Goodwin has written a letter to the editor."

My stomach felt as if I'd jumped out of an airplane with no parachute. "What now?" My eyes raced over the condemning words—the increased traffic, the lack of privacy on the beach, and the reference to the photo of one of the owners of The Beach House Hotel in a compromising situation. My dismay grew as I continued to read. "Is this what the community of Sabal wants? The Beach House Hotel should be more than a House of Ill Repute!" I closed my eyes as a trembling sigh left me. Brock had taken his battle with the Gold Coast Neighborhood Association board and us and made it into a foolish war.

Overwhelmed, I cupped my face in my hands.

Rhonda paced the room. "I could kill him."

I took a deep breath. "Me too. But in this case, maybe the best defense is no defense."

Hands on hips, Rhonda faced me. Her eyes burned with resentment. "I've thought that maybe we should say a little something. You know?"

I knew that look, that tone of voice. "But, Rhonda, rising to the bait will only make matters worse. After the whole mess with Vaughn, I've learned it's better to just lay low." If we didn't put a stop to it, our battles would become worse by being played out on the editorial pages of the paper.

Rhonda nodded, but I knew by the way her hands had fisted that she didn't like it.


Rhonda strutted into the office wearing a big grin. "You're gonna like this! Take a gander!" She handed me the newspaper.

I eyed her suspiciously. "Does this have anything to do with Brock Goodwin?"

"You bet your ass."

The whole editorial page was devoted to letters supporting The Beach House Hotel. Brock's reputation was called into question regarding his business dealings, as well as some community events in which he'd participated. I read with growing alarm.

She gave me a triumphant look. "Well? Pretty effective, don't you think?"

"Are all of these things they say about him true?" If not, we could be ruined by a costly lawsuit.

"They'd have to be true, or the paper wouldn't print them. The important thing is that the good name of The Beach House Hotel has been restored. That's what we wanted."

At her satisfied look, I ventured a guess. "Are these people all your friends?"

Rhonda nodded. "People I've done favors for in the past. Believe me; they were more than happy to write the letters. It turns out that behind the glam look, Brock isn't a very nice person. He's hurt a lot of people along the way. There's been a lot of gossip about him lately. Apparently, he's got all sorts of problems with his business."

My feelings were mixed. It was nice to have our

reputation restored, but Brock was a formidable enemy, and this assault on his character was bound to come back to haunt us. I decided to say nothing more about my worries. But I knew that sooner or later, Brock would try to get back at us. It was his very nature to do so.

Work kept me busy during the day, but nothing could keep my mind off Vaughn at night. Then, images of him gazing at me intently and dark curls framing his handsome face haunted me. I could still feel his lips on mine, imagine his arms around me, hear his ragged breath as our passion swept us away. Still ... I could not call him.

Tim, who managed our website for us, confessed he'd deleted some negative comments about me, Vaughn, and the hotel. I couldn't jeopardize the success of the hotel any further by making contact with Vaughn. Let sleeping dogs lie, I told myself, wishing with all my heart that things were different.

The metamorphosis of our small hotel continued. Some of the well-connected people in Sabal learned of The Beach House Hotel's role in the negotiations between Senator Snyder and his colleague and were now eager to use the hotel in the same manner. Word spread across the country at top levels. Bookings grew, making it seem as if Vaughn had been right all along, and people had all but forgotten about the story of us in the pool together.

More and more in the weeks that followed, I found myself taking on the role of hostess to small groups while Rhonda supervised the daily kitchen activities. We'd hired cooks from other hotels, but Rhonda still wanted to oversee the kitchen until she found the right person to take over. Tim turned out to be a wonder, handling the small, day-to-day details of keeping things running smoothly and keeping an eye on the in-house staff. Dorothy was now helping out part-time five days a week and loving it. Manny and Paul kept busy maintaining the physical plant and the landscaping.

When the *Sabal Daily News* ran an article about the different kinds of people who were moving into the area, my eye caught the familiar name of Jean-Luc Rodin. He'd run a well-known French restaurant in Boston when I'd lived there. I read the article about Jean-Luc with growing excitement.

"What'cha reading?" Rhonda asked, breezing into the office.

"Listen to this. It's in an article about all the new people coming here: 'Jean-Luc Rodin, a retired chef from the *Chat L'Orange* restaurant in Boston shrugged his shoulder when asked if he might open a restaurant in the area. "I'm retired," he said, "but a chef is always a chef. It's in his blood. But I wouldn't want the responsibility of owning a restaurant again. Perhaps, I will cook omelettes now and then in one of your little breakfast cafes, *non*?"'

Rhonda's eyes grew big. "Are you thinking what I'm thinking?"

I grinned. "Let's give him a call. What could it hurt?"

As we led Jean-Luc through the kitchen, I twisted my hands nervously. Rhonda explained the equipment we'd recently added to the kitchen, and at Jean Luc's nod of approval, beamed at him.

We showed him both dining rooms and the outdoor kitchen near the pool. After the tour, we sat in the library with him and sipped a delicious, French red wine.

Jean-Luc leaned back in his chair and crossed his legs.

"So, tell me about this hotel. It's new, yes?"

I nodded. "It's officially been open less than a year, but the building is from the '80s."

"I bought and renovated it. Together, Annie and I have converted it to an active hotel. And if I do say so, it's become *the* place to be in Sabal," Rhonda said proudly.

"We've been able to draw successful people to it by assuring them of privacy," I explained. "Everything we provide needs to be of top quality. That's why we're talking to you."

He raised a hand to stop us. "You don't have to sell me on the hotel or what you're doing. I see what you have, and I've checked around town. So, you're looking for someone part-time for evenings? I'm intrigued by this." He lifted a finger in warning. "However, if I'm to work here, you must add some new equipment and cooking utensils to suit me."

Dollar signs flashed in front of my eyes. I held back a groan. "What are we talking about in cost?"

He shrugged a shoulder. "A few thousand dollars. Maybe more."

I quickly reworked numbers in my mind. If we held off buying the towels, umbrellas, and robes we'd planned to purchase to sell, we could use that money for the kitchen.

"What about salary?" I held my breath. Adding him to the payroll would be expensive, but his reputation could boost the number of dinner guests.

He gave me a kindly smile. "For you, lovely ladies, I'll be reasonable as long as you allow me to cook what I want."

I turned to Rhonda, who'd been uncharacteristically silent.

"Can I cook with you from time to time?" she asked. "And Consuela too?"

He shrugged. "I don't see why not. As long as I'm in

charge of the kitchen and you listen to what I say and do as I say."

Rhonda nodded. "Okay. It's a deal!"

Jean-Luc grinned at her and turned to me with a questioning look.

"Deal," I said calmly, wanting to dance across the room.

The three of us shook hands. Observing his smile, I hoped his pleasant manner wouldn't change over time. He was exceptionally nice, but by tradition, chefs could be prickly in the kitchen. And after all, it was Rhonda's kitchen.

With Jean-Luc's assistance, we undertook catering to small, evening gatherings, providing a place where guests could hold elegant, personal dinner parties .

While the scenes in the dining room were quiet and peaceful, the activities in the kitchen were not. Rhonda, predictably, was having trouble allowing a man to take over her kitchen.

After one stormy fight, she came into the office, slammed the door, and threw her apron down on her desk. "That does it! He has to go!"

I gazed up into her angry face. "What's happened between the two of you now?"

Rhonda drew in a breath, trying to control that temper of hers. "Jean-Luc's trying to change *my mother's* recipe for an *Italian* soup! Can you believe it? What in hell does he know about Italian soup? He's a fuckin' French frog!"

I could hear Jean-Luc muttering to himself in French in the kitchen. Well aware of the response I was about to rouse from her, I rose out of my chair and went over to Rhonda. "I hate to see you so unhappy. The time has come to get rid of Jean-Luc. It's obviously not working out."

Rhonda's eyes widened. "Are you kidding? We can't do that! He's a wonderful chef! Our guests love him!"

I threw my hands up in the air. "Okay. The two of you are going to have to work it out."

Rhonda sighed. "Aw, Annie. You know me. I like to run the show."

"Really?" I teased.

She gave me a sheepish grin. "It's just that he's such a damn know-it-all."

"That's why we hired him. Remember?"

She nodded, grabbed her apron, and opened the door. "Jean-Luc? I'm back!"

"*Ah, oui,*" he answered pleasantly.

I smiled. As much as they quarreled, they really liked each other. And the food was delicious.

While Rhonda remained busy behind the scenes, I dressed up for the private dinners that were held more and more. I greeted guests, oversaw our new wait staff, offered drinks and wine, and generally treated our guests as if they were part of an exclusive event in a lovely estate. During some of these dinners, I met interesting, well-known people and was often privy to confidential conversations. It became exciting to see who I'd become acquainted with next.

Memories of Vaughn still lingered in my mind, but I tucked our wonderful moments of being together in the back of my mind.

Time flew by. As many times as possible during the day, Rhonda and I greeted guests on the front steps as they arrived. Now, as we awaited the arrival of Senator Byers, Rhonda and I chatted, happy for a few moments alone together.

As he stepped out of his limousine, the senator looked just as handsome as his photographs. A tall, muscled man in his early fifties, he exuded the self-confidence that skillful politicians do. He smiled up at us. Rhonda and I descended the front steps to greet him and his party. I approached him and paused when he blatantly stared at me, undressing me with his eyes.

Trying my best to ignore my discomfort, I offered my hand. "Welcome to The Beach House Hotel."

He clasped my hand in both of his. "That picture of you certainly didn't do you justice."

Put off by his words, I tried to pull out of his grasp. He hung onto me and lowered his voice to a whisper. "How about coming up to my room later? A senator learns a lot of things in Washington. More than most soap opera stars could ever dream up."

Shocked, I jerked my hand away from his and frantically looked around for Rhonda. She was greeting his other guests, but she caught my eye and hurried over to us.

"Greetings, Senator Byers. I'm Rhonda DelMonte."

I made my escape, went into the hotel to the office, and, still shaking, collapsed in a chair. I'd thought all that business with Vaughn was behind me. The idea that it was a senator of the United States who'd treated me that way made it even more humiliating.

Rhonda burst into the office. "Are you all right, Annie? I saw the way the senator was holding onto you."

I let out a shaky breath. "He told me the picture on the internet didn't do me justice. He wanted me to come to his room like some kind of whore." Tears filled my eyes.

Rhonda gave me a hug. "Aw, honey! He's an asshole! Just forget him."

I managed a weak smile, but I was mortified. This was a facet of the hotel business I hadn't expected. When I'd worked with Robert, no one had even hinted at making a pass at me. Now that I was a woman alone, it seemed the whole world had become a jungle.

# CHAPTER TWENTY-ONE

Rhonda came into the office one late-May morning and sat down with a sigh. "We're so busy at the hotel that Will and I have decided to postpone the wedding until September."

Alarmed, I asked, "Are you all right with that? Really?"

"Will and I spend all our free time together, so it isn't like delaying the wedding is keeping us apart. Jean-Luc and I are working better as a team, and I figure we hafta take advantage of the dinner business we've got."

I breathed a sigh of relief. With all my administrative duties on top of the new, social aspects of my job, I'd been feeling stretched to the limit. September would be slow and a good time for Rhonda to be away on a honeymoon.

The girls came home from school for a few days before once again going off to their New Hampshire camp as counselors for the summer. And then, too quickly, I was alone again.

On a slow afternoon, Rhonda found me in the library. "There's a call for you, honey. It's something I can't handle, but I'm pretty sure you can."

At another interruption, I let out a groan and picked up the phone. "This is Ann Rutherford. May I help you?"

"I hope so. I'm at a charity event in Orlando, and I was wondering if I could get a room at The Beach House Hotel this weekend. I'd like to fly over there Saturday night."

My heart pounded so fast I grew dizzy and dropped the phone. I grabbed it up. "Vaughn? Is that you?"

"Hi. Ann. I've got a couple of free days, and I've missed you. I've been flubbing my lines like crazy on the show, and everyone knows why. Roger told me not to come back until things were settled between us."

Elation filled me. Over the past six months, no matter how much I'd told myself to forget him, I never could. "Don't worry. We'll make space for you. I can't wait until you're here," I said breathlessly. "But, Vaughn, I have to warn you that Rhonda and Will are going to the Keys this weekend for a well-deserved break. I'll be very busy on my own."

"That's okay. I want to see you. And if you need an extra hand, maybe I can do something to help. Anything."

I grinned. "Well, I know you're good at carrying suitcases," I teased. "I've seen you haul a few of your own."

"Right now I feel like I could move mountains, just knowing I'll be seeing you!" he replied playfully.

Amused, I laughed. "Oh, Vaughn, it will be so good to see you!"

We hung up, and the day seemed brighter, more beautiful.


Rhonda and Will left for the Keys in a flurry of activity. Flanked by Consuela, Manny, and Tim, I stood on the steps of the hotel waving goodbye to them. After their car disappeared through the gates, I turned to the others. "Okay, we're on our own. The house is full. Let's do a terrific job for Rhonda."

Tim placed a hand on my shoulder. "Don't worry, Ann. Just because Rhonda is gone, it doesn't mean the whole place is going to fall apart."

I gave him a sheepish grin. "You're right. We're a good team. The chef is lined up for dinners, and with the extra help we've hired for the weekend, we should be fine. I'll be in the office if anyone wants me."

I was deep in paperwork when the phone rang. My mind was still on the latest pricing package from the printer when I reached over to answer it.

"Hello there," came Vaughn's rich voice. "I just wanted to check in with you. It looks like everything is on schedule, so I should be there late tomorrow night."

His arrival couldn't come soon enough. "How's the Mayor? And all your sinful children?"

"As tired of me as I am of them," Vaughn replied. "I'm going to skip out of tomorrow's reception by nine o'clock and catch a private flight over. Then, I want you all to myself."

A tingle of sexual anticipation traveled through me. "I've planned a light supper for us at my house. I intend to enjoy as much time with you as possible."

"Great. That's what I was hoping to hear."

I hung up, lost in sensual thoughts about him—things we could do for each other, things I'd never done with Robert. My body responded with a need only Vaughn could fill.

Tim poked his head in the doorway. "You'd better come take a look at the laundry room. It's a mess!"

I was brought back to earth in a dizzying rush. "What's wrong?"

"Something broke on one of the washing machines. There's water everywhere." He wore a worried frown. "It looks pretty bad."

Heart pounding, I hurried out of the office and followed Tim to the commercial laundry area in the garage.

Ana was standing in the middle of the laundry room. Water swirled over the tops of her sandals as she tried to push it with a mop toward the drain in the middle of the concrete floor.

"It's not a broken hose. I checked. And I've shut off the water to the machine."

"Better help Ana mop. I'll run inside and see if we can get someone to come and take a look at the washer right away."

A few minutes later, I returned to Tim in the laundry room. "I've called everyone I could think of. No one can come until Monday to fix the machine. I even offered to pay somebody extra on the side." I let out a ragged sigh. "Everyone I talked to has a list of repairs a mile long. We should have paid the maintenance contract fee."

Tim frowned. "There should be enough clean sheets for today. We can try to make it through with the two other machines we have."

"We'll just keep plugging away at it. That's all we can do."

The day rattled along like an old wagon with a wobbly wheel. Paul called me from I-75 to tell me the limousine had a flat tire, and he'd be late picking up the guests at the airport in Ft. Myers.

I checked my watch. "How long do you think it'll take you to fix it?"

"I'm not sure. The spare isn't here."

I groaned. If this was an indication as to how the whole weekend was going to go, I was in trouble. Big trouble.

"I'll send Tim out in the van. He can pick up the passengers at the airport and bring them here. By then, I will have ordered a new tire for the limo, and he can bring it back out to you."

"Thanks," said Paul. "I'll go ahead and jack the car up so it'll be ready."

I hung up, shaking my head. Paul should have made sure the limo was in good shape before taking off. I'd have to speak to Manny about it.

For the rest of the day, I held my breath, wondering what

was going to happen next. Aware things came in threes, my superstitious soul quaked.

That night, after seeing that guests were checked in and settled for the night, I crawled into bed, tired to the bone. I flipped on the eleven o'clock news, realizing I had no idea what was happening outside my little world. As I tuned in, the weatherman was pointing to a line of stormy clouds on the map. A severe storm warning had been issued for most of the southwest coast of Florida. Heavy rain and high winds, he explained, were part of a cold-air system moving down the peninsula, aimed directly for us.

I rolled out of bed and called Tim, who was manning the hotel as a night clerk. "We'd better get out candles, matches, and extra flashlights. If we lose electricity, the emergency lighting system will illuminate the exits, but not the rooms themselves. I don't want to take a chance on anyone being hurt. Be sure each guest room has one of the large emergency lanterns placed in it."

"Okay, will do. The palms are already dancing up a storm. These Florida weather systems are something else."

"Call me if you need me. I'm going to try to get some sleep so I can come in early and relieve you. I'm exhausted."

Caught in frightening dreams, restlessly reaching for deep sleep, I tossed and turned. Some time later, I woke in a sweat. The room was warm and stuffy. I sat up in bed and automatically checked the digital alarm clock. Nothing. An unnatural stillness was broken by the sound of rain hitting the glass windows with the force of strong wind behind it.

Reaching for the flashlight I'd placed next to my bed, I flipped it on and quickly dressed by the single beam of light. I found my slicker and slipped it on.

Outside, the wind stole my breath, leaving me gasping. The fronds of the nearby palm trees rustled noisily in a frantic pattern. The salty air shook the leaves of the bushes along the walkway. I slowly fought my way through the wind and rain to the hotel. I'd just reached the front steps of the hotel when the headlights of a car broke through the darkness at the street entrance. A taxi rolled up and came to a stop in front of me. The driver hopped out of the cab, raced around to the trunk, and lifted out two suitcases.

A white-haired gentleman opened the passenger's door of the cab and assisted a small, fragile-looking woman into the stormy weather. "Hurry, Ethel! It's pouring," he cried.

I rushed over to help them. "You're staying here at The Beach House Hotel?"

"Yes," the man answered, wiping the rain from his brow. "The name is Keene. My wife and I were supposed to be here several hours ago, but our flight out of Atlanta was delayed. We're lucky we found a cab when we finally arrived."

"Come right inside. Here, let me help you with your wife." I steadied the tiny wisp of a woman on her feet.

The cabbie carried the suitcases up to the front door. While Mr. Keene paid him, his wife and I slowly made our way up the front steps. The wind buffeted us about as the rain continued to fall in driving sheets, drenching us.

I seated the weary guests in the foyer and hurried off to find Tim.

He was in the kitchen. "Glad to see you! It's as bad as they said it'd be."

"Help me! We've got guests in the front hall. The Keenes. They're soaking wet. We've got to take them to their room."

Tim grabbed a couple of flashlights and followed me out to the foyer.

I quickly checked their reservations, Then we led them upstairs and helped get them and their luggage settled in their room.

Downstairs again, I set up battery-lit lanterns along the stairway. "I'll stay on one of the sofas in the living room. Who knows what might happen next."

Lying on a couch, I tensed each time the wind rattled the windows and prayed the storm wouldn't do a lot of damage to the property. Our budget couldn't stand it.

As dawn was trying to make its presence known, I opened my eyes and sat up, disoriented. Realizing where I was, I scrambled to my feet. The wind had died down considerably. I hurried over to the doors leading to the pool and looked out. Chair cushions were scattered everywhere, a table lay on its side, and the umbrellas on the rest of the tables had blown open and hung at crazy angles in the lingering breeze.

I walked to the front door and opened it. Tree branches lay on the lawn along with several palm fronds. The hibiscus blossoms in the front hedge were hanging in pink, knotted, wind-blown clumps, still dripping water. Rainwater puddled in the driveway in a series of miniature ponds. The putting green had a few stray leaves lying on top of the grass but looked fine otherwise. I breathed a thankful sigh.

In the kitchen, I turned on the gas range to heat water, grateful we'd be able to provide our guests a hot breakfast. "It could be worse," I murmured.

"What could be worse?" Tim appeared at the door in rumpled slacks and shirt.

"We've no electricity, and the phones are out, but we can rustle up a hot meal."

Tim yawned and stretched. "What's it like outside?"

"We'll have to replace the umbrellas on the lanai, and some of the furniture as well, but everything else seems to be fine. I'll take a closer look after breakfast."

Tim sat down at the table looking as if he hadn't had any sleep at all. I knew how ragged he felt. "I'll make us breakfast before we get too busy to have one. Once the guests are up, we'll be hopping."

I scrambled eggs and broiled toast in the gas oven.

Tim plugged a big coffee pot into one of the small generators we had, and soon the aroma of coffee added to my growing hunger.

We sat, sharing breakfast companionably. I liked Tim. He was a hard worker who didn't complain when something unexpected came up. With Will and Rhonda away, I realized how much both Rhonda and I had come to depend on him. He was a gem in today's world where nobody seemed to be willing to start out at the bottom.

After breakfast, Tim headed outside to survey damage to the landscaping, and I listed the tasks we'd need to take care of inside. I was glad to have insurance coverage for damage to the FF&E but worried about the deductible.

The sound of someone calling my name caught my attention. I leaped up from the table and hurried into the front hall, just as Tim came through the front door.

"Mr. Keene! What is it?"

The elderly gentleman was standing on the stairway in his pajamas, beckoning to me. "It's my wife! It's Ethel! She's ill!"

I took the stairs two at a time. Tim followed on my heels.

Inside their room, Ethel Keene lay on the wide bed. Her face was drained of color, her lips tinged with blue.

*Heart attack?* I took hold of her hand. It was cold, clammy. "How are you feeling, Ethel? Any pain anywhere?"

She nodded. "My jaw and my chest."

"We're going to get you some help. You'll be fine." I turned to Tim. "Call 911. I'll stay here."

Tim nodded grimly and raced from the room. He returned moments later. "They're on their way."

Waiting for the ambulance, I helped Mr. Keene into

clothes. The EMTs arrived, and we stood by as they checked Mrs. Keene's vitals, hooked her up to monitors, and placed her on a stretcher.

I handed Mr. Keene his coat and took hold of his hand. Remembering the horror of Wilkins Jones' death, I whispered a frenzied prayer for Mrs. Keene's life.

"I'll drive you to the hospital," I told him. "We'll meet them there."

Tim pulled the hotel van up to the front circle. We got Mr. Keene settled into the passenger seat, and I slid behind the wheel.

The wind and rain continued as we got underway. I soon discovered the streets of Sabal had become an obstacle course. I gripped the steering wheel so tightly my knuckles turned white as I picked my way around debris. The trip to the hospital, which should have been only a matter of minutes, seemed to take forever. *Mrs. Keene, please don't die*, my mind screamed over and over.

Finally, the emergency entrance to the Sabal Community Hospital appeared before me. I pulled the van up to it, jumped out, and helped Mr. Keene inside. He took a seat in front of the desk of an admissions clerk, who was ready to take his information.

I parked the van and took a moment to call Tim. "Manny and Consuela are due to arrive at the hotel any minute. Last night, they stayed at their daughter's house outside of town to babysit. They're supposed to ride in to the hotel with Rosita and Ana. See if you can call them. Heaven knows what destruction they may have had in their area."

"Okay," said Tim. "I'll get breakfast going, but Consuela better get here soon or we'll have a lot of unhappy guests. My cooking isn't that great."

I hung up and took a seat in the waiting room.

Mr. Keene finished with the admissions clerk and sat down next to me, his face creased with worry.

I patted him on the back. "She'll be all right." I silently prayed it was so.

We kept a silent vigil.

After a while, the emergency room doctor approached us. "Mr. Keene? Your wife is going to be okay. We're working to get her stabilized now. As far as we can tell, it was not a heart attack, though there are irregularities in the heartbeat. My guess is that she's a perfect candidate for a pacemaker. We'll do extensive testing later."

"Can I see Ethel now?" Mr. Keene asked. Tears filled his eyes. "I need to make sure she's all right."

The doctor nodded. "Okay, but don't be alarmed by all the wires and machines you see. We're monitoring her carefully."

The relief on Mr. Keene's face was touching, and I realized how much he loved his wife. I watched him leave with the doctor. If it were possible, he'd aged ten years since last night. I couldn't help wondering if Vaughn and I would ever know that kind of devotion to one another.

When I told him I had to go back to the hotel, Mr. Keene opted to stay at the hospital. After making sure he understood he could call me for a ride anytime, I left him.

Driving back to the hotel, I saw more clearly how many trees had come down. Big branches were scattered everywhere. Earlier, I'd been too focused on driving to take a better look around.

The hotel was still dark when I arrived. As I opened the front door, I inhaled the smell of bacon cooking. I stepped into the kitchen and stopped.

Two of our female guests were running in and out, carrying platters of food. Tim and a guest from Minnesota, a man by the name of Mr. Kirk, stood at the stove cooking. They turned to me with wide smiles.

"What'll you have?" Mr. Kirk said. "I'm doing fried eggs and omelets."

I grinned. "I'm fine as I am, but thanks."

"Where's Consuela?" I asked Tim.

Tim gave me a worried look. "I don't know. I couldn't reach them. And none of the crew from that area has shown up yet. And you know Manny—he's never late for anything."

I frowned. Tim was right. It wasn't like them not to check in.

A woman, Julie Snyder from Pennsylvania, if I recalled correctly, came into the kitchen. "You guys have more eggs and bacon? We have some big eaters."

Tim smiled at me. "I've put a few people to work. They're doing a great job."

Another woman entered with an empty platter. Her face was flushed.

"Do you want to sit down? I'll take over for you," I said, unable to hide my concern.

"Are you kidding?" she chuckled. "We're all having a ball. I haven't waited tables since I was in college too many years ago."

"I used to be a short order cook in the army. This is a piece of cake," said Mr. Kirk, winking at the woman beside me.

She laughed. "We own a little stock in restaurants, but we agreed that was as close as we'd come to owning one. Right, hon?"

Mr. Kirk laughed good-naturedly. "You got it."

"Well, we really appreciate your help." I understood all too well the endless work of running a restaurant, even a small, limited one like ours.

I went into the dining room. Someone had placed candles on the tables. The room glowed with warmth, defying the gray, windy, cool weather outside. As often happens in adverse circumstances, guests who might not have spoken before now chatted together like old friends. The room vibrated with their easy bantering.

Relief, warm and sweet, traveled through me. What could have been a nightmare had turned into something memorable. It was at least one thing that seemed to be going right.

I went back to the kitchen to speak to Tim. "When things calm down here, would you be willing to drive to where Consuela and Manny are staying? I'm very concerned about them."

"Sure. I'm worried too."

I left him heating water to wash the dishes and went to check on the status of the downstairs rooms. I fluffed pillows, picked up magazines, and tidied up as much as possible. Then I set to work on what guest rooms I could clean, freshening bed linens and replacing dirty towels as I went.

Tim tracked me down. "I'm going to leave now to find Consuela and Manny and the others."

"Okay. Drive carefully. It's pretty bad out there."

I'd been working for some time when I heard Tim call my name softly from the hallway. I sighed with relief. Help was here.

"Ann?" Tim stood in the doorway of the room I was cleaning. He face was white, his eyes suspiciously red.

My body turned cold. I dropped the pillow in my hand. "What's the matter?"

"It's Manny and Consuela. They were in an automobile accident with Rosita and Ana." His voice broke. "I guess it was pretty bad."

My mouth went dry. "How bad is it?"

"Manny's in the hospital with a broken leg and Ana ... Ana's hurt real bad!" He choked. "She's going to live, but they tell me she's not coming back here for a long time. It's some sort of back injury. Rosita and Consuela are shaken and bruised, but they're okay. Paul's fine."

The blood drained from my face. My knees gave way. I staggered into the room and sank down on the bed, feeling as if my whole world had exploded.

"Ann?" Tim wiped at his eyes. "Consuela's son-in-law said he'd call you when he could, but what'll we do now?"

I took a deep breath. "I'll work something out." But at the moment I didn't know exactly what I'd do.

He left me, and I sat numbly, thankful lives had been spared. I wondered what the injuries would mean for Manny and Ana and how it would impact us. *One moment can change lives forever,* I thought sadly.

Soon, my practical mind took over. We'd have to hire extra help to replace Ana. Manny, too. In the meantime, Tim and I would do the best we could. There was no way I was about to ruin Rhonda's vacation. She was as exhausted as the rest of us on our staff, and after postponing their wedding because of Sal and the hotel, she and Will needed some time to themselves.

Downstairs in my office, Tim and I discussed the situation.

"Maybe Consuela's daughter, Maria, can take Ana's place," I said. "She's helped at some of the breakfasts. Any suggestions for someone to take Manny's place? At least until he gets better?"

Tim shrugged. "Maybe. A guy I used to know from school called me last week wondering if I knew of any job openings.

He was kicked out of school a while back. Low grades, I think. Now, he's down here looking for work."

Feeling desperate, I said, "Go ahead and call him, and ask him to come in for an interview as soon as possible. With all the damage from the storm, we need someone to help Paul clean up this mess."

"Okay." Tim rose. "After I call him, I'll go outside and start on the lanai."

"Thanks. I'll help you." The pool area was the least of our worries.

Tim left a message for his friend, and then we both went outside to see what we could do. The sun peeked out from behind clouds and hid again in a child's game of Hide and Seek. We straightened the furniture by the pool, taking the useless, bent umbrellas down and wiping the furniture clean with rags. It was tedious work, but I was happy to keep busy while I waited for a call from Consuela's family.

I left Tim fishing flower petals and other debris from the pool and headed for home, praying no damage had been done there. I might have received all the money Robert owed me, but it had already been used to pay my share of our improvements.

Approaching my house, I was relieved to see that no windows were broken. In the back of the house, a section of the pool cage lay twisted on the ground. The outdoor furniture was scattered but didn't have any major damage. Two of the pots holding flowers were cracked and broken, leaving their contents in sad lumps on the surface of the lanai.

As I started the process of straightening, my cell phone rang. Esteban, Consuela's son-in-law, called to say that Manny would have to stay in the hospital for a couple of days. They were still waiting to hear about Ana. The sting of tears blurred my vision. It seemed so unfair this had happened to such good people.

I went inside to change. Reflected in the glass of the sliding door in my bedroom, a rumpled stranger gazed back at me. I stared at my image. My hair was tangled and windblown around my flushed, sweaty face. My clothes were rumpled and soiled. But it was the ache of worry about the others that had creased my brow and caused my spirits to droop.

Emotionally drained, I went into the bathroom to repair the damage, feeling as if Rhonda had been gone for weeks, not two days.

# CHAPTER TWENTY-TWO

I opened the door to Manny's hospital room a crack and peeked in. Manny's brown, weathered skin was unusually pale as he lay among the white bedding of the hospital bed. One of his legs, encased in an adjustable, lightweight cast, lay on top of the sheets. I tiptoed inside.

As I approached the bed, his eyes flickered open. "*Buenos*," he murmured, staring at me with glassy, medicated eyes. "What are you doing here?"

Tenderness filled me. "I could ask you the same question. What happened?"

"*Ay! Dios mio!* As I drove down the road, a big branch came loose above us. I stepped on the gas to get out of the way, and when I tried to put the brakes on, I skidded right into a tree."

I took Manny's hand in mine. "I'm glad you're okay. Just relax and get well."

"What about my job? Will I lose it?" His eyes peered at me fuzzily, but he wore a pleading expression.

"How can you fire family?" I gave his hand an encouraging squeeze. "Of course, you're not going to lose your job. We'll just have to take on some extra help for a while—until you're back on your feet."

"Even with a cast on, I can do lots of things." Manny squinted as if trying to focus on me while fighting a drug-induced sleep. "You'll see." He closed his eyes.

As I turned to go, Consuela walked slowly and stiffly into the room. Seeing the purple bruises that marred her features, my eyes filled with tears. I reached out and hugged her gingerly.

"How are you doing? I'm so sorry about the accident."

"I'm sore, but I'll be fine," she said with her usual determination. Then, her face crumpled. Tears ran down her cheeks, leaving silvery trails behind. "You heard about Ana? It's her back. It's broken."

A lump filled my throat. "I'm so sorry. As soon as Rhonda comes back, we'll see what we can do to help the family. I understand she won't be able to work for some time."

Consuela grasped my hand. "I can come back to work right away. I'm sore, yes, but I can work. Rosita, too. She's home now. And my daughter can help. She needs the job. Okay?"

"That'll be fine, but don't push yourself, Consuela. You've been through a lot of trauma. Just come back to work as soon as you can. We need you."

Leaving Consuela, I went to check on Mrs. Keene. She was sleeping. Mr. Keene napped in a chair beside her bed. I tiptoed away from them.

When I returned to the hotel, the lights had come back on. Soft, soothing music played on the sound system, and things seemed to be running smoothly. Jean-Luc had made it in and was prepping the dinner.

Tim greeted me. "Ana's neighbor is going to come in tomorrow to help with the laundry. Paul will bring her when he comes."

"Good," I smiled, grateful that tomorrow would be easier. Best of all, Vaughn was due to arrive that night.

While Tim set to work with the vacuum cleaner, I sorted through the piles of laundry in the laundry room. Maybe, I thought, taking a load out of the washer and putting it in a dryer, it was time for a professional laundry service. I'd talk to Rhonda about it.

As it was turning dark, I made the rounds at the hotel to make sure our guests were settled for the night. Two of our part-time kitchen staff had made it in to help Jean-Luc prepare dinner. Most of our guests had decided to stay on site after Jean-Luc announced the menu selection—Filets of Beef with a cracked pepper crust, Roasted Oriental Chicken, Rack of Lamb with a mustard crumb coating, or Pistachio-Encrusted Pompano.

Mr. Keene returned to the hotel and informed me that Ethel would stay in the hospital for a couple more days. We gave him an early dinner so he could go to bed.

Tim set up a rollaway bed in the office for him to be on hand if anyone needed anything during the night.

Tired to the bone, I wished him goodnight, plucked a single white rose from the arrangement in the front hall, and left to go home.

I dragged myself inside my house and prepared for the evening. First things first, I reminded myself and went into the bathroom to draw water into the soaking tub. I took off my grubby clothes and tossed them in a hamper. As I lowered myself into the hot water, I leaned back against the end of the tub. The water caressed my body, loosening muscles that had tightened with tension, making me feel deliciously lazy. I lay there remembering my first meeting with Vaughn and how I'd felt watching him kiss someone else professionally on the show. How I'd wished it'd been me. And now he was coming to see me. It seemed such a fantasy.

Smiling, I recalled making love with him. An undeniable wave of desire surged through me. It had been as wonderful as I'd dreamed it would be. Even better. I'd wanted him from the beginning. His sexy, warm smile had touched me in a way that was new to me. As I thought of the way he made me feel, I still found it hard to believe someone as famous and handsome as Vaughn could possibly be interested in someone like me.

After I emerged from the tub, I toweled myself off and spread my favorite lotion over my skin, delighting in the flowery essence of its perfume. In anticipation of Vaughn's touch, I sprayed the matching perfume on my wrists and between my breasts and slipped on a silk robe. I set aside a pair of sea-blue linen pants and a matching silk shirt. He'd once mentioned he liked me in blue. Just before his arrival, I'd put them on.

In the kitchen, I set out wine glasses for the chardonnay chilling in the wine cooler, took French brie cheese from the refrigerator, and placed it on a serving platter. Crisp French bread sat on the counter ready to be sliced and warmed. I washed greens for a nice, light salad. Vaughn had told me he enjoyed a light, late meal like this. I set the table and placed the white rose in a crystal bud vase in the middle of it, adding a bit of romance to the scene. Satisfied, I went into the living room.

The ten-o'clock news showed pictures of the unpredictable storm. It had caused havoc up and down the west coast of Florida but had just missed the Keys. Glad Rhonda and Will were safe, I switched over to a concert on the public television network and sat back to listen, counting the minutes until Vaughn arrived.

"Ann!" a soft voice called to me in my dreams. "It's Vaughn. I'm here."

I stirred and held out my arms, still caught in a fantasy world where Vaughn's lips pressed down on mine, filling me with soaring happiness.

"Hey, sleepyhead! Wake up!" Vaughn's amused voice startled me.

I opened my eyes. My arms were wound tightly around Vaughn's neck, and he was smiling down at me.

Suddenly shy, I released my grip on him. "I thought I was dreaming!"

"I like it when you dream," he whispered and gave me a lingering kiss.

I lay there, so happy to see him that tears sprang to my eyes.

"Hey! What's this?" He wiped the corners of my eyes tenderly.

"I'm so glad you're here." I sat up. "I'm sorry. This isn't starting out as I'd planned. It's been an unbelievable time with the storm and the accident."

He drew me to him, making me feel so protected. "I know," he murmured. "Tim filled me in on the details when I stopped by the hotel."

His gaze traveled down the length of me, and I realized my robe had fallen open, revealing the fact that I wore nothing underneath it.

I started to rise. "The supper ..."

"Mmm, I'd rather have you," he murmured. He stretched out beside me and kissed me. His lips felt so good, tasted so good.

He stroked my body in all the right places. I lay back among the cushions, thrilled to be alive, in this place, with this man. I'd dreamed of it for so long.

We went from the couch to my bedroom, becoming reacquainted all over again. As we made love, the need to talk evaporated. Our hands and lips and tongues did it for us. I couldn't get enough of him. When he finally entered me, I was trembling with need, a need he was happy to fulfill.

Sated, I lay in his arms, pleased I'd given him as much pleasure as he'd given me. I now believed in soul mates, because I was certain I'd found mine.

Later, I stirred in bed, confused by my inability to shift positions. In the dim early morning light, I stared at the length of the man who'd entrapped me with his long legs. His strong, familiar features were relaxed now, smooth with contentment. Smiling to myself, I touched his dark curls, deceptively silken to the touch. Vaughn roused long enough to pull me closer, shifting, so my body was molded into the curve of his. I felt him harden against me and filled with satisfaction at having such power over him.

I slept briefly, and when I awakened, pink fingers of color in the sky beckoned through the open blinds with the promise of a better day. I gently touched Vaughn's earlobe with the tip of my finger.

"It's going to be a beautiful day," I whispered into his ear.

He opened his eyes and smiled lazily at me. "I'm not ready for the day; the night was too fantastic."

I laughed and disentangled myself from him. "I promised Tim I'd be over there before breakfast. I've got to go. But if you want to stay here, do. We can meet up later."

I turned away, but I wasn't quick enough to escape his grasp. He sat up and drew me onto his lap.

As I leaned against him, I loved the feel of his skin against mine and inhaled the manly smell of him. I recalled how easily his softness had turned hard and demanding, and wondered how I could leave him even for a short time.

He nuzzled my neck. "I'd dreamed of spending another night with you, but I had no idea that it could be even better from what I remembered. You're something else."

Satisfaction spread through me. I stroked his cheek. "You're not so bad yourself. In fact," I teased, "I would say you're the best."

"Compared to what?" His dark eyes twinkled with mirth.

I chuckled. Making love with Vaughn was very special, and we both knew it. The words he spoke, the things he did to make me cry out with pure, ecstatic release were responses that couldn't be compared to anyone else.

He kissed me, and I leaned into him, realizing I couldn't leave him after all.

A while later, I climbed out of bed, laughing when Vaughn grabbed my hand. "I mean it this time, Vaughn. I have to go over to the hotel to make sure everything is set for breakfast. Jean-Luc promised to come in, but I need to know for certain things are okay."

"Does your work always come first?" Vaughn teased, patting my bare behind.

I grinned. "I've just proved that it doesn't. But seriously, I do need to go over there. C'mon! I'll race you to the shower."

I stood under the hot running water of the shower and reveled at the sight of a naked man in the bathroom with me. My body came alive as I soaped the areas Vaughn had so easily aroused. I was almost afraid of what he could do to me. I became a woman obsessed in his arms. Robert had never been as free and creative in his lovemaking as the remarkable man who stood at my sink.

We dressed and headed out. A light breeze rustled the leaves of the plantings around the house. The last of the gray storm clouds skittered across the sky, leaving a pale blue behind. Soon, the sun would change the sky's color, brightening it to a tropical hue.

I moved with the ease of a well-loved woman and glanced over at Vaughn, strolling beside me. He was a wonderful man, sure of himself, careful with others, kind, and tender. As if he'd read my thoughts, he caught my hand and lifted it to his lips. He gazed into my eyes and gave me a sexy, crooked smile.

I blinked. I'd seen him look exactly like that before—on television—causing thousands of women to swoon over him.

I frowned and stopped. Was this whole scenario as real to him as it was to me?

"You okay?" he asked, giving me a curious look.

"How do you separate reality from the acting you do on television? I'd hate to think what we had together might seem unreal to you."

"Did I give that impression?" His voice was deceptively soft, though I knew him well enough to know I'd touched a nerve.

"Nooo," I admitted.

He held both of my hands in his and looked down at me, his expression grave. "I need to know I can be me with you. Not the mayor of that crummy little town he lives in. Not the television star. Just me—Vaughn Sanders from Chicago, Illinois, the kid growing up who was too tall, too skinny, and too ungainly to do sports. That's why I became an actor. What I say to you and what I do to you comes from me— nobody else. Okay?"

I realized how difficult a career like his could be, and how it could affect his whole life. Reality was the thing that kept an actor grounded, while at the same time, it was his ability to go beyond it that gave him his success. I knew now how important it was for him to keep that balance.

I stretched up on my toes and kissed him tenderly on the lips. "Yeah, it's okay with me, Vaughn Sanders from Chicago, Illinois."

His eyes brightened, and the frown on his face disappeared. "Good."

We entered the hotel, and I headed for the kitchen while

Vaughn went to look at the pool. At the entrance to the kitchen, I stopped in surprise.

"Consuela! I didn't expect to see you here!" I gave her a careful hug. "How are the others doing? Any word?"

She smiled. "Manny called me this morning. He's feeling better. He's talking about coming home. Already, he's asking when he can come back to work. The doctor says it will be a while, but he doesn't know Manny. Rosita is going to be okay, too. They think Ana will walk again, but it's going to take her time to heal."

Her eyes grew misty. "Annie, I have it all figured out. Maria brought me here. I thought we could show her what Ana used to do. Then I'll take over for Rosita when Jean-Luc comes in. Paul is bringing Ana's neighbor in for the laundry. Her name is Lourdes. She's real nice."

"Sounds good." I was pleased she'd taken such initiative.

Maria walked into the kitchen, carrying a tray of dirty dishes. I smiled at her. "Thank you for your help. I understand you'll be with us every day now."

She nodded. "*Si. Gracias.* My parents and I are grateful for your help."

"I'm so sorry about Ana, but I'm very glad to have you here." Maria was a taller, thinner version of Consuela and quiet like her father.

After grabbing a quick bite to eat with Vaughn, I spent a good hour with Maria, showing her exactly what we wanted to be done in the rooms. "Lourdes will come to take care of the dirty sheets and towels." I checked my watch. "She should be here soon."

"Don't worry, Annie, I'll see that things are done right," said Consuela, joining us. I believed her. No one would get away with less than excellence with her.

Downstairs, I skimmed through emails and checked in

with Tim at the reception desk. He gave me a sly smile. "Go home and enjoy your guest, Ann. I'll call if anything important comes up. After yesterday, today will be a gentle breeze."

I groaned at his sense of humor, and we both laughed, sharing our relief that the bad weather had disappeared in a blaze of sunshine. Our guests were outside enjoying the pool and the beach.

Paul and Lourdes drove in the driveway as Vaughn and I walked toward my house. I waved and brushed aside any lingering concerns about the hotel. Things were in order, and I was nearby if anyone needed me.

The rest of the day passed in a haze of lazy happiness. Vaughn was a relaxing companion, content to read or help me out with a word or two on the *New York Times* crossword puzzle. Each time I glanced over at him stretched out in a lounge chair by the pool, I had to remind myself that he was really here beside me and not a figment of my imagination.

Later, as we sat on the steps in the cool water of the pool, sipping bubbly water, making small talk, a man in uniform came into view and continued on his way.

Vaughn smiled. "I'm glad you have those guards around. I'm pretty sure my photographer friend didn't make the trip this time, but it's still a good feeling to know a security guard is keeping an eye on things."

"The scandal with you was a horrendous experience for me," I said. "It continued long after you left. How can you stand losing your privacy like that?"

"It's not easy," Vaughn admitted. "You do your best to arrange your life, so you aren't in the limelight all the time. That's why it's so important to me to find someone who's content to live simply."

I nodded thoughtfully. "I can understand that."

"Any idea how crazy I am about you?" Vaughn drew me to him, and even in the coolness of the water, I could feel heat building between us.

He grinned. "I can prove it to you right here."

I laughed and pushed him away. There was no way I was going to disrobe in my pool, not with the memory of scandal so sharp in my mind. "Beat you to the end of the pool!"

He set his bottle of water down, and I took off. He caught up with me at the end of the pool and grabbed me to him. He grinned. "You can't get away from me!"

I threw my arms around his neck and wrapped my legs around his torso. "You don't understand," I whispered in his ear. "I don't want to."

I felt his body harden.

As we stood in the water, his lips came down on mine. When we finally drew apart, we both were breathing fast. "I want you with me. We're good together."

His lips settled on mine again, and lost in the urgency of his kiss, I felt as if we were the only two people in the world.

Vaughn pulled away. "Let's go inside." His voice was husky.

Smiling, we climbed out of the pool and hurried into my bedroom.


As I dressed for dinner, I reflected on the afternoon. It had been one of the most pleasant times I'd ever had. I'd only had to take two phone calls from Tim, allowing me plenty of time with Vaughn. He was right. The two of us *were* good together.

I heard Vaughn moving about in the other room and smiled. He made me feel young and vulnerable at the same time I felt wise and worldly. His gentleness, his easy-going manner, and his eagerness to share his ideas with me were so endearing.

"You almost ready?" He came into the bedroom, and I was sorry we'd agreed to have dinner with Roger Sloan and his wife, Darlene. Vaughn's producer had decided at the last minute to come to Sabal. Though Roger couldn't book a room at the hotel, he wanted to dine with us. I told myself the least I could do was to be gracious about the invitation. Darlene had spread the word about The Beach House Hotel among a wide circle of people in New York. And Vaughn had informed me that he was in the midst of contract negotiations with Roger for next year's show, and this dinner was important to him.

*Business is business*, I told myself as I greeted Roger and Darlene Sloan and their friends, Bob Masterson and Lily Dorio at one of the nicest restaurants in town.

At dinner, I was seated opposite Vaughn, next to Roger Sloan. I tried to hide my dismay when Lily, sitting next to Vaughn, made a show of hanging onto Vaughn's every word. She batted her eyelashes at him in what fast became a parody of infatuation. I might have been tempted to laugh at her adoration of Vaughn, but as it was, I was having trouble feeling part of the group. The conversation centered on mutual friends in New York and gossip among the theater group. When talk finally turned to the right of free speech and creativity versus violence on television, I perked up.

Roger went into a tirade against those who wished to control artistic endeavor. "Everyone should be allowed to express themselves however they want, regardless of how it affects others."

Vaughn turned to me. "What do you think, Ann? Do you agree?"

I was grateful to be included and looked around the table. "I'm wondering where common sense and good taste play a part in all this. Creativity should not be stifled, nor should government attempts to control it be tolerated. It's simply a matter of personal responsibility."

Roger snorted at me. "You don't know anything about the television business or what it's like to try to arrive at something at the bottom line that makes sense. People today want blood and guts and gory, weird, kinky stuff. Look at some of the reality shows and talk shows. Those fools are willing to spill their guts about anything."

I persisted. "That's where responsibility comes in. Too many television programs appeal to the baser qualities in people ..."

Lily cut me off. "You're very naïve, Ann. The world can be an ugly place, filled with rotten people. What's wrong with showing it that way? That's what people want, just like Roger says. They don't deserve anything better."

I glanced at Vaughn, wondering if he was as irritated by my remarks as the others.

Vaughn winked at me, and I let out the breath I'd been holding. Robert would have been furious with me for making waves.

"I think Ann has something there," Vaughn said. "I've thought a lot about it recently. I believe you'll see a change back to more traditional movies and programs. Oh, I don't mean we'll go back to the overly simplistic ones of long ago. Life has become much more complicated, after all. I just think some people are tired of all the aimless violence without apparent artistic purpose."

"Are you tired of it?" Darlene asked, entering the conversation.

Vaughn nodded and gave her a steady look. "Yes, I am."

"Do you mean to tell me that if a great part came up, one that involved a lot of violence, you'd turn it down on principle alone?" Roger's tone was scornful.

Lily laughed and pushed at Vaughn playfully. "No, he wouldn't. He would look so adorable playing the tough guy, he couldn't resist. Right, darling?"

My lips tightened at the way she leaned into him, resting her ample bosom on his arm.

Vaughn glanced at me and turned to Roger. "I might. I just might turn it down." He glanced at me again and smiled.

The conversation remained on show biz. I turned to Darlene, sitting on my other side. She'd been especially quiet. I had the uneasy feeling she and Roger had been fighting. They'd ignored each other all night.

When it was time to leave, I was more than ready to go. Lily was still draping herself across Vaughn, and I was having a difficult time accepting it. She knew Vaughn and I were together, and she'd come with Bob Masterson. I couldn't understand why she was acting this way. Was this how it was in show business?

Vaughn and I drove back to the hotel in silence.

He pulled my car into my garage and turned to me. "You're awfully quiet. Is everything okay?"

I shrugged. "I was thinking about the dinner conversation. I hope people like Roger Sloan, who have the power to make some changes in programming, have the courage to do so. Even though we didn't agree on the issue of violence and television, I think he's a bright man."

Vaughn gave my hand a squeeze. "I was proud of the way you handled yourself tonight. You were well-spoken and honest. Not many people will stand up to Roger Sloan."

"Hopefully, things will change, even if your *very dear friend*, Lily Dorio, doesn't think so."

Vaughn chuckled. "Do I detect a note of jealousy here?"

My cheeks turned hot. "Should I be jealous?"

"Of Lily?" Vaughn's expression turned incredulous. "Not on your life."

I let out a confused sigh. "Then, why did you let her hang all over you tonight?" I couldn't hide my dismay.

"It was harmless, believe me. She does that to any man she thinks is attractive at the moment. It doesn't mean a thing."

"I see." I got out of the car and turned to go inside.

Vaughn stopped me. "Hey! Wait a minute! You're not going to let that bother you, are you?" A trace of annoyance crept into his voice.

I shook my head. "No. I'll just put that in the same category as the newspaper article and try to live with it. You're used to all of this. I'm not. C'mon, let's go in and have an after-dinner drink and relax."

Vaughn grinned. "That's my girl."

We sipped Kahlua over ice and sat in companionable silence before going to bed, where Vaughn proved to me Lily Dorio definitely wasn't on his mind.

Long after Vaughn had fallen asleep, I lay in bed wrestling with my thoughts. Honesty forced me to face the fact that many things threatened a long-term relationship with Vaughn Sanders. I liked him; I loved him. I needed him; I didn't want him to interfere with my goals. I loved being with him alone; I hated being part of an entourage around him in public.

# CHAPTER TWENTY-THREE

The moment came to say goodbye to Vaughn. We sat at the kitchen bar at my house, facing each other, sipping coffee.

I felt like weeping. During our short time together, I'd given him my heart. With his departure, I'd be left empty and cold. "I wish you didn't have to leave."

The brown in his eyes darkened. "I wish I knew what's ahead for us. I have no idea how the contract negotiations are going to go. *You* can't leave your job. *I* can't leave mine. It's sort of crazy, our being together, but it's what I want. At this point, I can't promise you anything except to tell you how much you mean to me."

His honesty stung, but what else could he say? As always, our future was uncertain.

The ride to the airport was quiet, the air between us filled with unspoken words.

After he'd boarded the small, private jet carrying him, the Sloans, and Lily, I stood forlornly inside the terminal of the Sabal airport. Though I knew he couldn't see me, I wiggled my fingers in a final sign of farewell. He'd promised to return in time for Rhonda's wedding, but I didn't know how I could survive those interminable weeks without him until then.

I walked slowly back to the car. Vaughn's presence had filled me and my house with a vibrant, passionate love. I already felt at loose ends.

My work at the hotel helped keep me busy. Rhonda and Will were scheduled to return that afternoon, and I wanted everything to be in order by the time she showed up. Her weekend away was a test of sorts to see how things would go when she and Will went on their extended honeymoon.

Joey Howard, Tim's friend from school, came for an interview. His unkempt appearance was a far cry from Tim's neatness. As we talked, I reminded myself that he wouldn't be in front of the guests, but working behind the scenes assisting Paul with the landscaping. Physically, he appeared to be more than capable of doing heavy yard work.

"It's important to have the grounds of the property looking their best at all times. Manny, our landscaper, has been in an accident. In his absence, you are needed to work beside his nephew, Paul. Anyone hired for a job at this hotel must sign a confidentiality agreement, keeping the names and faces of our guests private. Are you willing to do that?"

Joey shrugged. "Sure. So, how much does the job pay?"

"Twelve dollars an hour." It would cost at least that much or more through a temp agency.

He frowned but nodded. "Okay."

After Joey filled out the paperwork, I called Tim in, grateful to have one less problem to worry about. Tim agreed to introduce Joey to Paul and to show him where the garden supplies were kept.

A couple of hours later, I was in the office, working on figures, when I overheard voices in the hallway by the dining room.

"I'm not taking any more orders from a Mexican!"

I stopped and sat quietly, listening for a reply.

"Paul is a good guy," Tim said with surprising firmness. "He works hard, and he knows a lot more about landscaping than either you or I do. It's his uncle who's really in charge of all that around here, but he's out of work with a broken leg. That's why you got the job."

"Well, I don't like it," Joey grumbled.

"Look, do you want the job or not?" I silently cheered at the disdain in Tim's voice.

"Okay, okay, I'll do it," Joey said. "Jeez! You don't have to be such a hard ass about it!"

"Yeah, well I'm the one who recommended you, so you'd better do a good job," snapped Tim.

They moved away, and my estimation of Tim rose even higher.

The phone rang, and when I saw who it was, I smiled and picked it up. "So how was it?"

Rhonda laughed. "Perfect. Just perfect. We should be there in another hour. We heard about the storm on the radio. How's The Beach House Hotel?"

"We were lucky. No real damage. Hurry home. I can't talk now; someone's here to see me."

Sarah Patten, a young lawyer from New York, looked unhappy as she sat in a chair opposite me.

"What can I do for you?" I asked her.

"I asked for a room close to the beach, but I've been put in one overlooking the front circle. That's not what I want."

I groaned inwardly. Thirty-two guest rooms and she had to end up in one she didn't want. "Let me check the reservations." I opened up the reservations file on the computer and tried to figure out who I could shift around. "Okay, I can move you to a beachside room, but it sits in the middle of the wing. Will that do?"

She nodded. "That would be much better. Can you have someone move my things for me?"

I forced a smile. "I'll be happy to help you. Anything else?"

"Yes. You know the flowers you put in the room? Well, I think I might be allergic to them. So I don't want any fresh flowers in my new room. And the bottle of water, could it be sparkling instead of still water? And could I have three packages of mixed nuts instead of two?"

I reminded myself this was the hotel business and hid my irritation.

I'd just finished helping Sarah get her things into her new room when I noticed the time and hurried downstairs to wait for Rhonda and Will. All was in order for their arrival, including the repairs in the laundry room.

Moments later, Rhonda and Will pulled through the entrance. I ran down the front stairs to greet them.

Rhonda climbed out of the car and grabbed me in one of her bosomy hugs. "Good to be back home!" Releasing me, she stepped back and glanced around. "But, Annie! We had no idea things were so bad around here—so many trees and branches down." Her cheeks turned a pretty pink. "We didn't even turn on the television over the weekend, and you didn't call like you promised you would if anything bad happened."

"There was no way I was going to interrupt your time with Will. You told me it was a pre-honeymoon trip."

"Oh, honey! Was it ever!" She lowered her voice. "He's even hotter than Sal. How did I get so lucky?" Rhonda's cheeks turned even redder, and I smiled. She was positively glowing.

Glancing at Will, I noticed he wore a look of satisfaction himself.

Rhonda elbowed me. "So how did it go with you and Vaughn? Knowing you two were together again, I almost hated to leave."

It was my turn to be flustered. "Well ... it was ... well ... wonderful!"

Rhonda threw her arms around me. "I knew it! You two are great together. Maybe I'd better save my notebook of wedding ideas. You might need them."

"Whoa! That's not going to happen anytime soon, if ever. He's in New York, and I'm here."

"Right," scoffed Rhonda. "And I'm thin as a rail."

I grinned. The idea of marrying Vaughn was startling, but not totally unreasonable. Was it?

With Rhonda back at the hotel, things settled into a more relaxed routine for me.

Paul maintained control of the yard and gardens with much conferring from Manny, who, Consuela informed me, quizzed the boy unmercifully each evening. I kept an eye on Joey, but as far as I knew there were no further problems between Paul and him.

Then, after I received a complaint about Joey from one of our guests, I called him into the office.

"Yeah? You wanted to see me?"

I gritted my teeth at his insolent manner. "Please sit down."

His attitude as he slouched in a chair with a bored expression sharpened my tongue. "You have signed a statement of confidentiality that we expect you to honor. I understand you told one of our other guests that Shelly Saxton was due to arrive. Comments like that are inappropriate and will not be tolerated. Actors, along with our other guests, have a right to their privacy. No such information about any of the people staying here will be discussed by any of our staff. You are to remain silent and do your job. Is that understood?"

Joey rolled his eyes and nodded.

"You can imagine my embarrassment when one of our guests brought this matter to my attention," I continued. "What you see and hear on these premises is confidential. Period."

"Is that all?"

"For now. If anything else comes up, we'll have to let you go." I knew our confidentiality policy wasn't always easy to keep, but it was important. I'd been shocked a few months ago when a tall, good-looking, young man-of-the-cloth arrived at the hotel and had literally discarded that persona, along with his clerical collar. I became even more flabbergasted when he lounged at the pool flirting with a stunning, young woman who had, to my knowledge, remained at his side throughout his stay. He departed wearing clerical clothing and a satisfied smile. In keeping with our policy, no one had spoken a word to him or anyone else about it—except Rhonda, who had said plenty to me in the privacy of our office.

Joey left, and I went into the kitchen for a cup of coffee. Fresh cookies were cooling on the counter. I snatched one.

I'd just finished eating it when Rhonda called and invited me up to her suite to see new items she'd just purchased for her trousseau. I happily climbed the stairs. Rhonda was throwing herself into her wedding preparations, enjoying all the things she'd been unable to do the first time around. She greeted me at the door wearing a white cotton dress. Cutwork edged the hem of the full skirt and accented the bodice. "What do you think?" She twirled around. "I was talking to this fashion consultant the other day. She wants me to tone down a bit. She even suggested I let my hair go dark." A wistful expression crossed Rhonda's face. "You know, I think she's right. With Will being in the accounting and investment business, I should really look the part of his wife."

I read uncertainty in her eyes and glanced at the beige outfits lying on Rhonda's bed. They were so wrong for her. Not wanting to hurt her feelings, I hesitated.

"Well? What do you think?" She moved from foot to foot impatiently. "Tell me the truth."

Rhonda subdued was not Rhonda at all. And the Rhonda I knew was perfect. "I think the fashion consultant doesn't have a clue who you are and what you're all about. I remember how insulted I felt when you accused me of being too beige. Now, why do you want to be like that, when you're going to Tahiti for your honeymoon?"

"Really, Annie? Is that what you think?" Rhonda broke into a broad smile. "Boy! Do I feel better! She had me worried." Her expression grew serious. "But I do want to look nice for Will. Maybe I'll tone down just a bit."

I went over to her and gave her a hug. "That's up to you, but I think you're wonderful just the way you are—and he does, too."

Rhonda's eyes turned shiny with emotion. "You're the best, Annie. Honest, you are."

I smiled. When I'd first met Rhonda, I'd been bowled over by what I thought of as her self-confidence. Now, I understood she used her flamboyant manner to cover up the insecurities she had. Our friendship had done us both a lot of good.

The wedding drew close. Liz and Angie arrived home, looking tanned and healthy from their second summer as counselors at the camp in New Hampshire.

Humming, I cooked one of Liz's favorite things for dinner—a chicken and lemon dish she'd always loved. Watching me, she sat at the kitchen bar telling me about some of her favorite campers.

At dinner, Liz toyed with her food. "You told me Vaughn was going to come back for Rhonda's wedding. What's up with that? Is it serious?" Her gaze met mine.

I squirmed uncomfortably. *Was this how Liz felt when I quizzed her about her dates?* "We're good together. We want to see how things evolve in time." I knew Liz wanted me happily settled, but I couldn't make it seem so easy. Vaughn and I had a lot to work out between us before anything more serious could happen.

Liz smiled. "I can tell you really like him, Mom. Is he as nice as Nell says?"

I nodded. Every day without him was agony for me. I was a planner, someone who wanted to know where she was headed. The hotel business had taught me I couldn't do that anymore. With Vaughn, it was even more unpredictable.

"Did I tell you about the guy I met in Boston? He's hot. Really hot." Liz launched into a description of the senior at Harvard who'd hosted a party she'd attended, and I let out a sigh of relief. I was off the hook—for the moment.

After dinner, Liz took off, and I went into the office to send an email to Vaughn. Over the past few weeks, we'd kept up a pretty regular exchange of messages. The more I learned about him, the more I liked him.

Liz came in before eleven o'clock and plopped down on my bed. I put aside the book I'd been reading and smiled. "Have a good time?"

She shrugged. "Not too much going on. It was good to see some of the kids, though. And Angela and Tim have a thing going on. Tim's great, but that Joey guy is a loser. He even tried to hit on me."

"Really? He's on the reception desk tonight. He asked for a chance to do it so Tim could have some time with Angela.

Was he there?"

"Yeah, but, Mom, he's a pothead or worse. A total jerk."

I drew myself up. "Really? I should've caught on to that. Well, let's see how he does with his new responsibilities."

Liz lay next to me, her head on the pillow like she used to do as a little girl. "Mom? I'm not sure I want to go back to college this year. I might want to take some time off. Dad's making noises about how expensive it is, and I'm not sure what I want as my major. I keep changing my mind, and that makes Dad mad."

I took a deep breath. "Liz, you have a wonderful life ahead of you. It's important for you to have your degree. You can choose any career you want. As far as your father is concerned, he should have no worries about the cost. The money has already been set aside for you."

Liz rolled over and looked at me. "You think it's that important for me?"

"Oh, yes. I want you to have all the choices in the world and to be able to do anything you want. Go for it, Liz."

She grinned. "And if I want to become a lawyer?"

Thinking of the additional cost of law school, I held back a groan.

She giggled. "Tricked you, Mom. I'd never become a lawyer. I promise."

I laughed and gave her a hug. "Seriously, Liz, I want you to stay in school."

"I know, I know. Kandie is the one who doesn't want Dad to spend money on me."

I bit back a reply. I was not about to be enticed onto that emotional merry-go-round. I'd heard from an old neighbor in Boston that Robert and Kandie fought a lot. Robert had, in fact, confided to my neighbor's husband that marrying a much younger woman wasn't all it was cracked up to be.

### # # #

I dressed and slipped out of the house eager to see how Joey had performed on the evening shift. As I entered the hotel, I was greeted by the tantalizing smell of freshly baked cinnamon rolls. I stopped at the reception desk and checked for notes. Joey hadn't left any. I opened the cash drawer, where we normally kept a bank of four hundred dollars and counted the money. Frowning, I counted it again. My stomach clenched. We were missing one hundred dollars. I lifted the bill tray out of the drawer, thinking a big bill might have been placed underneath it. No such luck.

I headed into the kitchen. "Good morning, Consuela. Have you seen Joey?"

Consuela shook her head. "He hasn't come in yet. And if you don't mind my saying so, Annie, he isn't doing a very good job with the outside work. Paul complains to Manny about him, but he won't complain to you."

"Well, I don't think Paul will have to worry about him much longer." I checked my watch. "Joey's supposed to be here now."

Some time later I heard Joey come in. I rose from my desk chair and went to meet him.

"May I see you inside my office?"

A sullen expression crossed Joey's face, but he followed me inside and took a seat.

I shut the door and sat opposite him. "Joey ..."

He jumped to his feet. "Look, I'm sorry I'm late! All right?" he cried, already on the defensive.

I reined in my temper. "Sit back down. We need to talk. We're missing one hundred dollars from the cash drawer. What do you know about that?"

"You're accusing me of stealing? No fucking way. You'd

better count again." The smirk on his face sent a rush of heat to my face.

Seeing him differently, I noticed his glassy eyes. Why hadn't I realized he had a problem? A problem that was bigger than we could handle. I wanted to slap the belligerent smile off his face, but I forced my voice to be controlled, steely.

"I think we both know my count is accurate."

I waited for him to deny taking the money, but he merely sat, silently fuming.

I reached into my desk drawer. "I've made out a check to you for the full amount of money you're owed, including the hours you worked last night. As of this moment, you are no longer employed by The Beach House Hotel. I want you off these premises immediately."

Joey's lips curled. He jabbed a finger in my direction. "Yeah, well I don't want to work here anyway. This place sucks."

I stood and faced him. "I'm not reporting you to the police, but I am notifying Bob Silvia at the police department that your presence at the hotel is no longer wanted. Take the check, Joey, and don't return here for any reason."

Joey snatched the check I held out to him and gave me a murderous glare. Fear shot up my spine. I struggled to keep my voice steady. "Leave now, Joey, and don't hang around."

"Fuck you!" He stormed out of the office.

I gripped the edge of my desk and lowered myself into my chair, shaking. Never again would I be too quick to hire someone.

Rhonda came into the office. "What's up? Joey stomped right past me without saying a word! What's he all upset about now?" She stopped and stared at me. "What's wrong, Annie?"

"It's Joey." By the time I finished telling her the whole story, she was pacing the floor.

"That little bastard! He was too cocky for his own good."

"I never should have hired him."

Rhonda shook her head. "Don't take that on, Annie. We both had growing concerns about him."

She left, and a few minutes later, Tim burst into the office. "Okay, where's Joey? Paul is still waiting for him to begin work outside."

"He's gone. I fired him. One hundred dollars is missing from the drawer, and he didn't deny taking it."

"Hey, I'm sorry." Tim brushed a hand through his hair. "I thought he was working out his problems. I didn't know how bad it was."

"It's something I'll watch out for in the future." I decided to chalk it up to another learning experience, mentally adding it to a long list of them.

The rest of the day went more smoothly. I left the office around six and decided to take a walk. The beach, where Vaughn and I had shared such magical moments, beckoned to me. At home, I checked on Liz, changed into a bathing suit, and headed out to the sand. It felt good to set a pace and move quickly down the shoreline, loosening muscles, letting hotel-related concerns escape into the onshore breeze. Lost in thought, I slowed my steps. No matter how much I tried, I couldn't see a future with Vaughn. Not if I was totally honest with myself. Our lives were so different.

I turned to go back to my house and noticed Brock Goodwin heading my way. He lifted a hand in salute, and I sighed. There was no way I could ignore him.

I tensed as he drew closer to me.

"Hey, Ann! Glad to see you."

His pleasant manner caught me off guard.

He gave me one of those smiles I'd once thought so charming. "I know we've had our disagreements in the past, but that doesn't mean we can't be friends, does it?"

I shook my head. "Rhonda and I just want to be able to run our business in a way that hurts no one. I'd hoped you'd understand that."

He shrugged. "As it turns out, you've kept your promises about no unsightly messes and no unnecessary disruptions to the neighborhood. But most people in your position wouldn't do that, especially if it meant more money."

"The Beach House Hotel is different from most. We don't want messes and loud noise."

"Hey look, no hard feelings. I was merely doing my duty as head of the Gold Coast Neighborhood Association. I've been voted back on the board. Maybe we can get together sometime."

I shook my head. "Rhonda and I are both very busy."

He stared at me a moment, nodded, and went on his way.

I headed back home thinking about Brock. His old charm had resurfaced, leaving me wondering at his change of heart. I didn't trust him and never would.

# CHAPTER TWENTY-FOUR

The week before the wedding, the hotel became Rhonda's home once more. As predicted, it was a slow time for the hotel. We set aside beachside rooms for her brother Richie and his family. We rearranged the dining room so it would comfortably seat all fifty people for the wedding reception. Rhonda spent hours in the kitchen with Jean-Luc going over recipes, deciding which individual cakes she wanted for each guest, and how she wanted them decorated. Sandra Marle at Tropical Fleurs in downtown Sabal met with Rhonda and the party planner to coordinate colors of the flowers for the garden-party theme of the reception. Through it all, Tim and I handled the few guests who came and went, unaware of all the activities taking place behind the scenes.

The wedding festivities officially began with the arrival of Rhonda's older brother Richie and his family a couple of days ahead of time.

As planned, Rhonda and I stood at the top of the stairs and greeted them sedately, as if they were VIP guests. Then, unable to keep up the pretense, all hell broke loose. Rhonda gave a shout of glee, hugs were given all around, and everyone talked at once. When Rhonda introduced me, I quickly found myself embraced by Richie, then his wife, Margaret. Their three teen-age boys stood by awkwardly. Angie and Liz appeared, and more shouts and hugs were exchanged. Angie introduced Liz to everyone and then she and Liz and the boys took off for the beach.

While Paul and Tim helped with the luggage, Rhonda and

I led Richie and Margaret inside.

"It's so fancy," Margaret exclaimed over the small dining room.

"Wait'll you see the other dining room," said Rhonda proudly. "It's not as fancy, but it's a lot bigger."

We toured the inside, and then we took them out to the garage to show them the laundry area, Consuela and Manny's apartment, and Tim's quarters.

Richie elbowed Rhonda's side. "Now I know where Marg and I can live when we give up the butcher shop."

Rhonda let out a loud guffaw. "Ha! The only way you can stay there, brother dear, is if you do all the work that Manny and Consuela do."

They laughed together, and I studied them. Richie was large and big-boned like his sister, but his dark features seemed oddly misplaced after seeing those familiar features surrounded by a mass of blond curls on Rhonda. There was no mistaking they were related and no doubt about their closeness. Watching them laugh and tease one another, I felt a pang of envy. It had been lonely for me, an only child living with my strict grandmother.

Margaret came over to me. "It's great you and Rhonda have turned this huge place into a hotel. I've never seen Rhonda so happy."

I smiled. "It's a lot of hard work, but we're holding our own. It's Will who's made Rhonda very, very happy. Wait until you meet him. They're perfectly suited for one another."

She frowned. "He's quiet, right? It would be too zany if they were exactly alike."

I laughed. I agreed with her. Two people like Rhonda would be one too many.

Will arrived at the hotel promptly at six. Cocktails were served by the pool before we gathered in the small dining room. Consuela had prepared a special meal of traditional, lesser-known Mexican dishes. Everyone dug in.

Toward the end of the meal, Rhonda rose to her feet. "I'd like to give a toast to my brother. He's the best." She winked at Richie. "Well, almost the best."

We lifted our glasses and sipped.

Rhonda stayed on her feet. "And now I'd like to toast the one who is the best— Will. See, he's not like my brother at all." The outrageous sexy look she gave him made us all laugh. Richie's laugh was loudest of all.

Rhonda's cheeks flushed. Her eyes began to fill. "Seriously, I love you both."

She gave Will a lingering kiss that made it clear how unlike a brother Will was to her. The three boys whistled and hooted while the rest of us clapped. Red crept up Will's neck, onto his cheeks, and spread to the tips of his ears.

Everyone clinked glasses and took another sip of the special, Italian red wine Richie had brought as a gift. Margaret and I exchanged happy smiles. It was nice to feel part of this close-knit family group. I couldn't wait to share this with Vaughn.

I stood among the crowd at the airport waiting to greet the arrivals, eagerly searching for Vaughn among the passengers exiting the gate area. The memory of his face, tanned and happy, lingered in my mind.

When I finally spotted him, I let out a gasp.

Vaughn was wearing dark sunglasses that hid his eyes. But they couldn't hide his gray-looking skin or his drawn cheeks. He walked slowly, hunched over as if he were ill. My heart pounded with shock.

I waved and called to him.

He came right over.

"I'm so glad to see you." Wondering at his appearance, I held him tight. "You look as if a bit of Florida sunshine might do you some good."

He let out a sigh that spoke volumes. "Dealing with the personalities and politics involved in a long-running television show can become impossible. I couldn't wait to get away."

I slid my arm around his and smiled up at him. "Well, I couldn't wait to have you here. After you relax by the pool, the whole world will seem better. C'mon!"

We picked up his luggage and headed to my house. On the drive home, Vaughn leaned his head back against the passenger's seat and closed his eyes.

Worried, I kept glancing at him, wondering what I could do to help. He looked terrible. I'd never seen him so exhausted, not even during the filming when he was working so hard.

We arrived at the hotel to find the place hopping with activity. Two of Richie's boys were tapping golf balls on the putting green. Liz and Angie and two boys I'd never seen before were playing a game of tennis. Richie was tossing horseshoes with a man I hadn't yet met. Rhonda, Margaret, and another woman sat on the sidelines in chairs drinking sodas and talking. A young boy and girl headed for them wearing bathing suits.

Rhonda jumped up from her chair when she saw us and signaled me to stop.

I noticed Vaughn's wary look. "Don't worry," I said quietly. "I promise I'll rescue you from all this."

Rhonda leaned into the car window, a grin on her face. "Hi ya, Vaughn. My cousin and sister-in-law can't wait to meet you. Are you going to have lunch with us?"

Vaughn and I shook our heads together. "He isn't feeling well," I explained. "Do you mind? We'll join you for dinner."

She studied him with concern and turned to me. "Okay. See ya later."

I silently blessed her for understanding how real the situation was and drove on to my house.

Inside the house, Vaughn took his suitcase to the guest room to unpack. That's how we'd decided to play it with Liz home. I fixed him a ham sandwich and took it, along with a cold bottle of beer, to his room.

"I thought you might like a little lunch." I set the plate and the bottle down on the table next to the overstuffed chair in the room. "I can't imagine the food on the plane was worth eating."

"What food? First class doesn't have real food anymore." He walked over to me and gave me a quick kiss. "Thanks."

After he finished eating, I opened the sliding door of his room and led him out to the lanai. A refreshing onshore breeze was picking up.

He stretched out on a chaise lounge. "Ahhh, this feels great!" He took a deep breath and gave me a worried look. "Ann, I need to talk to you about something."

"Why don't you wait a bit?" His eyelids were drooping. "I know how tired you are. Whatever it is, we can talk later."

Vaughn gave me a grateful smile and closed his eyes.

I left him sleeping, returned to the kitchen, and went into my home office.

Liz found me there. "Is everything all right? Rhonda said Vaughn isn't feeling well."

"I guess he had a horrible week. He looks like he hasn't slept for days. He's asleep in a chaise lounge outside. I'm going to let him rest there. What's up with you?"

She smiled. "One of Angela's really cool friends, a guy

named Mike Westerly, has invited us to go for a boat ride this afternoon. His family owns a yacht. We're taking two of Richie's boys with us. We won't be back until dinnertime. Rhonda says it's fine with her. Okay, Mom?"

"Sure, hon. Just be careful."

Liz put her hand on her hip and frowned at me. "Mom, I'm twenty years old. You don't need to tell me to be careful. For your information, Mike has his captain's license and is a very safe boater."

I chuckled. "All right, old lady, I won't worry about you."

She leaned over and gave me a kiss. "See you later."

Through the window in my office, I watched her leave the house, swinging her towel as she walked down the path to the main house. A mental image of her as a little girl doing the same thing made me smile.

I went back to work. In the midst of my number crunching, warm lips nuzzled the back of my neck. I started in my seat and turned to find Vaughn behind me, grinning. I stood and went into his embrace.

"I feel like a new man," he murmured. "Thank you for giving me that time to recuperate. I needed it."

He lifted my chin and settled his lips on mine, thanking me in a very different way. My heart hammered with desire. New man or not, this was the man I wanted. I responded to the increased pressure of his lips, the strokes of his tongue.

He pulled away. "Are we alone?"

I nodded.

He took my hand, and we headed to my bedroom. Knowing what lay ahead, I felt like dancing on my toes as I skimmed along beside him.

Later, lying beside Vaughn on my bed, gloriously fulfilled, I playfully tugged on a few strands of his chest hair.

He pulled me closer and stroked my face. "You make me

feel alive. Know that?"

I smiled up at him. "The Florida sun and fresh air have already started to work its magic on you."

"No, it's you." His smile disappeared. "I need to talk to you."

He was obviously worried about something, but I didn't want to let anything destroy the tenderness of the moment. "Later," I murmured. "Kiss me now."

His lips claimed mine, and we lost ourselves in one another's arms.

Checking the bedside clock later, my eyes widened. "It's late! We have to get going. I don't want Liz to find us like this." I hadn't come that far from my upbringing.

Showered and dressed, Vaughn and I sat in the shade of the lanai, sipping drinks. It felt so right for him to be near me, enjoying a relaxing time at home.

"It's good to be here. Back to reality and sanity." Vaughn lifted his frosty glass of vodka and tonic in a salute to me. "But, Ann, we have to talk about something."

"Okay, but here comes Liz. Can it wait?"

Looking unhappy, he shrugged. "I guess it'll have to."

As Liz got closer, I noticed her face was a mask of fury. Alarmed, I set down my drink and rose.

I met her at the entrance to the pool deck. She brushed past me and marched over to Vaughn. "You bastard! How could you!"

"Elizabeth Rutherford! What are you doing?" I grabbed her arm, but she brushed me off. "No, Mom! You don't understand!"

"Understand what?" I felt as if I were caught up in a scene from his television show.

Liz turned to me, her eyes glistening with tears. "I'm talking about a brand new internet story about Vaughn and some lady named Lily Dorio. Mike asked me all about it when we were alone in the cockpit of his boat. He didn't know Vaughn was here with you. The dirty double-crosser!"

Feeling ill, I staggered back into my chair. Liz came over to me and put her arm around me. "While you've been mooning for him down here, it seems Vaughn's been fooling around with someone else. You deserve better than that, Mom." She shot Vaughn another nasty look. "A lot better!"

I felt faint as I turned to Vaughn. "Is it true? Lily Dorio? The woman who kept throwing herself at you the last time you were here? You're seeing her?"

Vaughn's jaws worked, the muscles on the side of his face flexing in a rhythmic pattern that set my heart to pounding. He looked from me to Liz and back again. "No. It isn't true. It's all part of something I can't discuss right now. God help me, I know that sounds like a lame excuse, but there it is. You have to believe me."

Though I wanted to run and hide, I forced myself to answer. "If it's something you can't discuss with me, why should I believe you? The whole world must think it's true. Why shouldn't I?"

He stood. "Because you, of all people, know how those damn papers and internet reports work. They don't tell the truth!"

I looked up at him, my body too weak, too cold to confront him standing. "They don't tell the whole truth, but there's always some tiny particle of truth to their stories. Enough to prevent lawsuits."

Liz stood in front of me, inches from Vaughn. "How do you explain the fact that the story shows a picture of you kissing that Lily woman who is, according to the report, pregnant?" Her voice cracked on the last word.

I grabbed hold of the arms of the chair to keep from

slumping to the floor. *Lily pregnant?* The whole world tilted. I closed my eyes. "Liz? Why don't you change your clothes and go on over to Rhonda's? Vaughn and I will join you later."

"Are you going to be all right, Mom?" Liz grabbed hold of my hand and squeezed.

"I don't know," I whispered. "Vaughn and I need to talk, to work this problem out between us. Liz, I know how angry you are, but I'm asking you not to say anything to anybody else. Chances are, nobody here will see the story with all the wedding stuff going on. I don't want to ruin this happy time for Rhonda. It's so important to her. Agreed?"

Liz drew a deep sigh and glanced at Vaughn with undisguised fury. "Okay, but I don't like it. I'll tell Angela to keep quiet, too."

"Thanks." This scene was a replay of the news I'd received from Robert and was almost as hard on her as it was for me.

After Liz left us, I covered my face with my hands, gasping aloud. Pain, sharp as tiny razors, cut through my heart. My nightmares had come to life all over again. First, Robert's deception. Now, Vaughn's.

"Ann?" Vaughn stepped toward me.

I held up my hand. "No!"

"God, Ann, I'm so sorry! I never meant to hurt you. I know how wounded you've been in the past ..."

"No. You. Don't!"

"Please, Ann." He drew me up in his arms.

I stood helplessly and finally let myself relax in his embrace, needing it so much.

"Don't cry, honey. Don't cry," he murmured. "I'm sorry."

I gathered my strength and pushed him away with unexpected force. "Don't cry?" Fury rippled through me. "You know how betrayed I felt by Robert. Now, you're doing the same thing. How dare you tell me not to cry?"

Tears welled in Vaughn's eyes, surprising me. "I swear to you, it isn't true. It has nothing to do with me. I believe all of this is because of Roger Sloan."

"Roger Sloan, your producer?" I snorted my disbelief. "Why would he have anything to do with you having an affair with Lily Dorio?"

Vaughn gritted his teeth. "I did *not* have an affair with Lily Dorio! I only saw her once. You've got to believe me. You've got to trust me."

My temper flared. "Trust you? How can I trust you or any man? Am I always to be betrayed?" I pushed myself away from him.

Vaughn stopped me with a hand on my wrist. "Listen to me! I'm caught up in the middle of something I can't control. I have most of the pieces in place, but not all of them. I need you by my side. I once asked you if you'd be willing to fight for our relationship. The time has come for you to decide. I promise you I didn't lay a finger on Lily. You've got to believe me!"

Seeing the misery on his face, I took a shaky breath. "I want to believe you. I really do. But I'm not sure I can."

Vaughn ran a hand through his hair, the same curls I loved to touch. He shook his head sadly. "I hope you can trust me on this. Without absolute trust in each other, we'll have no chance of making anything of our relationship. Especially with me in the business I'm in. I tried to tell you. Dammit! I love you, Ann."

I blinked in surprise. *Loved me?* He'd never said those words to me before. I saw the pleading in his eyes and hesitated. He was an actor. Was this just another scene to him? But then I recalled our lovemaking and knew no one could fake what had happened between us. He filled a need in me I hadn't even known existed before I met him. If it turned out to be another lie, I didn't think I could bear it.

"I do love you. I think you know that," said Vaughn. "I wouldn't be here now fighting for you if it weren't true. You know me well enough by now to realize that what I say is true. Stay with me. Everything will be all right in the end. I promise."

He held out his hand to me and, God help me, I took it and allowed myself to be drawn into his embrace, where I let tears of pain and relief flow.

We made it to the rehearsal dinner at the hotel just as cocktail hour was coming to a close. I'd waited to leave the house until the swelling around my eyes had gone down and I could cover my blotchy face with natural-looking makeup.

Vaughn took my hand as we entered the small dining room. Margaret and Rhonda's cousin Annette surrounded him, asking questions about the show. I went over to Liz.

She gave me a hug, and I whispered in her ear. "He says there was no affair with Lily and I believe him. He'll be able to tell me the whole story soon and I'm going to give him time to do it."

Liz's nostrils flared. She glanced at Vaughn. "He'd better be telling the truth."

I clasped her hand. "Give us both time, Liz."

She stared at me and finally nodded. "Okay. I'll do it for you, Mom."

Angela called her name. Shoulders bowed, Liz left me to go to her.

"Hey, Annie!" Rhonda came over and threw her arm around me. "You're sure you and Vaughn don't want to stand up in front of the church with us?"

I forced a laugh. "Tomorrow is your day, partner. I wouldn't change that for anything."

Rhonda lowered her voice. "Is Vaughn okay? He doesn't look so good."

"He's got some problems at work," I said in as non-committal a tone as I could muster.

Rhonda indicated the crowd with a sweep of her arm. "Annie, I can't believe all this is happening to me. How lucky can I get?"

I gave her a hug, squeezing back sentimental tears. "I'm so happy for you, Rhonda. I really am."

"Hey, Sis!" Richie called from across the room. "Are you women going to stand around talking all night or are we gonna eat?"

Rhonda laughed. "Ok, bro. Let's break bread."

After everyone was seated and wine and water were poured, Will rose. "I'd like to make a toast to my lovely bride. Rhonda, you're everything I've ever wanted. I thank you for agreeing to be mine."

Rhonda dabbed at her eyes and lifted her glass.

Watching the look of love pass between them, my heart contracted. Their love was so sweet, so genuine. I felt eyes on me and looked across the table to find Vaughn gazing at me, his expression full of tenderness. My pulse quickened. He's right, I thought, if we're to have any meaningful relationship, we must trust each other. I fervently hoped it wouldn't prove devastating to me.

He seemed to sense my decision and gave me a subtle wink that brought a smile to my face. More sure of myself, I lifted my fork. Vaughn was not Robert.

After dinner, Vaughn and I walked over to the house with Liz. It was important to me that the three of us come to some sort of understanding. I didn't want Liz to think Vaughn was like her father.

At home, Liz grabbed a bottle of water from the

refrigerator. "It's late. I'm going to bed."

Determined to bring up the topic that hung between us like a cloud of doom, I cleared my throat. "Vaughn has promised me that he and Lily Dorio were not having an affair. I'm going to trust him on this while he takes care of some personal problems concerning it. I want you to trust him too."

"Yeah? Well, I've seen what happens when guys lie and take off with someone else. It's not easy for anyone." Liz's face grew flushed, and I knew this was as much about Robert as it was about Vaughn.

"My children have suffered through a lot of false rumors," said Vaughn. "I'm sorry for that, but it's something that sometimes happens in my line of business. I would do nothing intentionally to hurt them, and I'd do nothing to hurt your mother or you. You can talk to Nell about it if that would make you feel better."

"Yeah? Maybe I will." She turned to me. "Goodnight, Mom."

"And?" I waited. She'd talked about being grown up. Was she?

She rolled her eyes. "Good night, Mr. Sanders."

She left, and I shook my head. Okay, so maybe she wasn't so grown up after all.

"Good night, Mrs. Rutherford." Vaughn gave me a tender smile. "I'll make it easy on everyone and go on to bed. I could use the rest."

"Good night." I was too tired physically and emotionally to do more than blow him a kiss as he left the kitchen.

# CHAPTER TWENTY-FIVE

The day was crystal clear and pleasantly warm, without the hot stickiness that September can bring—perfect for Rhonda's wedding, set for four o'clock in the afternoon.

Vaughn joined Will and the other men for an early round of golf at one of the clubs. Liz, Margaret, and Annette worked in the large dining room, helping the party planner decorate the room for the wedding reception. Rhonda and Angela took off for the beauty parlor.

At three forty-five, I stood outside the church greeting guests and introducing Rhonda's brother and sister-in-law to friends. Through my work at the hotel and in the community, I now knew most everyone who'd been invited to the small wedding.

Vaughn arrived with Will, and then it was time to enter the church.

Holding hands, Vaughn and I walked into the cool interior of the church and were ushered to one of the front pews to sit with Liz and the family. Dorothy, I noticed, had a seat two rows behind me on the aisle. Tim, Manny, and Consuela sat beside her.

I took a calming breath and admired the stained glass windows. Lowering my head, I prayed for the inner strength to give Vaughn the time he needed to make things right. I was still so insecure from Robert's betrayal.

Organ music announced the bridal procession.

I rose with the rest of the congregation and turned to face the bridal party. Vaughn smiled at me and squeezed hand .

Angela preceded her mother down the aisle. I drew in an admiring breath. She wore a simple, tea-length dress of pale-rose organza that showed off her petite figure. With each step forward, her brown hair swept the top of her shoulders. She carried a small, simple bouquet of off-white hydrangeas with the barest touch of rose. Green leaves added color. She glanced at Tim standing beside Dorothy, and a pretty smile lit her face, accentuating her beauty.

The music grew more dramatic.

I turned my gaze to Rhonda walking down the aisle with Richie. At the sight of her, my eyes grew misty. Rhonda wore a tea-length dress in ecru silk, covered with scattered, hand-worked silk flowers made brighter by pearl and crystal centers. With its simple, soft-flowing lines, the dress was perfect for her. A cluster of matching silk flowers nestled among the curls at the crown of Rhonda's head. In her hands, she carried a large bouquet of hydrangeas like Angela's. The hint of color was just right with the dress.

Rhonda exuded a mixture of awe and unrestrained enthusiasm. I held back a chuckle as Richie tugged on Rhonda's arm, silently exhorting her to slow down. It was so typical of Rhonda to be in a rush, even for this. She looked over at me and winked, and my heart filled with joy for her.

Will stood at the front of the church alone, waiting for Rhonda to join him. His dark suit was molded to his trim build, and I thought he looked much younger than his fifty-two years. The sweet way his face lit up as Rhonda approached him sent people scrambling in their pockets for tissues. I dabbed at my own eyes.

Vaughn grasped my hand and caressed my palm with his thumb. I held on tight. Though I continued to gaze at Rhonda and Will, I was very aware of the man beside me.

After the final words had been spoken and Will had kissed

Rhonda, she turned to the audience and raised a fist in the air. "We did it!"

Will laughed with the rest of us. Rhonda grabbed his arm. Amid clapping and cheers, they marched up the aisle.

Outside, Will led Rhonda to a white, open-air carriage. It had been trimmed for the occasion with red roses that offset the red-velvet seats of the carriage. A ring of red roses hung around the neck of the gray-dappled horse that pawed the ground impatiently.

A coachman, dressed in bottle-green livery, assisted Rhonda and Will into the carriage and climbed up in the driver's seat. Amid a shower of red rose petals, they pulled away from the curb.

"Great wedding, huh?"

I turned to find Brock Goodwin at my elbow. Vowing to keep my good humor, I smiled and nodded. Rhonda had decided it would be good PR to have him around, but he was the last person I wanted to see at that moment.

Limousines carried us to the hotel. At the entrance to the dining room, I stood and gazed around with pleasure. Tiny sparkling lights and off-white trimmings had transformed the room into a fairyland.

"Nice," murmured Vaughn as we found our table. Manny and Consuela were seated there, along with the mayor and his wife.

We greeted everyone and took a seat. Manny and the mayor got into a discussion about the use of fertilizers. I turned to Consuela. "What a nice wedding."

"Rhonda was so pretty," gushed Consuela. I nodded, watching with interest as the mayor's wife grabbed hold of one of Vaughn's hands and complimented him on the show. He glanced over at me and, understanding how it was, I smiled.

I took a moment to study the crowd. Jean-Luc stood next to the dining room entrance, critically observing the waitstaff we'd hired for the event, making sure everything was done to his satisfaction.

For all their squabbling, he and Rhonda were fond of one another, and he'd worked hard on this event. The prime filet of beef was cooked to medium-rare perfection, the sea bass gently baked and sauced with a subtle blend of ginger and cream. For dessert, each of us was given a miniature white wedding cake, topped with a pink flower.

At the end of the meal, Will rose and gave a toast to the chef. Jean-Luc blushed at the loud applause he was given, but he deserved every bit of praise. The chocolate mousse cake beneath the stiff white icing had melted in my mouth.

Rhonda and Will made the rounds to each table, thanking the guests for coming. At our table, Rhonda greeted the mayor and his wife, hugged Manny and Consuela, and turned to me. "Here." She placed her bouquet in my hands. "I'm not leaving it up to chance. Your turn next." She eyed Vaughn meaningfully.

Vaughn grinned good-naturedly and gave me a look that told me he wouldn't mind that one bit. If I didn't already love him, I would have fallen in love with him right then. But I knew we needed more than love to make such a union. Our relationship was complicated by others.

Will shook hands with Vaughn and gave me a peck on the cheek. Rhonda embraced us both. "You two take good care of The Beach House Hotel. We'll see you soon!"

We all followed them outside. Tim and Angela sat in the limousine, which was decorated with white ribbons. Rhonda turned to Will with a smile. "Ready? Let's go!"

Inside the limo, Rhonda opened her window and leaned out. "Remember, Annie, you're next!"

As the limousine pulled out of the driveway, Liz came up beside me. "Didn't Rhonda look great? Angela too!"

"Yes, it was lovely, wasn't it?"

"But, Mom—" Liz lowered her voice and gave Vaughn an anxious glance. "Are you really going to be next?"

"I'm taking it one day at a time, Liz." I put my arm around her. "Now that the wedding's over, we have to think about getting you back to school. I'm going to miss you, Liz, but I'm glad you're going."

She shrugged. "Yeah, well, I guess I have no choice."

She walked away to join Angela's cousins. Watching her, I couldn't stop a sigh of frustration. Robert had given her an opening to quit school.

"Kids. They're always a worry," said Vaughn, joining me.

I smiled. "I guess that's what makes us parents."

"What do you say we go back to your house?"

"Let me check with Paul and Maria, then I'll be ready to go." I couldn't wait to go into the pool and take a night swim. With Liz at home, we'd be restrained, but after she left for school Vaughn would be alone with me for the whole week. We planned to make the most of it.


I rose and quietly dressed, managing to tiptoe out of the house without waking either Vaughn or Liz.

When I arrived at the hotel, Consuela and Maria were already in the kitchen preparing breakfast. Richie and Annette and their families were due to fly out mid-afternoon. Liz and Angela were on a different flight a half-hour later.

I checked email and voice messages and went back to the kitchen, drawn by the unmistakable bouquet of brewed coffee. Richie was seated at the table sipping coffee and munching on a sweet roll. By now, I was used to seeing

Rhonda's face on his shoulders and didn't feel the least bit awkward when he stood and gave me a bear hug.

"Annie, you gonna be able to tackle this joint alone or do ya need me to stay behind with ya?" He laughed Rhonda's raucous laugh, and I chuckled. He was almost as outrageous as his sister.

I smiled. "Vaughn and I are going to be fine." Rhonda and I had been surprised by the number of reservations that had unexpectedly been booked, but I was comfortable about running the place with the staff.

"Sit." He waved me to a seat at the kitchen table. "I want to tell ya how damn much it means to me to see Rhonda so happy. A lot of it has to do with you being here, supportin' her if ya know what I mean. Anytime you need somethin', you tell me. That's how we keep it in our family. Hear?"

"Thanks." It meant more to me than he knew. I'd never had a real family. My grandmother would abhor his rough language, but there was nothing but heartfelt emotion behind his words.

We chatted for a few minutes longer, and then I hurried away to take care of business.

After a late lunch, we loaded the family's luggage into the van, the trunk of the limo, and even my old Honda. It was quite something to see how we managed to fit everything and everyone in the vehicles. We headed for Ft. Myers like a gypsy caravan, with Tim and Angela in the limo and Vaughn driving the van. Liz and I were alone in my car, along with luggage that had been loaded inside it. I was glad for the private time with her.

We'd gone only a short distance when she turned to me. "Mom? Make sure Vaughn doesn't hurt you. Did you see all those women at the wedding? They couldn't stay away from him."

"It's not easy to get used to, but as he says, it's all part of the scene. It really doesn't mean anything to him personally. He learned that long ago."

"I talked to Nell ..."

"You did?" I couldn't hide my surprise.

She gave me a sheepish smile. "She told me to back off. Guess Nell really likes you."

I gave her a reassuring smile. "Liz, I'm not going to do anything foolish."

"It's just that my whole life is upside down. First, Dad. Now, maybe you." She looked younger than her years. My heart went out to her. I patted her hand.

"The one thing that won't change is how much I love you."

Tears sprang to her eyes. "I know. Sorry, I was such a jerk to Vaughn."

She turned away from me, and I realized it would be a while longer before Liz accepted the fact that I was on my own and about to enjoy it with the most exciting man I'd ever met.

We got the luggage inside the terminal, and then I had one last chance to hug Liz before she and the others stood in the security line to go out to the gates.

I raced back to my car and led the parade of vehicles back to the hotel. As I passed through the gates to the hotel, Manny waved frantically to me from the front entrance. I pulled the car to a stop in the front circle.

"What's wrong?"

"You'd better come, Annie! Dorothy needs to see you!"

It could only mean another problem. Heart pounding, I got out of the car and rushed up the steps.

Dorothy looked up from behind the front desk, her eyes huge behind her glasses. "Oh, there you are, Ann. I don't know what to do! I just got a call from one of Roger Sloan's friends, a big movie producer by the name of Robert Bronson. He's at the airport in Chicago with his wife and another couple. They're catching a plane to Sabal, and he wanted us to know he and his group of four would be arriving by six o'clock tonight. I looked on the reservations list, but they aren't there."

My lips thinned. "And I know why. They never sent us a deposit as we requested or called to confirm their reservations. I told him when we talked that we wouldn't hold a room without a deposit."

"What are we going to do?" Dorothy wrung her hands. "I didn't know what to say, so I told them okay. And now they're on their way!"

We were in trouble. I didn't want someone like Robert Bronson turned away. It would kill too much goodwill . I checked the reservations schedule.

"We've only got one room available. A large group from the east coast booked rooms for a special event this week. We'd better pray one of our other guests can't come at the last minute. Otherwise, we'll have to walk the Bronson party to another property, and I'd hate to do that."

Dorothy clucked her tongue. "I'm so sorry."

"You'd better go ahead and call the other hotels to see if they have any availability, in case we need the room. Let me know."

Carrying an inspection checklist, I climbed the stairs to check on Maria and Rosita. Each room had to be spotlessly clean, with fresh flowers in vases and a basket of amenities that included bottled water, crackers, and nuts.

After I left them, Vaughn met me downstairs. "How's it going? I told the party planner I'd help take down the decorations."

I filled him in on the latest news and returned to the office to check with Dorothy.

"There's a big boat and fishing exhibition along with a contest or some such thing. The other hotels, at least the ones we'd choose, are pretty well booked." Dorothy gave me a worried look. "I'm sorry, Ann. I really am."

"Don't worry. We'll work something out," I said, but I wondered how.

As each guest arrived, I checked them off my list. With time running out, I realized the only space available was Rhonda's suite in her wing of the house. After deciding to live in Will's bayside home, where they'd have more privacy, she'd pretty much moved out of it.

Maria and I checked the suite to make sure it was clean and that nothing of Rhonda's personal property was in danger of being taken.

Observing the tall ceilings, the crystal chandelier hanging from it, and the marble fireplace, I thought the elegant bedroom with its large sitting area overlooking the Gulf was exquisite by anyone's standards. Using this room might be a great marketing tool for us, sort of like the Presidential Suites of larger hotels.

I turned around to get a better sense of the room. The pale-blue tones of the walls and the assorted fabrics in the room were duplicated by the shades of the water outside, while the deep-magenta accent colors in the Oriental rug were echoed by the bougainvillea displayed so colorfully in the landscaping.

I checked the bathroom. The brass fixtures gleamed. Maria set to work on the enormous shower, which featured six shower heads. I leaned over the spa and looked out of the crescent-shaped window to the view of the Gulf.

"Mr. Big Producer and his wife better appreciate this," I grumbled and went about setting out flowers and amenities.

By six-thirty, all the reserved rooms but the two set aside for the producer and his group been filled. I heaved a sigh of relief. It had all worked out.

Paul had already left to pick up the producer, his wife, and their friends. Tim would officially greet them. Jean-Luc was in full swing in the kitchen with his new assistant, who'd done a spectacular job with the wedding.

I peeked into the living room. Consuela and Rosita were serving wine and appetizers to several of our guests. Everything was in order.

"Go home!" Tim gave me a big grin. "Rhonda told me she'd skin me alive if you didn't have any free time with Vaughn."

I smiled happily. "Thanks. You know where I am. Give me a call if you need me."

"No problem. Go!"

I all but skipped along the path to my house. The lights in my house shone a welcome. Best of all, Vaughn was waiting inside. My steps quickened.

I burst through the front doorway. "Hello! Anybody home?"

"Just me!" Vaughn lunged at me playfully from behind the door and drew me into his arms. His lips pressed down on mine.

I closed my eyes, reveling in the feel, the touch, the taste of him. At that moment, being with him like this was all that mattered to me. He drew me closer, and I could tell he was as ready for me as I was for him.

Vaughn stepped back and looked at me with such a tender expression, tears stung my eyes. He offered his hand, and I took it.

In my bedroom, I pushed thoughts of Lily away. I wanted to prove to Vaughn that our relationship was worth fighting for. Making love with Vaughn never ceased to amaze me. He was creative and gentle and rough and tender and so, so generous.

Much later, we returned to the kitchen. Vaughn sat at the kitchen bar and watched while I fixed a crisp green salad and sliced cold, blackened chicken breast to put on top. I handed him a chilled bottle of sauvignon blanc. He opened it and poured out two glasses of the white wine.

We sat side by side at the bar, relaxed with each other as we ate our supper.

"Liz told me she talked to Nell," I said.

Vaughn's eyebrows lifted. "And?"

"Nell told her to back off."

Vaughn laughed. "At times, she's so much like her mother. My son, Ty, is more like me."

I sobered. "Do you still miss Ellen? She sounds like such a nice person."

Vaughn nodded. "Yeah, it was a real blow to the gut to lose her, but I'm ready to move on." He leaned over and kissed me.

I didn't know much about his wife, but I was grateful to her for making Vaughn so happy and teaching him what a woman wants.

We took our wine outside, and I relaxed in my chair, enjoying the clean, salty evening air. A sliver-shaped moon hung suspended above us. Whimsically, I thought of it as the night sky smiling down on the love we shared.

Vaughn took the last sip of his wine, set down his glass, and turned to me. "While you were working this afternoon, I wandered down to the beach to take a walk. There's something wonderful about doing that. It helps bring things into perspective. I'd like to tell you about Lily Dorio now."

My stomach clenched as I faced him. I remembered the

lies I'd heard from Robert and gripped the arms of my chair.

Vaughn reached over and gave my hand a squeeze of encouragement. I gazed at the love in his eyes, and the tension that had gripped me eased. I settled back to listen.

"You remember Roger Sloan, the producer of the show? As you know, his wife, Darlene, is in the fashion industry and has become quite a force to be reckoned with. Her business now does over one billion dollars a year. She works very hard at it, and she's been very successful."

Vaughn leaned back in his chair and took a deep breath. "When Roger and Darlene flew over here with me in July, I was surprised to find Lily Dorio and her date with them. Lily is well-known in theatrical circles as someone who enjoys a fantasy world for the right price, if you get my meaning. I didn't think much more of it because Darlene and Roger have always been a close couple. I didn't know then that Roger's affair with Lily had already begun."

I sat up in surprise. I remembered how Lily had hung onto Vaughn's every word during our dinner together, how she'd brushed up against him with her ample breasts.

Vaughn looked uncomfortable. "That's why Lily kept throwing herself at me. She didn't want Darlene to suspect anything was going on between Roger and her."

"Surely Darlene would have known something was up when she was right there with them," I said, and then recalled how fooled I'd been by Robert's need to stay at the office.

"Apparently, Darlene suspected something along the way. Roger cashed in some stock he owned in the company, and when Darlene discovered it, she was furious. Roger tried to cover it up by saying the show was starting to get stale, and he needed the money for it. Actually, it was to pay off Lily."

"Pay her off? For what? The affair?"

Vaughn shook his head with disgust. "Roger decided he wanted out. Darlene threatened divorce and Roger is no dummy—he didn't want to give up his lush lifestyle with her. He told Lily he couldn't see her anymore. Lily threatened to tell Darlene all about what their little games had produced unless he kept her living in style. As long as he paid her, she wouldn't tell anyone that the baby was his. That's when Roger came to me."

"Why you?" I asked, thinking life is sometimes the best and worst soap opera of all.

"You may remember my mentioning my contract was up for renewal. It expires in October, and we'd already begun negotiations. Through my agent, I let it be known I wanted a special release from the show to do some movies. I had an offer I wanted to be able to think about. The big guys didn't like that one bit, Roger included. So when he came to see me, he offered me a deal. If I'd talk to Lily, he'd talk to the network's bigwigs about the movie clause in the contract and convince them to give it to me. I agreed to do it. What did I have to lose?"

"And so you went to see Lily. And I imagine she tried to latch onto you, a handsome, single man. Is that it?"

Vaughn's cheeks grew red. He nodded. "If you knew Lily, you'd know she's not one to let grass grow under her feet."

"Going for the green can be a never-ending pursuit," I said sourly. "She's just the type."

Vaughn gave me an abashed look. "Yeah, well, she tried, but I wasn't interested. She seemed to take it in stride, almost as if she was expecting it. She walked me to the door of her apartment to show me out. Just as I was leaving, a photographer popped out of the bushes. Lily grabbed me before I could stop her. The picture in the news shows her in a filmy gown of some sort, clearly displaying the fact that she was wearing nothing underneath it despite her pregnancy, and made me look like a love-sick schmuck in her arms."

Vaughn's eyes flashed. "The picture came out the day before I left to come here. I was furious. It was a set-up if I ever saw one." He stirred angrily in his chair. "I went to see Roger and asked him what the hell was going on. I thought he was going to break down and cry. He gave me this song-and-dance routine about how he could never let Lily go. It seems he's hooked on some of the weird stuff she does—stuff I wouldn't even tell you about. He admitted he arranged for the photographer to be there so Darlene would be convinced there was nothing going on between him and Lily. He wanted her to think that Lily was having an affair with me."

"Nice of him," I commented.

Vaughn shook his head. "While you were at the hotel this morning, I called a few people I know in New York. It seems the loser's trying to scrounge money from anybody he knows to keep Lily happy. Believe me, I've been so disgusted with the whole thing, I was ready to quit the show. But I've had time to think about it. As bad as this is, I don't think I could leave the show forever. Acting is my work."

I frowned. I was still trying to absorb the impact of what Vaughn had told me. "Didn't Roger realize that other people would be hurt by what he'd done? Your children? Your friends? Me?"

Vaughn snorted. "I guess he just doesn't give a shit. I've talked to Nell about it, and she's okay. Ty's great about it too. My son is pretty liberal about things like that. It's you I've been worried about. I know how you feel about scandals. I'm trying to prove to you that I can be trusted, and then something like this comes along to ruin it. What can I do?"

"You've already begun to do it." Touched by his sincerity, I clasped his hand. "You've told me what happened and how you feel about it. That's a good beginning."

Vaughn gazed into my eyes. "I want you with me. I need you. When I come home at night, I want you there. I don't want to talk to you on the phone or exchange emails. I want you in my arms. Will you give me, give us, this chance to be together? Will you come to New York and stay with me for a while?"

My racing heart bumped to a shocked stop. "You're suggesting that I come and live with you for a short, trial period?"

Vaughn nodded, smiling at me. "To be sure you'll be happy there—with me."

Alarm filled me. "But, Vaughn, I don't want to live in New York. I'm happy here. I love you. I really do. Why should it be up to me to leave my home and business?"

"I can't change the location of my work. Surely, you know that."

I sat silently, wondering why things couldn't ever be easy.

Vaughn rose and drew me up into his arms, tilting my chin so his lips could meet mine.

My body responded to his kiss even as my mind fought to make sense of the situation.

"I'll tell you what," Vaughn murmured in my ear. "Let's just take it one day at a time and enjoy our week. We can come to some decision later. Okay?"

I nodded, still uncertain where we were headed. But we had a precious seven days, and I didn't want to waste a moment.

# CHAPTER TWENTY-SIX

Vaughn and I started our days off cuddling in bed and a whole lot more.

In an effort to keep physically active outdoors, Vaughn approached Manny about doing some light landscape work. When he told me about the surprising arrangement, Vaughn explained that he enjoyed gardening and liked the idea of doing something for the hotel.

It was amusing to me to see Manny and Vaughn working together—small, wiry Manny hopping around with the use of his cane, conversing with Vaughn in a mixture of Spanish and English. I caught glimpses of Vaughn as he trimmed bushes, planted fresh flowers in the wide flower beds surrounding the house, and helped Manny direct Paul and others to perform heavier labor. I loved the idea that Vaughn was a temporary part of something that meant so much to me.

Most days, I managed to meet Vaughn for a quick lunch. I marveled at the changes in him. His skin had turned a nutty brown. The worry lines that had creased his face upon arrival had disappeared. His body moved in a more relaxed way as he worked around the grounds, whistling and humming. He confessed to me he'd never felt better, even when he was forced to soak in the pool spa to relax sore muscles.

Too soon, Saturday arrived. The following day, Vaughn would return to New York.

At lunch, Vaughn announced he was taking the rest of the day off.

Planning a romantic meal in my head, I went back to the hotel. We'd opted to stay in for dinner. My house had become a haven for us. Neither of us wanted to change that.

As the sun began its descent, giving the sky a pink kiss, Vaughn and I floated in my pool and swam leisurely, encouraging our bodies to unwind from the busy day.

"Come with me." Vaughn held out his hand. We climbed out of the pool, and still in our bathing suits, we walked out onto the sandy beach to watch the sunset. Standing with him, watching the bright red orb slip below the horizon, an overwhelming sadness enveloped me. I squeezed Vaughn's hand. We'd become as close in spirit as any two people could.

Vaughn turned to me. "I love you."

"I love you, too." I blinked back tears, wondering how I could bear to have him leave me. But I had no choice. My life, my work was in Florida.

I sighed, and we turned to go home.

Vaughn wrapped an arm around me. "I don't want to let you go."

I lifted my lips to him, needing another chance to store the touch, the taste, the feel of him in my memory for the time when he'd be gone.

We returned to the house and quietly got dressed, silently agreeing to make love later when nothing but morning stood in the way.

Fighting misery, I set the table on the lanai.

Vaughn came up behind me and kissed me on the nape of my neck, sending shivers of delight through me.

"I bought us a bottle of bubbly. Care to have some champagne?"

I turned and smiled. "It sounds lovely."

"Have a seat. I'll bring it out."

Smiling broadly at me, he brought out a bottle of Dom

Perignon nestled in an ice bucket and set it on the table. He expertly opened it, giving me a satisfied look at the soft pop the cork made as it came loose. I watched his every move, memorizing them for the time ahead when he'd be back in New York, and I'd be achingly alone.

He handed me a tulip glass of champagne and lifted his own to me. "Thank you for one of the best weeks of my life." His resonant voice washed over me, filling me with deep contentment.

He pulled a thin, black leather case out of his pocket and handed it to me. I smiled at the look of excitement on his face. "This is just a small token of my love. I hope you'll wear it close to your heart."

With trembling fingers, I opened the case and gasped with pleasure. Nestled against the black velvet lining was a gold necklace that took my breath away.

"It's beautiful!" I said softly, lifting the woven, gold chain out of the case. I stared at the pendant dangling from it. The right side of the letter A served as the left extension of the letter V, entwining them. A bar of five large, white, round diamonds ran horizontally across the middle, binding them together.

"It's gorgeous! I won't ever take it off!"

Vaughn held the pendant in his hand, studying it. When he looked up at me, love shone in his eyes. "I designed it. The five diamonds are for the family I want—you, me, Liz, Nell, and Tyrone. I want us to be a real family. I'm tired of being alone."

"I am too." My gaze caressed the man I loved with all my heart.

His mouth found mine and all doubt about the future melted away in the heat of his kiss. Somehow we'd find a way to be together. If we couldn't, a part of me would die.

### 

Vaughn went back to New York, and though the business of running the hotel kept my mind whirling as guests came and went with their own special demands, I ached for him.

A series of postcards arrived from Tahiti. The staff and I shared them with each other, laughing at all the exclamation points in Rhonda's handwriting, emphasizing the good time she and Will were having.

I was in the midst of doing a food inventory with Consuela when Dorothy came to find me. "You have a phone call, Ann, and whoever it is, he didn't sound too happy. He was actually rude to me."

I frowned. *A disgruntled guest?*

I answered the phone. "Hello?"

"I need to talk to you, Ann. About money."

My heart sank. Robert. "What about money?"

"Something's come up, and I don't have the funds to pay for Liz's tuition."

"What do you mean?" The blood in my veins turned cold. I waved Dorothy out of the office and took a seat at my desk. "We had that money invested. No one was to touch it. It was all set aside for Liz's education. That's what we agreed upon."

"Well, I had to borrow some of it." Robert's tone was harsh, defensive. "If I hadn't had to pay you off, that might not have happened. As it is, I had no choice. And now it looks like I won't be able to pay it back. I'm calling you, so you can take care of it."

"Me? How? You're the one who's supposed to do it. It's all in the legal agreement we signed." My breath came out in little nervous gasps. I didn't have the money. My money was tied up in the business.

"I'm trying to tell you I can't do it," said Robert, sounding as if he was about to explode with anger. No doubt, in his twisted mind, he was blaming me.

Fury turned my clipped words to ice. I knew damn well who was at the bottom of this. "It's because of the house, isn't it? You and Kandie are building some huge place, and you used Liz's money to help you do it. Maybe it's time to sell the house."

A tense silence followed. "Too late. The bank is taking it back."

Shock coiled through me. *What had he done? Had he lost everything?* "What about the business, Robert? It was a solid business when I left. There must be money there."

"You know what the economy has been like," Robert snapped at me. "Can I help it if nobody is hiring consultants anymore?"

"Did you initiate some of the new marketing strategies we talked about two years ago? You didn't want to hear it then, but I thought you might change your mind!"

Robert's tone turned nastier. "You think you've got all the answers, don't you?" he screamed. "Well, you don't know a thing about my business anymore! So, don't go blaming me!"

I was too angry to speak. My body burned with rage. This was an old argument. He was too proud, too vain to accept anyone else's advice. It had always been that way. And now he couldn't make things right.

"Ann? Are you there?"

I drew a deep breath. "I'm here." My mind raced. How in the world could I come up with any money? There was no way I'd even consider asking Rhonda or Vaughn for it.

"Ann, you work out something. Your hotel is doing well. I hear about it all the time. You've got all that money. You take care of it."

"Robert, that isn't right, and you know it!" I said hotly.

"I've had to start a business of my own, and that's taken all my money. It's not fair to leave it up to me. I'm not able to do it."

"Come now, Ann, you've been very successful. I'm really disappointed in your attitude." Robert's words made my stomach turn. In the past, I hadn't wanted to disappoint him or anyone else. But I'd broken away from that kind of manipulation.

"I guess it might have something to do with that actor friend of yours. Jilted again." Robert's tone was snide. "Kandie told me all about it. She saw it in one of those movie star magazines."

I laughed bitterly. "You can't believe everything you read, Robert. I've never been happier in my life." I hoped the news would go straight to the core of his ego and hurt him as badly as he'd once hurt me. "Anyway, it's no business of yours. We were talking about our daughter's life, not mine. Obviously, Liz is not important to you anymore."

I listened to his harsh denial, as I'd done so many times in the past. Now, I had no pity for him. Whatever I might have once felt for him was gone for good. My only concern was for my daughter's welfare.

"The ball's in your court now," he said. "It's up to you."

Shaking with fury, I slammed the phone down. A part of me wanted to call Liz and tell her exactly what her father had done, but I decided to say nothing to her. She was already questioning her schooling. Fair or not, I was determined to try to come up with a way for her to continue. I wanted her to have a degree and to be able to do things on her own that I hadn't been allowed to do. I wasn't going to let Robert's selfishness destroy my daughter's future.

I punched in Syd Green's number to let him know what had happened.

"I understand how angry you are, Ann, and I don't blame you," said Syd, after hearing me out. "Suing him probably won't do you much good. I've heard rumors that Robert's business is about to close down. Legal action at this time would probably not provide the results we want."

My breath left me. "I didn't know things were that bad. I guess you're right. We'd get nowhere. Still, it infuriates me that once more Robert has cheated Liz and me."

"As it should. I wish I could offer an easy solution, but there isn't any. It's good that you've done so well with the hotel. It was a big risk, but you made it work."

We hung up with the promise to stay in touch.

Pacing the floor, I tried to think of alternative financing for Liz. When no new ideas came, I finally decided to wait for Will's return. He knew more about my money situation than anyone else.

I was getting ready to leave the office when Liz called. "Hey ..." she paused. Her voice sounded strained. "Dad called and told me you're going to pay my tuition this year. What's going on? I thought you told me Dad was responsible for my college education."

I clenched my teeth to keep from telling her that Robert didn't know the word responsible, that he was a selfish man not fit to be her father.

"Mom?"

"I'm here, Liz. Somehow the money is gone, but I don't want you to worry about it. Your tuition will be paid. I'm trying to make the arrangements now. You'll be able to finish school."

"It's Kandie," said Liz. She let out a snort of disgust. "I bet he took the money and spent it on that fancy house of theirs. Well, neither of you need to worry about it. I have some ideas of my own. Everybody's pressuring me to declare a major, and I'm not sure what I want to do. I need some time to think."

"Liz..."

"Wait, Mom. Hear me out. I want to take a year off from school to let me consider some options and decide what I want to do with the rest of my life."

"Oh, Liz, no! Once you leave, it's so hard to discipline yourself to go back to school."

"Lots of kids are doing it, Mom. It's what I want to do. Don't worry. I won't end up without a degree. It means too much to me. It's my decision, Mom. I hope you understand. Dad's silly games just make it easier for me to do it."

I thought of all the hopes and dreams I'd had for her. "Liz, please don't make a snap decision like this. Promise me you'll do some more thinking about it before any final choices are made."

"It's not a snap decision. I've been thinking about it for some time. I'm not going to change my mind. I've already talked to Nell about finding an internship in Washington. I was impressed by what I saw there at Thanksgiving. If I like it, I might major in political science."

"Think about what I said, and we'll talk tomorrow. I love you, Liz, and want the best for you. I really do."

"I know. Love you too."

As we hung up, I shook my head. Life never seemed to work out the way you thought it would.

I clutched the pendant Vaughn had given me, letting the coolness of the metal soothe me with its promise of love and commitment. Our children were already coming together. How and when could we?

Later, talking to Vaughn about it, he calmed my fears. "Liz is a bright girl. She's not going to want to live a life without choices of her own—good choices. Have faith in her."

I took his words to heart.

Liz called the next day to tell me the dean was okay with her taking a year off, and that she'd be welcomed back.

Remembering Vaughn's words, I succumbed to the idea. Liz would be all right. She was going to bunk in with Nell for a while. Nell even thought she might have found a job for her. Things had a good chance of working out. But inside, I blamed Robert for his willingness to harm our daughter.

Vaughn continued to be a source of comfort to me as we discussed the happenings at the hotel.

"So what's the deal with your negotiations?" I asked him one night.

"Sorry, I can't discuss them."

There was a firmness to his response I couldn't ignore. Telling myself he needed a sense of trust from me, I worked very hard not to pressure him. But I waited and worried.

# CHAPTER TWENTY-SEVEN

Rhonda returned in a flurry of activity, with hugs and gifts for everyone. Tanned and beaming, she looked as lovely as I'd ever seen her.

"We had such a good time," she declared, giving Will an impish grin. "But, Annie, I kept wondering how things were here. Will told me he promised you I wouldn't call. Did you make out all right without me?" She gave me a warning look. "Don't you dare say yes or I'll be crushed!"

I laughed and told her the truth. "I missed you like crazy! We all did."

She grinned. "Good."

Later, Rhonda and I shared a cup of coffee at the little table in our office. "You look terrific, Annie. Now tell me about you and Vaughn." She shook a finger at me. "And you'd better not leave anything out."

I told her everything I could, including my worries that with him in New York and me in Florida, things might not work out.

Rhonda studied the pendant around my neck. "Are you going to leave The Beach House Hotel?"

I shook my head. "I can't. This is my life now. Living here, sharing the business with you."

She clapped a hand over her heart. "Oh my God! I was so scared you'd say yes. If you walked out on me now, I'd die, Annie. This hotel is proof that I can do something right, and you? You're the sister I never had." Tears glistened in her eyes.

I patted her hand. "Oh, hon, I'd never let you down. We're much, much more than business partners. Right?"

She nodded and rose to give me a hug.

Our days fell into a smooth routine, giving me a chance to catch my breath. Each morning started with a phone call from Vaughn, making it seem as if he were a part of my daily life. At night, we talked on the phone, making love with words.

"How are the negotiations going?" I finally asked, unable to hold back one of the questions that never left my mind.

"They're coming to a close," he answered. "I can't say anything more about it."

I remained silent, finding this test of trust next to impossible to endure. I was a planner, a doer, not someone who drifted along without a charted course.

When I complained to Rhonda about the situation, she gave me a pat on the back. "Hold on, Annie. Good things come to those who wait, and Vaughn Sanders is worth waiting for."

After more agonizing days of wondering about the negotiations and how their outcome might affect our future plans, Vaughn called. "I need you to do something for me today." I heard a lilt in his voice.

"Sure."

"Watch the show. I know you can't always view it, but it's very important for you to see it today. I need to know what you think. Promise?"

"Yes. Can you tell me why?"

"Nope. I've got to go. I'll call you right after the show."

Puzzled, I shrugged. "Okay. Good-bye. Talk to you later."

That afternoon, promptly at three o'clock, Rhonda and I

curled up on the couch in my living room, waiting for the show to come on.

The theme music for *The Sins of the Children* came through the television, and I shifted in my seat.

My heart leaped when Vaughn's image filled the screen. He still had a trace of tan and looked more handsome than ever.

During the show, when his face took on an angry expression as he stared down the ex-boyfriend of his television daughter, I grew amused. He'd worn the same expression when I'd told him about some of Robert's antics. Becoming involved with the dialogue, I leaned forward.

"I've warned you to stay away from my daughter! You may be the father of her child, but she's chosen not to marry you." Vaughn said. "She and the child are going to live with me."

"Nobody has the right to take my family away from me!" the distraught young man shouted at Vaughn. "Not you! Not nobody!"

Susannah Scoville, the female lead, entered the room as Vaughn's daughter, Esmeralda.

"What are *you* doing here?" she asked the angry young man.

He stopped shaking his fist at Vaughn and turned to her. "I'm here to get my family back. You and little Nicola are my family. I want you with *me*, not *him*!"

"Look here!" said Vaughn. "She isn't your family. She's my daughter, and as long as she wants to stay with me, she can. As far as Nicola is concerned, I can give her a much better life than you ever could."

"But she's my baby girl," the young man cried. "She's the only family I've got. I'm not going to give her up."

Her eyes blazing, Esmeralda stepped forward. "She isn't yours, you fool. I only told you that so you'd stay with me while I got on my feet. I don't even know who the father is. Now, get out of here before I call the cops!"

His features twisted with fury. He pulled a gun out of the pocket of his black leather jacket and pointed it at her. "I know she's mine. She's all I've got, you bitch! You're not going to take her away from me!"

Vaughn stepped between his daughter and her angry lover. "Now see here, think of Nicola, not yourself. Just put the gun away, and nobody need ever know about this ... this disagreement."

"This ain't no disagreement, as you call it," the young man shouted, still pointing the gun at Vaughn and Esmeralda. "This is my life, my family!"

Esmeralda flung a long lock of blond hair over her shoulder and sneered at him. "Who's to say she's yours?" She smiled smugly as she stepped from behind her father. "You don't think I stayed home alone all those nights you were working, do you?"

His eyes widened with surprise. "Do you mean that Dave guy upstairs and you were lovers, not just friends?"

She gave him a smile that let him know he was right.

He cocked the gun. The clicking sound it made froze everyone in place. "That's it. It's all over, you little slut!"

At the exact moment the gun was fired, Vaughn moved to protect his daughter. Pumping blood, he crumpled to the floor.

Panicking, the young man fired another shot. Vaughn's body jerked from the impact.

"No!" I gasped as the camera focused on the blood oozing onto the floor.

"Holy Shit!" Rhonda's face turned white.

"My God! He's dead!" I gasped, facing her. "He's dead!" Still in a state of shock, I turned back to the television. The scene had faded to a solid gray, but the image of Vaughn lying on the floor with a bullet through his heart played over and over in my mind.

I laughed nervously through my tears and wiped my eyes with a tissue. "I know it's just a show, but it seems so real!"

"What does it mean?" Rhonda dabbed at tears of her own.

"I don't know. I really don't know." My voice trembled at the horror I'd witnessed.

The theme music for the show played, ending the show.

The phone rang. I got up to answer it on legs gone weak.

"How did you like the show?" Vaughn asked.

"Oh, Vaughn! I'm so glad to hear your voice. I know it's just a television program, but I'm still shivering. It seemed so real. I would just die if anything happened to you. I wish I could put my arms around you, to know you're alive and well."

"Great. I'll hold you to it. I'll be there in a few minutes."

My eyes widened. "Where are you?"

Vaughn chuckled. "I'm at the airport. Tim is on his way over here to pick me up. See you soon!"

"What does all this mean?" I asked. Hope burned brightly inside me, giving voice to my silent prayers.

"It means one dead mayor needs some work. Got any ideas?"

I couldn't resist. "Some."

"There's just one catch. I want room and board and all the privileges of my last stay. But this time, we're going to make it official."

I let out the breath I'd been holding. Tears of happiness welled in my eyes. "Do you mean it? Hurry! I'll be here, waiting for you out front."

I told Rhonda the news. She waved her fist triumphantly in the air. "Yes! I knew it!"

Laughing and giggling, we raced each other to the hotel to wait for Vaughn's arrival.

Dorothy stood at the top of the front steps, waving frantically to us as we approached.

"I've been searching all over for you!" she cried, looking as if she were about to burst with an excitement of her own. "Hurry! Come quickly! It's a phone call from someone who says they're calling for the mayor of New York. I don't know if it's a joke or not, but you'd better answer it."

Rhonda and I looked at each with widening eyes.

"There's only one way to find out. Beat you to it!"

We rushed up the stairs and into the hotel, where Dorothy, having delivered her exciting message, sank down into a chair to catch her breath.

Shrieking like schoolgirls, Rhonda and I hurried past her to the reception desk. Rhonda reached the phone first.

"Hello? This is Rhonda DelMonte Grayson, one of the owners of The Beach House Hotel," she managed to say between puffs of her breath. She looked over at me and winked. "It *is* the mayor's office? Really? November 17th and 18th, you say? Just a moment, please, while I check the date."

Rhonda pressed the hold button and turned to me with a look of awe. "Annie! Annie! It's the mayor's personal secretary calling. The senator from California, who was with us over Labor Day, told him all about the hotel, and she's calling to see if they can book the whole place for November 17th and 18th for a birthday party for him. She even asked about my cinnamon rolls for breakfast. Can you believe it?"

My breath caught, even as my mind raced. The truth was, I *could* believe it after all that had happened to us. Our hotel had attracted people I'd only read about earlier. Now, I was on a speaking basis with a number of famous people and had discovered they were no better or worse than any of us. This call was another example of the magic we'd created.

I hurried over to the computer to check the reservations schedule. Punching in the date, I waited for the data to pop up on the screen and then let out a disappointed sigh. "The Williams family has already booked and confirmed twenty-two rooms for that entire weekend. Their daughter is getting married right here on the property. It's been on the books for a while now."

"But what do we say to the Mayor's office?" Rhonda fluttered her hands in front of her, looking as if she was about to take flight.

"We say the only thing we can, that we're booked for those nights, but if they would like to make reservations some other time, we'd be most honored to have him stay with us."

Rhonda stared at me in disbelief, then slowly nodded. A look of pride crossed her face. "We've come a long way, baby!"

I gave her a high-five. "You bet your ass!"

Her jaw dropped. "Why, Annie Rutherford, I didn't think I'd ever hear such words coming from *your* mouth!"

I laughed, and she joined in. The joyful sound of it echoed merrily in the large, seaside estate we'd successfully turned into a hotel.

We hugged. Many things had happened to me in the last

two years. My life had changed, I'd changed. The lonely, uncertain nights in Boston seemed a long time ago.

At the sound of the limo pulling into the front circle, I hurried to the entrance of The Beach House Hotel. My pulse raced gleefully. My triumph at the hotel didn't compare to the happiness I felt at the bond of love I'd formed with Vaughn.

I grinned at the sight of him bounding up the stairs to greet me. The smile he gave me melted my heart. He swept me into his arms and pressed his lips on mine, and I knew our future together at The Beach House Hotel would be as bright as the sun that shone down on us.

I hope you've enjoyed Ann and Rhonda's story in *Breakfast at The Beach House Hotel*. My readers demanded more of their stories; *Lunch at The Beach House Hotel*, *Dinner at The Beach House Hotel,* and *Christmas at The Beach House Hotel* are now out as well. If you enjoyed this book, please help other readers discover it by leaving a review on Amazon, Goodreads, or your favorite site. It's such a nice thing to do for any author.

Enjoy an excerpt from my book, *Lunch at The Beach House Hotel* (Book 2 in The Beach House Hotel Series).

## CHAPTER ONE

I'd just stepped out of the shower when my business partner, Rhonda—Rhonda DelMonte Grayson, as she proudly called herself—phoned in a tizzy.

"Annie, you've got to get over here right away. Something's come up."

She hung up before I could ask her about it, but I knew I'd better get moving. In the hotel business, there were a lot of "somethings"—some good, some bad.

My mind whirled with possibilities as I quickly dried off and dressed. After brushing my hair and dabbing on some lipstick, I took a moment to put on the chain and pendant Vaughn Sanders had given me. He wouldn't return from filming for another six weeks, and I missed him like crazy. The gold pendant spoke of so many things. His initial V formed one side of my A. Across the middle of it was a bar with five diamonds—a symbol of us, our collective three children, and the hope that we'd all share a life together.

I left my house on the hotel property and headed toward the hotel. Warm air wrapped around me, caressing my skin in silky strokes, and I joyfully inhaled the tang of the salty air. After living most of my life in Boston, I relished the tropical setting along the Gulf Coast of Southwest Florida.

As I approached the front of The Beach House Hotel, I paused to stare at the beachside estate Rhonda and I had turned into a small, upscale hotel. The pale-pink-stucco, two-story building spread before me at the water's edge like a palace, regal and splendid. Wide steps led to carved-wood, double doors that invited guests inside. Potted palms sat on either side of the doorway, adding a tropical elegance to the entry. Along the front of the hotel, brilliant pink hibiscus blossoms vied for attention with bougainvillea and other colorful plantings and softened the lines of the building.

Gratitude filled me.

In the troubling days following my ex's dumping me for his receptionist—Kandie with a K as she called herself—I would never have imagined being part owner of such a beautiful place. We'd started out better than expected, but the fear of failing kept me working day and night to make sure the hotel succeeded. So many didn't. And though I loved Rhonda, it was sometimes frustrating to be left with most of the detailed, follow-up work she disliked. Doing it as cheerfully as I could while she stayed busy doing the most-fun stuff was a way to pay her back for all she'd done to help me.

Rhonda appeared at the top of the stairway. Dressed in one of the light-weight, colorful caftans she loved to wear, she urged me forward, flapping the green sleeves of her dress like a tropical bird about to take flight. *Or more like the early bird who got the worm,* I thought wryly, as I got a closer look at the grin on her face.

She placed her hands on her ample hips and shook her head at me. "Annie Rutherford, how can you look so freakin' beautiful and put together at this early hour? I swear, if you weren't my best friend, I'd hate your guts."

I laughed. Rhonda was known for speaking her mind. It was amazing we even got along—we were as different as two people could be. My strict grandmother, who'd raised me after my parents died, would shiver in her blue-blooded Boston grave at the language Rhonda used. I'd gotten used to it, which was a good thing because Rhonda didn't even notice it. She'd come from a loud, Italian family in New Jersey.

"What's up?" I asked. "It better be good. I haven't even had my coffee yet."

"Oh, it's good all right. We have a decision to make—an important one that can't wait."

"And?" I prompted, giving Rhonda a dubious look.

"And I promised Valentina Marquis' agent we'd call her right back. She's at LAX, ready to put Valentina on a private jet to us."

"Oh, no!" My heart thudded with dismay. "Are you talking about the same Valentina Marquis who co-starred with Vaughn in that awful short film, the one he tried to get out of several times?"

Rhonda nodded. "The very same one. But, Annie, this could mean a lot of business for us."

As usual, talk of new business stopped me cold. Overseeing the finances of the hotel consumed me. At best, the hotel business was a series of ups and downs, fluctuating as bookings rose and fell. At worst, I had invested every cent of mine into my share of the business. Weather, dates of holidays, and fierce competition affected bookings for rooms reservations, which created a lot of uncertainty.

"Okay, you'd better tell me about it. Why does Valentina's agent want her to come here?"

An even bigger grin spread across Rhonda's face. Beneath her bleached-blond hair, her dark eyes sparkled with mischief. "You won't believe it! She's going to be shooting a movie in two months and has eight weeks to lose twenty-five pounds."

I frowned. "How's Valentina going to do that here? We're known for our delicious cuisine."

"The agent has requested us to provide a trainer to stay with Valentina, to keep an eye on her, and to guide her physical training. Because our guests know that The Beach House Hotel assures them total privacy, she figures the director and producer won't find out what shape Valentina is in before she loses the weight. Cool, huh?"

"I'm not sure." Vaughn, sweet guy that he is, had ranted and raved about Valentina's *prima donna* attitude on the movie set. He'd declared her self-absorption and treatment of the people around her deplorable.

"It could be a bit tricky," admitted Rhonda, "but it's been a really slow fall season for us."

I couldn't deny it. In the past, we'd had a lot of VIP guests from the world of politics, but, with the latest mess in Washington, they'd been forced to stay put. Not that I minded all that much. The politicians were as egotistical as any movie star.

"Okay, let's call her back," I said reluctantly. Her visit could boost our cash flow, and who couldn't use a better bottom line?

On the way to our office, which sat behind the kitchen, I stopped and grabbed a cup of coffee along with one of Rhonda's famous breakfast rolls. Sweet and buttery, filled with cinnamon and nuts, their enticing aroma filled the air.

These breakfast rolls had been instrumental in promoting the culinary reputation of the hotel since we opened it a little over a year ago.

After sipping my refreshing hot coffee, I carried it and the roll into the office and sat at my desk. A sigh of pleasure escaped me as I bit into the soft, warm breakfast sweet.

Seated opposite me, Rhonda dialed the number the agent had given her . I listened carefully as she informed Valentina's agent that we'd be delighted to have Valentina stay with us.

Rhonda stopped talking and then said, "Please hold. I'll check to see if we can make those arrangements." She turned to me. "Is it okay if I offer her the lower rooms at the far end of the hotel? If we give her rooms #101 and #102, Valentina will have the privacy her agent says she needs."

I quickly checked our online reservations system. "How long does Valentina's agent want her to use the rooms?"

"They want 'em for the full eight weeks, starting today. That takes us up to the Thanksgiving weekend."

I quickly looked at the reservations list. "We'll have to move a few people around, but we can do it." There were no full-house, wedding weekends planned during that time. Only smaller groups.

After she assured Valentina's agent she'd take care of everything, Rhonda hung up with a sigh. "It sounds as if this situation hasn't been easy for anybody. Valentina is getting on a plane within the next moment or two. We're to hire a personal trainer and meet her at the airport. She'll be traveling under the name Tina Marks, which I understand is her real name. And that's not all. I've agreed not only to provide special meals for her but to keep her out of the spotlight, so no one even guesses she's here."

"Okay, that's settled then," I said, suddenly overcome by

the horrible feeling that this might be one of the biggest mistakes Rhonda and I had ever made together. And there'd been a few.

Tim McFarland, our young assistant manager, agreed to pick up Jerry Brighton, the personal trainer we'd hired through an agency, and to drive him in the limo to the airport to pick up Tina.

Rhonda and I stayed at the hotel to discuss the details of Tina's upcoming stay. Then I began my daily ritual of reviewing revenue reports, staffing schedules, and reservations to update my forecast. The sales weren't as strong as I'd hoped, emphasizing how important Tina's stay was to us. I resolved to make her visit go well. In addition to paying for the rooms, her agent was paying a hefty price for the hotel to cook special, low-calorie meals for Tina and her trainer.

I'd finished making some financial projections when Tim called from the limo to say he was approaching the hotel with our guest. As part of our normal routine, Rhonda and I went to the front stairway to greet them. From the hotel's beginning, it was something we'd done as often as we could. Our guests liked it.

Rhonda and I were standing by the front door in our usual stations when Tim pulled the limo into the front circle.

"Here goes," Rhonda said, giving me a high-five.

As the car came to a stop, we watched closely.

Tim got out and raced around the limo to open the passenger door.

A foot encased in a high-heeled, gold sandal emerged. A

young woman quickly followed, dressed in a denim skirt so short I knew she was wearing a thong. Her white tank-top indicated she wasn't wearing a bra.

My gaze lifted to her face. Large sunglasses hid most of it. Blue hair piled in a knot atop her head added a few inches to her height but couldn't hide the fact that she was short and ... well, wider than normal in places ... for a movie star.

We started down the stairs.

"Welcome ..." I started my spiel.

"What a dump," Tina said, cupping her hands around her sunglasses for a better view in the sunlight. "I asked for a big, fancy, glittery place if I have to do this stupid Hollywood thing."

Beneath her normal tan, Rhonda's face turned red.

I held my breath. Nobody bad-mouthed the hotel in front of Rhonda.

"That little brat," Rhonda murmured.

I grabbed hold of her arm. "Don't!"

She jerked her arm out of my hand and hurried down the the stairway, her caftan flying behind her in a cloud of green.

Knowing what was coming, I raced past her. Tina might be a gigantic boor, but we would welcome her properly as my grandmother had taught me.

"Welcome to The Beach House Hotel," I said, elbowing my way in front of Rhonda.

A bald, muscular giant emerged from the car, looking like the smiling ad man on television who told viewers all about his cleaning products. Standing beside Tina, his bulk made her seem smaller than ever.

"I'm Jerry Brighton, the one you hired to keep tabs on Tina." Turning to Rhonda, he smiled. "This place is beautiful."

The lines of distress left Rhonda's face. She returned his

smile. "Thank you. I'm Rhonda DelMonte Grayson, and this is my partner, Annie Rutherford. Among other things, The Beach House Hotel has a reputation for good service; we're here to help you in any way we can."

"Great," he said.

Tina's red-painted lips formed a pout as she glared at us. "I don't need anyone watching over me. I can do this myself. And nobody can know I'm here at this fat farm," said Tina. "That would ruin me."

Rhonda drew herself up.

This time, I knew I couldn't stop her.

Hands on hips, Rhonda stared down Tina. "This is not a fat farm. This hotel is a lovely place where guests can find some of the finest food in Southwest Florida." She paused for emphasis. "If they're allowed to eat it."

Tina gasped and stamped a sandaled foot. "That's it! I'm leaving!" She ruined the effect of her tantrum by teetering on heels too high for her. She regained her balance and turned to climb inside the limo.

In one swift movement, Jerry took hold of Tina's elbow. "Hold on. Let's at least give this a try."

Tina's shoulders slumped in defeat, allowing me to see a vulnerability that touched me. It couldn't be easy for someone so young to have so many demands made of her.

"Okay. I'll show you to your rooms," said Tim, who up to now had been standing aside wringing his hands. He urged them forward.

After Jerry and Tina had followed him into the hotel, Rhonda gave me a sheepish look.

"I'm sorry, Annie, but that little brat deserves more than a scolding. She deserves a spanking."

"No wonder Vaughn found it so difficult to work with Tina," I said. "I hope this isn't how she's going to act for the whole eight weeks."

A frown creased Rhonda's brow. "We can do this, can't we? Keep Tina here and get her thin?"

"We're going to try our best," I said with determination, "but, Rhonda, she won't be our only guest. We'll have to keep everyone else happy too."

"Eight weeks seems like a long time, huh?"

I nodded. "More like an eternity."

# About the Author

Judith Keim was born and raised in Elmira, New York, and now makes her home in Idaho with her husband, their dachshunds, Winston and Wally, and other members of her family.

"Growing up, books were always present—being read, ready to go back to the library, or about to be discovered. Information from the books was shared in general conversation, giving all of us in the family a wealth of knowledge and a lot of imagination. Perhaps that is why I was drawn to the idea of writing stories early on. I particularly love to write novels about women who deal with the unexpected with strength and open their hearts to finding love, because no matter what our circumstances, we all need to love and be loved in return."

"I hope you've enjoyed this book. If you have, please help other readers discover it by leaving a review on Amazon, Goodreads, or the site of your choice. And please check out the Hartwell Women Series, the Fat Fridays Group, the Salty Key Inn Series, and the other books in The Beach House Hotel Series. ALL THE BOOKS ARE NOW AVAILABLE IN AUDIO on Audible and iTunes! So fun to have these characters come alive!"

Ms. Keim can be reached at www.judithkeim.com

And to like her author page on Facebook and keep up with the news, go to: https://www.facebook.com/pages/Judith-Keim/184013771644484?ref=aymt_homepage_panel.

To receive notices about new books, follow her on Book Bub - http://bit.ly/2pZBDXq

And here's a link to where you can sign up for her periodic newsletter! http://eepurl.com/bZoICX

She is also on Twitter, @judithkeim, LinkedIn and Goodreads. Come say hello!

# Acknowledgements

No writer writes a book alone–critique partners help, friends and family give support, writing groups exchange information, and sometimes, special people are available to help make the story the best it can be.

I wish to thank Stephanie Berget and Amity Grays for their willingness to look over this manuscript, all my writing friends new and old for giving me support, and my family for always being there. Most of all I wish to thank my husband, Peter, who supports me in all my efforts and gives me so much happiness.

Onward and upward!

Made in the USA
Columbia, SC
11 September 2018